WESTMAN LIONS MANOR

Diefenbaker for the Defence

Diefenbaker for the Defence

Garrett Wilson and Kevin Wilson

JAMES LORIMER & COMPANY, PUBLISHERS
Toronto, 1988

Photo credits: Unless otherwise indicated, photos are reproduced courtesy of The Right Honourable John G. Diefenbaker Centre, University of Saskatchewan.

Canadian Cataloguing in Publication Data
Wilson, Garrett, 1932-
Diefenbaker for the defence
ISBN 1-55028-104-6 (bound)
1. Diefenbaker, John G., 1895-1979. 2. Lawyers — Saskatchewan — Biography. I. Wilson, Kevin C. (Kevin Charles). II. Title.
KE416.D54W54 1988   345.7124'0092'4   C88-094508-7

James Lorimer & Company, Publishers
Egerton Ryerson Memorial Building
35 Britain Street
Toronto, Ontario M5A 1R7

Printed and bound in Canada
5 4 3 2 1 88 89 90 91 92 93

Contents

To Charles Wilson (in memoriam)
and
To Jacqueline

Acknowledgements

The confidence and trust of many made this work possible. The contributions of the following were especially helpful.

The generosity of The Canada Council enabled us to compile extensive files of the many cases tried by John Diefenbaker. The papers maintained by The Diefenbaker Centre at the University of Saskatchewan were invaluable, as was the assistance of the director, Sharon Mitchell, and staff members JoAnne Cadieux, Cathy Mitchell and Elizabeth Diamond.

The facilities and personnel of the Saskatchewan Archives have our deep gratitude. The depth and detail of their material, and their patience, are outstanding.

The archives of the University of Saskatchewan,and the College of Law, also have our appreciation.

The custodians of the documents in the Saskatchewan judicial system were extremely cooperative in searching out ancient files. In particular, Fred C. Newis, registrar of the Court of Appeal, and, in the Prince Albert Court House, Malcolm McNaughton, Ernie Birkham, John Krychuk and Marge Seufert deserve our thanks.

We are indebted to Professor Donald Swainson of the Department of History, Queen's University, for some of the material on the early days of the Diefenbaker/Bannerman families.

At Wakaw, Walter Chobuk and the Wakaw Historical Museum were most helpful. Old friend and former Wakawite, M.A. Hnidy, and Melva gave us both time and insight.

A number of John Diefenbaker's contemporaries and associates searched their memories and files. Retired Supreme Court Justice Emmett Hall has a remarkable recollection spanning seventy years of Saskatchewan legal history. Former members of the Court of Appeal, Justices R. L. Brownridge and Roy

L. Hall (supernumerary), and former members of the Court of Queen's Bench, Justices Walter A. Tucker and M.A. MacPherson, Jr., were gracious with their assistance. H.C. Reese, Q.C., and J.M. Goldenberg, Q.C., also added their remembrances of a bygone era.

J. Clyne Harradence, Q.C., Marcel R.C. Cuelenaere, Q.C., and Judge H.M. Ketcheson, Q.C., provided their recollections of life in the Diefenbaker law office.

Iain Mentiplay, Q.C., Secretary of the Saskatchewan Law Society, and his assistant, Ruth Armstrong, unfailingly responded to numerous requests for archival material and information.

The resources of the Prince Albert Historical Society and William Smiley were vital. Senator D.G. and Eunice Stuart were also a rich source of background on their former hometown. Two old friends, Gordon W. Kirkby, Q.C. and former mayor, M.A. Pereverzoff, must also be mentioned. Timothy O. Davis, a Calgary lawyer, kindly provided insight into the career of his uncle, T.C. Davis. Another former Prince Albertan, James Roche, also lent a hand.

For our description of 1920s politics and the Ku Klux Klan in Saskatchewan, we drew heavily upon two excellent theses: William Calderwood's "The Rise and Fall of the Ku Klux Klan in Saskatchewan," and Raymond J. A. Huel's "La Survivance in Saskatchewan: Schools, Politics and the Nativist Crusade for Cultural Conformity."

Arthur G. Cookson kindly expanded upon the recollections of the Bohun murder trial carried in his autobiography, *From Harrow to Hawk*.

Dr. David B. Rodger provided essential medical interpretation.

Allan and Myrna Roth added to the background.

Philip Derksen of the Wilson King law firm in Prince George unearthed much valuable material on the Atherton trial.

Heather Robertson, outstanding Canadian writer doubling as Lorimer editor, provided inspiration and guidance without which this book would never have been. We are very grateful for her insight and skills.

The partners and staff of the Wilson, Harmel, Drummond law firm in Regina were understanding and helpful over many months. May Pick deserves special mention.

Lesley Wilson, writer/researcher, assisted in both disciplines. Taralyne and Mark Ackerman, Florence Wilson, Sheila and Bob McMullan all gave their time, support and kind criticism. Moral encouragement came from Gail Gutwin.

Jacqueline Stewart, who endured the long months of writing and gave freely of her sure understanding, has a special place in the result.

Prologue

I first met John Diefenbaker in the early 1950s, when he was a distinguished lawyer and member of Parliament, but not yet leader of the Conservative Party or prime minister. I was one of a small group of law students whom he joined for dinner in Saskatoon one evening.

"Read biography," he advised us. The lives and accomplishments of famous men provided him with example and inspiration, he went on, telling us of those whose careers he had followed, parliamentarians such as John A. Macdonald, Laurier, Gladstone and Disraeli. We found him somewhat stiff and didactic.

A few years later, I was articled to an old political and professional friend of Diefenbaker's, Frederick Bagshaw, O.B.E., Q.C., who handled much of the Prince Albert lawyer's agency work in Regina. Bagshaw delighted in talking of his old friend and their experiences together. It was a matter of regret to both that, when the opportunity came, Bagshaw's age and health precluded his appointment to the bench.

During this time I came to know other such contemporaries: former Saskatchewan attorney general Murdoch A. MacPherson, Q.C., who contested with Diefenbaker for the leadership of the Conservative Party in 1942; and Everett Clayton Leslie, LL.D., Q.C., whom Diefenbaker refused to appoint Chief Justice of Saskatchewan because of a perceived slight at a dinner of the Canadian Bar Association, of which Leslie was then president. ("Lofty" Leslie got the last word in their dispute. Among a group of lawyers in the barristers' lounge in the Regina court house when word came in of the death of the former prime minister, Leslie, in his stentorian voice, commented: "Ah! His body has finally gone to join his mind.")

All of these outstanding lawyers, and others, spoke somewhat disparagingly of Diefenbaker's legal talents, although they were universal in their praise for his effectiveness before a jury. Initially, I put this down to professional jealousy, but that was too shallow an explanation, and out of character for the critics.

During Diefenbaker's years as leader of the Conservative Party, I attended two of his political meetings, one at the beginning of his term and one at the end. Both remain vivid in my memory.

During the 1957 election campaign, I attended a rally at the Regina Armoury where Prime Minister St. Laurent announced that the building of a large hydro-electric and irrigation dam on the South Saskatchewan River was not "in the national interest." (The dam, later built, impounds a large body of water known as Lake Diefenbaker.) St. Laurent went on to tell us that, if we did not agree with his policies, we could turn the job over to someone else. "But I don't know where you will find them," he concluded.

A few evenings later in the armoury, it was obvious where the alternative was going to be found. Conservative organizers had provided what was then an innovative change from the standard and dreary political backdrop. The stage was in darkness, except for three spotlights — two on large Red Ensign flags flowing in the breeze provided by fans, and one, in the middle, upon the speaker, John George Diefenbaker.

The props might well have looked cheap with another platform speaker, but not with the orator of that night. The effect was all the organizers could have wished; the audience was enthralled as the powerful voice rolled over them. Diefenbaker looked and spoke like a messiah.

Eight years later, in the fall of 1965, John Diefenbaker waged his last campaign as leader of the Conservative Party. The office of the prime minister, won in 1957, had been lost in 1963.

I was working in the Liberal campaign in the constituency of Assiniboia. It had been the last riding in Saskatchewan to fall to the Diefenbaker Conservatives, and the Liberals were hoping it would be the first to come back. To prevent that from happening, John Diefenbaker journeyed down to the town of Assiniboia to address a major rally.

Like many at that time, I believed that the former prime minister was through, that he was old and tired, already defeated. But I did not miss the opportunity to attend his rally.

It was glorious, though disappointing to me. It was clear then that the Liberals would not win Assiniboia as I had thought they would. The hall was filled with people I had naively believed were supporting the Liberal candidate.

John Diefenbaker was old; he had turned seventy that fall. He was tired; it had been a tough campaign and Assiniboia was a two-hour drive from the Regina airport. But the man on the platform was not defeated — the word was not in his lexicon — and the age and weariness disappeared as he spoke.

This was not the John Diefenbaker of 1957 who had spoken of the future, the brave new Canada. The John Diefenbaker I listened to in 1965 excoriated the Liberal government of Prime Minister Lester B. Pearson. He was magnificent as he ridiculed the embarrassments of the Liberal Cabinet and castigated their ineptness. He weakened even *my* confidence in anything Liberal.

After Assiniboia, I came to know that what I had seen there was John Diefenbaker doing what he did best. Before countless Saskatchewan juries, this prairie lawyer had developed to a fine art his talent for destroying the case of the other side, usually the Crown in a criminal prosecution. Taking that talent to the House of Commons, he had, in opposition, been extremely effective; when the opportunity came, he easily knocked the St. Laurent government out of office. That same talent, however, did not serve him well in the prime minister's office.

When the idea of a book on the early career of John Diefenbaker was proposed, my interest in the opportunity to delve into a fascinating period of Saskatchewan history was tempered by two concerns. Legends are usually larger than life, and I remembered the critical opinion of Diefenbaker's legal contemporaries.

I was reluctant to undertake a factual account that might be seen as the debunking of a legal legend.

I knew, too, that there might be certain inconsistencies in John Diefenbaker's own account of his early years. In the election of 1965, he had taken reporters to his family homestead near Borden, not far from Saskatoon. While there, he spoke of his boyhood, and of hearing the Red River carts creaking along the nearby Carlton Trail. My Irish Liberal father was incensed! He had homesteaded astride the Carlton Trail near Dana, Saskatchewan, some years before the Diefenbakers arrived at Borden, had personally plowed up the rutted cart trail, and had not been inconvenienced by the passage of Red River carts, already history. I intercepted an angry "letter to the editor" putting forth those facts, insisting that it was not in anyone's interest to set the record straight at that time.

It might not be now. And since I cannot escape my own time of involvement with the Liberal Party, I fully expect that there will be allegations of bias, and that some bias might, in fact, exist, even if only subconsciously. It would be impossible to remain completely free of opinion concerning such a controversial figure as John Diefenbaker.

Yet the belief that I have some advantages which at least equalize these liabilities, and the non-partisan encouragement of many, has carried me forward. My son and I have striven to produce an objective and accurate account of a determined gladiator making his way through perilous times. We hope that we have achieved some success.

Garrett Wilson
Regina, Saskatchewan
June 1988

1

The Opening Shot

It was a rough bicycle path, a cow path really, wending across the hilly and rutted pasture of rural Saskatchewan, but it was as good as any Nickola Sabadash had ever seen. The farm youth pumped vigorously as he bounced along through the darkening evening of August 5, 1919. He had stayed too long at the Fred Samborski farm, had stretched the chance for fresh conversation until now he was late for chores. Nickola turned onto the shortcut over John Chernyski's land, a new and strange route recommended to him by Fred Samborski. He wondered how he would explain to his father why he had taken more than two hours just to return Samborski's spade.

"*Coukin sin!*" Nickola cried out in fright and alarm. Two swift and silent shapes leaped out of the gloom, attacked his bicycle and threw him to the ground. As he gathered his wits, Nickola saw that two dogs had stopped him, and now held him at bay, one to each side of him.

"*Coukin sin,*" the Galacian cursed again, more annoyed than frightened as he identified his assailants. Damn dogs, he thought, I'll deal with them as soon as I find a stick. He crawled into the clump of bush behind him and emerged with a four-foot branch. Nickola swung at the dogs and, as they retreated, he recovered possession of the ground where his bicycle lay. The youth spotted a stouter stick and stooped to pick it up. He did not hear behind him the shouted command, "Sic 'em."

The shotgun blast took Nickola full in the left face and shoulder as he turned. He had seen no one. He yelled.

John Chernyski was aghast. The double-barrelled shotgun dropped from his hands as he absorbed the reality that he had shot his neighbour's son.

Chernyski's daughter, Hanka, had run into the house with the news that their dogs had cornered a wolf. Chernyski, with his son Mike, grabbed the gun and shells and ran to the scene, just a few hundred feet west of the house. With only a glance, he fired at the object between the dogs, then realized his terrible mistake as it called out and struggled to human height.

Hanka and Mike brought water to Nickola. He was badly wounded with fifty to sixty lead pellets in his shoulder and head. They helped the bleeding boy to his parents' home on the next quarter-section. John Chernyski, who had just stabled his horses after returning from a trip to town, went for help. He walked the long three miles back to Cudworth, a small village fifty miles south of Prince Albert, Saskatchewan.

Dr. Harry Venzke, rousted out of his Cudworth office after eleven o'clock at night, owned one of the few automobiles in the district. He went out to the Sabadash farm, and then drove Nickola and John Chernyski north to Wakaw, forty miles south of Prince Albert. At Wakaw, he installed Nickola in the hospital and took John — at the latter's request — to the year-old detachment of the Saskatchewan Provincial Police. By then it was five-thirty in the morning, but the two got Detective Sergeant George Harreck out of his bed.

Harreck listened to Chernyski's story, took a written statement from him, and placed the unhappy farmer under arrest. The charge: that he, with intent, did unlawfully cause grievous bodily harm to Nickola Sabadash by shooting him with a shotgun, contrary to Section 273 of the Criminal Code.

The policeman's investigation started with Nickola in the hospital, so bandaged he could not see and could hardly speak. Later in the morning, Harreck went out to the scene of the shooting. He took with him Corporal William Sulaty, a twenty-nine-year-old Russian Pole who, because of his fluency in those two languages as well as English, had been specially recruited to the

Wakaw detachment. Accompanying the two policemen was an intense young lawyer who had opened his office in Wakaw just the month before. He introduced himself to Harreck that morning, stating that he had been retained to defend John Chernyski. The lawyer gave his name as John Diefenbaker. John Chernyski was his first client.

John Chernyski spent a month in Prince Albert Gaol awaiting his preliminary inquiry, and very nearly stayed longer. Bail was not customary in 1919, and Wakaw Justice of the Peace J.H. Lewis, who presided over the preliminary inquiry on September 5, refused to grant bail. When the evidence was all in at nine o'clock that evening, Lewis, the Grand Trunk Pacific station agent in Wakaw, committed Chernyski for trial. He denied John Diefenbaker's reasonable request that his client be permitted to return to his farm until the case was heard.

Diefenbaker got busy with an appeal of Lewis's refusal, but not until September 17 was he able to bring the appeal before Prince Albert District Court Judge Algernon Edwin Doak. Doak allowed Diefenbaker's appeal, and fixed bail at $2,500. Two of Chernyski's neighbours guaranteed the bail, and the immigrant homesteader went back to his farm to await his trial at the next jury sittings of the Court of King's Bench at Humboldt.

John Chernyski had never been to Humboldt, sixty-five miles to the south-east, and had not before needed to know that his farm lay within the Humboldt judicial district. Some fifteen years before, he had come from his homeland in the Ukraine to the Wakaw-Cudworth district of Saskatchewan via the immigration centre in Rosthern, thirty-five miles west. He had to return to Rosthern to prove compliance with his homesteading requirements and secure title to his 160 acres, but otherwise he had no occasion to stray any distance from his new home. Scratching a subsistence from the Saskatchewan soil consumed all his energy and interest. He had no funds or time for leisure travel.

Like most of his neighbours, Chernyski was unable to read or write in any language, and was still uncomfortable speaking

English. But the farmer had no difficulty comprehending that he was in serious trouble over the shooting of Nickola Sabadash. He and his family and friends prayed that the confident young lawyer with the German name was up to the challenge before him.

Even that young lawyer, with no experience at all to draw upon, had no trouble spotting the defence to the charge against his client. Clearly Chernyski, in the dusk of the late summer evening, thought he was shooting at a wolf (or a coyote), and had no intention, criminal or otherwise, of shooting Nickola Sabadash, or any other human. It would, of course, be essential to establish that the light was so poor that Chernyski easily could have mistaken man for wolf.

Some of that line of defence was foreclosed when Ernest Gardiner, Crown prosecutor at Humboldt, received the file and prepared the formal indictment for trial. The prosecutor altered somewhat the charge laid at Wakaw by Harreck, and instead chose the equivalent of the present-day charge of criminal negligence. Framing his indictment in the cumbersome language of the day, Gardiner charged that John Chernyski: "did unlawfully wound and inflict grievous bodily harm upon one Nickola Sabadash by means of a certain weapon, to wit, a gun, by unlawfully discharging the said gun, the said John Chernyski being then and there in charge of or having under his control the said gun then and there loaded and knowing the same to be loaded which said gun in the absence of precaution and care might endanger human life...contrary to Sections 247 and 274 of the Criminal Code."

That charge, more appropriate to the circumstances, meant that Chernyski might be convicted if the jury found that he had been negligent and uncaring about what he was shooting at. In today's terminology, the question would be whether John Diefenbaker's client had shown "a wanton or reckless disregard for the lives and safety of other persons."

The young defence lawyer who studied his first criminal indictment so seriously had an intense and serious look. Above a frame that was tall and slender, almost slight, was a head that was arresting in its appearance. A finely-sculpted mouth and nose went almost unnoticed as the observer's attention was drawn to the strange, commanding blue eyes, piercing and questioning, that made one somewhat uncomfortable. Full black hair, receding in striking waves, unfashionable for the time, accentuated the effect of the eyes beneath. Dressed severely and formally in dark suit and vest, the lawyer was an outstanding figure as he strode the streets of Wakaw.

Just twenty-four years old, John Diefenbaker was unusually solemn and full of business. At first meeting, some assumed this to be a role adopted by the lawyer to compensate for his youth. They quickly learned that this young man took himself, and life, very seriously indeed, and expected the same from others. He was sensitive, and unforgiving of any slight, real or perceived.

The fall jury sittings at Humboldt were scheduled for the second Tuesday of October. Chief Justice James Thomas Brown assigned himself as presiding judge, perhaps looking forward to the modern facilities provided by the three-year-old court house. Brown had been one of the six justices of Saskatchewan's Court of King's Bench since 1910, and Chief Justice for a year. A tall and impressive man, he was also gracious, one of the great gentlemen of the prairie judiciary who always had time for, and an interest in, the younger members of the bar. Also, he was a duck hunter. These last two characteristics would prove to be a boon for John Diefenbaker and his client.

When Chief Justice Brown called Rex v. John Chernyski for trial at 10:00 a.m. on October 23, 1919, he noticed an ungowned colleague at the counsel table with John Diefenbaker. Emmett Hall, a former classmate of Diefenbaker's who was serving his articles in Humboldt, was sitting in to assist with the selection of the jury. His knowledge of the local people was limited, but still useful to the defence counsel. Hall returned to his office after the jury was chosen.

Once the jury was selected, Ernest Gardiner put the medical and police evidence before the jury, setting the stage for the testimony of the participants.

After lunch, Nickola Sabadash took the stand. He changed his version of the shooting somewhat from his evidence at the preliminary inquiry at Wakaw. Then he had described the incident in such a way as almost to concede that it was merely an unfortunate accident. Before the jury, however, he contended that Chernyski's action must have been deliberate, and told of trouble between the families. His mother, Nickola claimed, had had difficulty with Chernyski over a cow.

Diefenbaker went after Nickola Sabadash in cross-examination. He had examined the youth thoroughly at the preliminary, and was not about to accept the new and different description of the shooting. The lawyer was somewhat hampered, as all counsel then were, by the inadequacy of the handwritten depositions from the justice of the peace, the only record of the testimony at the preliminary inquiry. In spite of this, Diefenbaker succeeded in making it plain to Mr. Justice Brown and the jury that Nickola had given two seriously different versions of the shooting, both under oath.

Fred Samborski followed Nickola Sabadash to the stand. He described Nickola's visit to his farm, and his late departure. Samborski had told Nickola of the shortcut over John Chernyski's land that would save him time returning home. It had been about nine o'clock that evening when Nickola left, Samborski recalled. He was sure the lamps had been lighted. Fred Samborski's two sons confirmed their father's testimony.

Mike Chernyski was Ernest Gardiner's last witness. "It was dark," he said, agreeing with the defence lawyer. "I couldn't see very good."

This was the sort of evidence John Diefenbaker wanted. In cross-examination he secured admissions from all the witnesses as to the extent of the darkness at the time of the shooting. Diefenbaker's emphasis on how completely dark it had been bothered the trial judge as the Crown closed its case at 5:00 p.m. He adjourned court until the next morning.

Spotting Emmett Hall at dinner that evening in Humboldt's Arlington Hotel, Chief Justice Brown invited him to join his table. The student was honoured to do so. Since Hall was not involved in the Chernyski case, the trial judge felt free to discuss the progress of the evidence. The business of the darkness at the time of the shooting was a concern, he told Hall.

"I'm very fond of duck hunting," the Chief Justice said, "particularly in the early morning — before dawn. But as dark as Diefenbaker is making it out to have been, I couldn't hit anything, couldn't see to shoot, really."

The Chief Justice went on to criticize Nickola Sabadash for altering his evidence from that given at the preliminary inquiry. On the whole, he thought, the defence seemed to have a good case.

"I don't know whether the Chief Justice intended me to tell Diefenbaker or not," Hall recalls, "but, of course, I did."

The next morning Emmett Hall returned to the courtroom just as the trial was resuming. Seizing the handiest piece of paper, which happened to be a copy of the indictment, he turned it over and on the back scribbled a note to John Diefenbaker: "We were sitting & talking with the judge & he, in commenting on the case, said that the only weakness displayed in your case so far was that you had too much stress upon the darkness. I would comment upon it, but don't paint it too black. He is somewhat suspicious of your evidence as to the darkness — He is very favourable — he doesn't believe that the injured man is telling the truth about his actions — follows Crown line of argument re his position on the ground.

"He is very suspicious of the injured man on account of the discrepancies between his testimony here & at Wakaw. Referring to darkness, the judge is quite impressed by the fact the light was lit inside & when accused rushed out the darkness would appear greater."

John Diefenbaker read Hall's note as he was introducing John Chernyski's daughter as his first defence witness. Immediately, the lighting conditions at the time of the shooting improved from dark to dusk. Now it became reasonable for Chernyski to have taken his shot, but still possible for him to have made an honest mistake. This would be particularly true as he left a lighted room, and made his decision before his eyes adjusted to the dimmer outside light.

The accused's wife, Sophia, followed her daughter to the witness stand, and John Chernyski himself completed the defence testimony. He told the jury, with obvious sincerity, how the failing light caused him to make such a tragic mistake.

Whether due to innate good trial sense or first-time nervousness, John Diefenbaker's first jury speech was very brief, as was Ernest Gardiner's for the Crown. Chief Justice Brown, also, was concise when delivering his charge, and at ten minutes to noon the jury retired to consider its verdict.

Courts in 1919 did not waste time waiting for juries. It was not unusual for a trial judge to have two, or even three, juries out at the same time. When the Chernyski jury left the courtroom, Chief Justice Brown immediately proceeded with the next case, a charge of bribery of a public official.

The Crown case in the bribery trial was almost complete when it was interrupted at 3:25 p.m. to receive the Chernyski jury on its return. The verdict: "Not Guilty." John Chernyski was discharged, and returned to his farm a free man.

That evening, in the Arlington dining room, Chief Justice Brown laughed in delight at the sudden "enlightenment" that had struck the Chernyski trial.

"He had the idea that it was a legitimate defence," Hall says today, chuckling in reminiscence.

And John Diefenbaker had won his first case. Many more victories would follow, but none perhaps was more important to the establishment of his career and reputation than Rex v. Chernyski, which gave him his start at Wakaw.

James Thomas Brown served as Chief Justice of Saskatchewan's Court of King's Bench until his retirement in 1956. He was succeeded in that office by the same Emmett Hall with whom he had dined in Humboldt's Arlington Hotel on October 23, 1919, and who had become one of Saskatchewan's leading counsel. Hall went on to become Chief Justice of Saskatchewan, and then a member of the Supreme Court of Canada. All three of Hall's appointments were made under the direction of John Chernyski's former defence counsel, The Right Honourable John George Diefenbaker, Prime Minister of Canada.

But all that was in the future on that late October evening, as a happy country lawyer, just a month past his twenty-fourth birthday, made his way home to Wakaw, Saskatchewan.

2

Go West Young Man

One of the remarkable features of the settlement of the Canadian West was its success in spite of the complete unsuitability of so many of the would-be pioneers. Attracted by the romance and adventure as much as by the tales of sudden wealth and the prospect of free homestead land, thousands of gentle misfits ventured onto the western prairies. Although most homesteaders did not possess the $600 regarded as minimum for establishment upon the land, they had a chance at success if they had practical experience in wresting crops from the soil. A settler with neither capital nor experience was doomed, along with his family, to failure and privation.

But, as if by compensation of nature, even failure often had its reward. The years of struggle and pain instilled in some a determination to excel that manifested itself in achievements of a different kind. Whether homesteaders were defeated initially, or later by drought and depression, their sons and daughters frequently attained success that eclipsed the parents' original dream.

William Diefenbaker was one of the many who was destined to be vanquished by the harshness of the prairie frontier. He was a mild, gentle and bookish man, and his Ontario upbringing as the son of a Waterloo County carriage-maker did not equip him for the role of a homesteader. Neither had his several years of teaching school in the Bruce Peninsula where he had met and married Mary Florence Bannerman.

The Diefenbakers were Germans who had come to Canada in 1816 following a sojourn of a few years in Holland. Mary Bannerman's forebears were Scottish tenant farmers who had come to Canada at about the same time to join the Red River Colony. They retreated from the early Manitoba settlement after three years and finally put down roots at Port Elgin, Ontario.

William Diefenbaker was teaching in Neustadt, Ontario, when his two sons were born, both in a tiny, yellow brick house still standing on a back street of the southwestern Ontario village. John George arrived on September 18, 1895, and Elmer Clive two years later. The family moved twice in the next three years, to Greenwood (near Whitby) and, in 1900, to Todmorden, not far from Toronto.

The blandishments of Prime Minister Wilfrid Laurier and his interior minister, Clifford Sifton, who were engaged in populating the Canadian West, were not lost on eastern Canada. Although the government's advertising and recruitment of settlers was aimed mainly outside of Canada, at Europe and the United States, there was a heavy westward migration from Ontario and a lesser one from Quebec.

In the summer of 1903 William and Mary Diefenbaker succumbed to the lure of the frontier and, with their two young sons, joined the colonists heading into the North-West Territories. The thirty-five-year-old William secured a teaching position at Fort Carlton, near the North Saskatchewan River, roughly between Saskatoon and Prince Albert. Carlton had already achieved historic status, having figured prominently in the Riel Rebellion of 1885. It lay on the route of the West's most famous cart trail which had stretched almost twelve hundred miles from Winnipeg to Edmonton — the Carlton Trail.

William Diefenbaker was determined to be a homesteader and saw teaching as a means to that end. The year after his arrival he secured a better school at Hague, twenty-five miles south of Carlton, but by the end of 1904 had filed upon his 160 acres near Borden, on the north side of the North Saskatchewan River between Saskatoon and North Battleford. He continued teaching for two more years during which time he contracted to have thirty acres of his virgin land broken and built a small 332-square-foot frame shack into which the family moved late in 1906.

Failure came quickly. The Diefenbakers stayed on their land only three years. William supplemented his meagre farm income by teaching at a nearby school, but was never able to extend his cultivated acres beyond thirty or add more improvements. As soon as they qualified for title to their homestead at the end of 1909, the family moved to Saskatoon. That city was in the midst of a tremendous boom, particularly in real estate, but William Diefenbaker was through with risk-taking. Forsaking both farming and teaching, he secured a position in the provincial land titles office, transferring the next year to the federal civil service. William worked as a gauger in the Customs and Excise office until his retirement in 1938. His ability to acquire government employment so readily must indicate well-established credits with the Liberal Party, given the politics of the day.

The Diefenbakers' western dream had been demolished in six years. The erect and formal Mary, the more determined and tough-minded of the two, now transferred her ambition to her sons, particularly the eldest, John, who was already showing promise. In fact, it was the Diefenbaker boys and their need for better schooling than was available on the homestead that had precipitated the abandonment of the farm. They had been attending a one-room country school taught by their uncle, Edward Diefenbaker, quite a competent teacher, but their mother demanded more.

John Diefenbaker, eight years old when the family moved west, spent six precious boyhood years in the loneliness of the western countryside. Organized sports were then unknown for children and rare for adults. Social events were infrequent, occurring only when neighbours undertook the travel required to get together for dances and meetings.

The Diefenbaker family was close, but a growing boy could not escape the solitude, the ever present and sometimes oppressive loneliness of the open country. To make matters worse, neither of the Diefenbaker boys had a taste for the available and accepted activities of the West, such as hunting the gophers that infested the fields and pastures. John escaped into the books his father had brought west, most with an historical bent. The adventure novels of G.A. Henty, Ridpath's *History of the World*, Macaulay and Shakespeare were all available and gave the boy an insight into the achievements of the past and a rich vocabulary that remained with him all his life.

When they moved to Saskatoon, both Diefenbaker boys promptly took out newsboy licenses and learned something of huckstering on the streets of the western boomtown. John was accepted by Saskatoon Collegiate (later Nutana), graduating in the spring of 1912. Never robust, John's involvement with high school sports came no closer than helping manage the basketball team. He did compete in the school oratorical contest, and worked hard to win, but fell short.

An opening in a Saskatoon bank was offered to John by a friend of his father's, who thought it a great opportunity. John, too, was excited at the prospect, but Mary Diefenbaker squelched the proposal. John, his mother insisted, would not stop his education short of university. One of the reasons they had chosen to move to Saskatoon, she pointed out, was the new University of Saskatchewan under construction east of the city. William Diefenbaker acquiesced.

In September 1912, John Diefenbaker enrolled in the fourth freshman class of the young university. Able to attend his university classes while still living with his parents, John's first experience away from home did not come until his eighteenth summer.

In February 1914, the trustees of Wheat Heart School District, near Borden and not far from the Diefenbaker homestead, scraped together a minimum budget and advertised for a schoolteacher. They offered a salary in the pay range $65 to $70 a month. An application came in from John G. Diefenbaker, prepared to serve for $63 per month. Diefenbaker, just completing his second year of arts at the university, had no experience and no teaching certificate. The trustees applied to the Department of Education, secured a provisional certificate for Diefenbaker, and signed a contract with him, agreeing to pay "at the rate of $63.00 a month, from and after the 1st day of May, 1914....This agreement shall continue in force for seven months." The school would close for the winter on the first of December.

School opened in May and ran satisfactorily until September 9, when the school board was surprised to receive notice of their teacher's resignation, effective October 9. Diefenbaker proposed that his uncle, Edward Diefenbaker, who was qualified, complete his contract term as substitute. The board agreed on condition that the new teacher sign a fresh contract.

Of more surprise to the board, however, was the demand from John Diefenbaker to be paid for his five months of teaching at the rate of $75.60 per month, and referring the board to Section 155 of the School Act. In consternation, the board sought advice from the department. They learned that Section 155 provided that a teaching contract that lasted more than four months was to be treated on an annual basis. Since a school year was 210 days, they might be liable to pay John Diefenbaker at the rate of $756 per year, or $3.60 per teaching day, instead of the $3.00 they had contracted for. Twenty-one teaching days a month at $3.60 per day produced the $75.60 Diefenbaker was demanding.

On October 2, a week before the effective date of his resignation, John Diefenbaker advised the Wheat Heart School Board that he was leaving that very day, that he was placing Ed Diefenbaker in charge, and that the new teacher would sign a contract with the board the following week. The board accepted this situation, although Ed Diefenbaker never got around to signing a new contract.

When Ed Diefenbaker took over the school, he requested that the board continue to pay the $63 salary for the months of October and November directly to John. To their later sorrow, the board did so. Because of favourable weather the school continued to operate until the end of December, but then it closed for the winter.

In January the board received a new demand from John Diefenbaker, now back in university. This time the request was for the additional sixty cents per day for the period of 106 days he had taught, plus the same for the period of 40 days taught by his substitute during October and November. He wanted a total of $84.60.

Now the board felt they knew why Ed Diefenbaker had refused to sign a new contract. They complained to the deputy minister of education that "this was a trick to render the board liable to have to pay the additional salary due to the first teacher...for practically two months after his resignation had expired." Diefenbaker also wrote the Department of Education. His explanation was: "The board had me for these two months and I had my substitute."

The trustees stood their ground. They had a contract at $63 per month and "intended to pay the sum stated, no more, no less. Had they expected to pay him any higher salary than that stated, the Trustees would not have accepted Mr. Diefenbaker's application." Besides, they said, "there is not sufficient funds in hand to meet the claim, even if the Trustees admitted liability."

The Department of Education bowed out of the dispute. "The case appears to be rather complicated and one on which the Department does not care to give any definite decision. It may be necessary for you to obtain the ruling of the courts in this particular case," the deputy minister advised John Diefenbaker. The one-time teacher, about-to-be-lawyer, threatened to do so, and as late as May 1915 was still pressing his claim, but then he gave up the case and went on to other things.

John Diefenbaker decided early upon a legal career. In his second year of university he combined with his arts program two law classes, jurisprudence and contracts (the latter possibly of assistance in his dispute with the Wheat Heart school board). In 1914 he was admitted to the university's law program and he took a further law class. He also received credit in the law college for some of his political science classes.

During his last undergraduate year of 1914-15, Diefenbaker joined the arts college debating club, which conducted all of its sessions in the form of a non-partisan mock parliament. He participated as leader of the opposition, representing an untitled party. On May 6, 1915, John Diefenbaker was awarded his Bachelor of Arts degree.

The April issue of the student newspaper, *The Sheaf*, carried a humorous article by one of Diefenbaker's fellow graduates. Musing psychedelically (he claimed to have gone into a trance after smoking something) about the whereabouts of his classmates ten years in the future, he saw some of them in outrageous vocations. One of his kaleidoscopic views was of the House of Commons where the minister of defence was "explaining the necessity of raising another $100,000,000 for defence purposes. Near him, the Premier, Sir A.L. Robinson, was smiling across at J.G. Diefenbaker, the leader of the Opposition, who was restraining himself with difficulty in the face of such expenditure."

Diefenbaker intended to return to university in the fall to take a Masters degree in arts, but gave up teaching as summer employment. Instead he elected to become a travelling salesman for the John A. Hertel Company of Chicago, publishers of biblical literature with such titles as *The Chosen Word* and *Catholic Bible Symbols*. Hertel recruited many of its salesmen from universities across Canada and the American Midwest.

The nineteen-year-old Diefenbaker joined forces with fellow arts graduate Stanley Mighton, later a successful lawyer in North Battleford. After a short "field training," the two drummers sallied forth into their territory. Their first destination was Watrous, then a town of about eight hundred, some seventy miles southeast of Saskatoon.

From Watrous, Diefenbaker moved south into the area that, in years to come, he represented in Parliament, then east as far as

Yorkton. He occasionally slept in barns, straw stacks, or rinks closed for the summer, and was often cold and wet.

According to "Field Echoes and Pointers to Success," a weekly bulletin published by Hertel "for the benefit and encouragement of its representatives," Diefenbaker and Mighton did rather well. Both quickly achieved the rank of "Top Notcher," the highest classification in the Hertel incentive system, with Diefenbaker in first place and Mighton in fourth. Their sales for the ten day reporting period were $327.15 and $273.65 respectively.

By the end of July, Hertel was referring to Diefenbaker and Mighton as "our Western Giants," and the two had won suitcases for their sales totals. Diefenbaker, according to Hertel, on one day in June "made the most remarkable record ever made by anyone selling *Chosen Word*. He took 9 orders out of 9 calls, 5 in the best binding. His sales for the day were nearly $60.00, his profits nearly $24.00." Diefenbaker attributed his success to the motto: "Stop bawling. Get right in and do some mauling."

The sales pitch Diefenbaker employed has been preserved. Presumably developed under the direction of Hertel instructors, but written by the hand of the door-to-door Bible salesman, it is a cunning appeal to the better instincts of the mothers who answered his knock.

"Good morning, Mrs. Jones. You have some boys and girls in your home, haven't you? I am working in the interest of Sunday School and Home Bible study among the children just the age of yours. I'll just step in and show you what I'm doing.

"(a)(Start talking of a subject of common interest to both in order to allay suspicion.)

"(b) As I said at the door, I am working in the interests of a scheme which has as its purpose the increasing of people's interest in bible study, more particularly in Home Bible study.

"Now, Mrs. Jones, do you think there is as much real, earnest and persevering study now as there was some fifteen or twenty years ago? (No.) You have heard of Marian Lawrence, the General Secretary of Sunday School Association, and Dr.

Hamill, the President of the Association? Both these men have asked themselves, 'What is the reason for the decrease in the desire of children to read the bible, and in what are children really interested?'...The idea occurred to these men that, if the bible were presented in some pictorial way, interest would arouse the children and they would commence to read the bible...I have a few sample pages.

"(Move chair over with apology. Right angle to lady. On opening book say,) Nothing more nor less, Mrs. Jones, than a picture puzzle...I know you'll be enthusiastic over it. (Hesitate before reading. Read page running along word line and hesitate before pictures.)" As Diefenbaker began to close his sale, he swung into another part of his prepared script, "Last Part of Talk — Decision." He anticipated problems with price.

"The astonishing fact is the cheapness of the volume. Some people think it would cost some $12.00 or $15.00, but it comes at the reasonable price of $4.90. I came into town two days ago and called on your minister and here is his recommendation, but the thing which I prefer is the names of the mothers who have endorsed the work."

If resistance to the price was strong, Diefenbaker was ready.

"(Any objection — must first let her be surprised by your reception of it. Be glad she is so particular with money.)

"You know your financial affairs better than I do. Isn't it true that, the smaller amount one has to spend, the better judgement we must use in spending it? The question really resolves itself into whether an article is a luxury or a necessity.

"Now, Mrs. Jones, do *you* consider the religious training of your children — training given them on the approved methods laid down in a work of this kind — to be a necessity or a luxury? Now I am convinced that you regard this training even of greater necessity than the training received in the public schools.

"Just at this moment, I am reminded of a home on which I called some days ago. The mother had two little girls the age of yours. I showed her the work just as I showed you. She told me that she had a place for all her money, and no money left for herself or anything else. And she said to me,

"'Mr. Diefenbaker, when I put my money in a work like this I am not spending it — I am investing it. How could I better invest my money than in the lives of my children? Long after they have grown up I can see the result of that investment in their lives. The interest on the investment, as it were, will come back years after they have left my home.'

"And so, Mrs. Jones, as the lady of whom I spoke did, surely you'll do, by investing this small sum in the lives of your children, and so if you will just put your name under Mrs. — , I will bring a copy when I come."

The season concluded with John Diefenbaker in fifth place overall in the Hertel organization and Mighton in fifteenth, with weekly sales averages of $223.60 and $172.80.

Successful though the two had been, the Hertel salesmen received their commissions only after the orders sold had been filled and paid for. Thus the charming story originated that Mighton, a pool shark disguised as a Bible salesman, on more than one occasion had to augment their living expenses by out-hustling the locals in their own pool hall. Diefenbaker enjoyed a game of pool but had not the skill for serious play. Mighton did.

When John Diefenbaker returned to the campus in the fall of 1915 after his stint with Hertel, the First World War had been underway a year. Almost as soon as the conflict began, the university, in a burst of patriotism, agreed to give credit for a full year's work to every undergraduate in arts, agriculture and law who went to the front. The exemption applied not only to attendance, but, strangely, also to examinations. Diefenbaker was to make good use of this exemption, together with a similar one granted by the Law Society of Saskatchewan.

During his Master's year, Diefenbaker enrolled in the army and underwent initial training along with his classes. In the spring, following his graduation with an M.A. in political science and economics, he attended the Infantry School of Instruction at

Winnipeg. On May 27, 1916, he was commissioned as a provisional lieutenant and attached to the 105th Fusiliers at Saskatoon.

The fledgling officer then took his first steps towards securing qualification as a lawyer. On June 12, 1916, John Diefenbaker (together with his father because John was not yet twenty-one) entered into Articles of Clerkship with Russell Hartney, a Saskatoon lawyer. Hartney, an Englishman, practised alone, usually without even a secretary. His habit of bicycling to work long before that was accepted transportation for a professional man was one of his several eccentricities.

Under the Law Society rules, the articled student would be required to remain in his principal's office for three years, minus such time as he might spend in law school, but with one full year of service after graduation. The Law Society, no less patriotic than the university, had decreed that active military service would count as time served under articles.

The new student's legal studies were soon interrupted. The carnage in Europe was decimating the British Army's officer ranks and a call came from England for three hundred junior officers to reinforce British regiments. On August 21, John Diefenbaker answered the call and applied for overseas service. He was accepted the next day. Within a week, although after a furious debate with his father, who strongly disapproved, Lieutenant Diefenbaker was on his way back to Manitoba, this time to Camp Hughes (present-day Shilo).

The young volunteer, not yet twenty-one, began a "war diary" as he embarked upon the great adventure. His entries are frequently poignant and occasionally display self-pity.

September 5. Felt quite lonesome.
September 7. First morning ever spent in camp. Most lonesome ever have been.
September 14. Very cold in tent at night.
September 16. Dull till 11 a.m. Orders from Major Young to go overseas at midnight. Embarked on journey at 12:30 a.m.

September 18. (Aboard train to the east) Twenty-one years of age today and away from home as usual.

Diefenbaker was accompanied by two other Saskatoon law students, Hugh Aird and Allan McMillan. On September 23 they embarked on S.S. *Lapland*, which landed them in Liverpool, England, on October 6. First posted to Shorncliffe, near Dover, they were soon assigned to the Military Training School at Crowborough, near Sussex.

There began one of the more mysterious episodes in John Diefenbaker's career. Four months later he was back in Canada, having been found "permanently unfit for service" by a military medical tribunal. In his later years Diefenbaker described having been seriously injured by a trenching tool accidentally dropped upon him when he was in a training trench. The spade-like implement, he said, caught him on the spine, causing a haemorrhage at his mouth and throwing his heart out of alignment. This version is inconsistent with the fairly complete evidence available.

The young soldier's diary for the period of his stay in England portrays the comfortable life of the officer class during the First World War. Lectures, light drill and training occupied most of the weekdays and weekends were available for sightseeing, dining and the theatre. Diefenbaker took full advantage of his opportunities, touring London and Glasgow and enjoying the culture of the "old country." On November 14, five weeks after arriving in England, his diary tells us that Diefenbaker underwent a medical examination, passing "with weak heart and defective eyesight." He was exempted from drill and two days later sent to hospital in Brighton to have his eyes tested. He spent Friday night in the hospital and was then released, devoting the rest of the weekend to sightseeing in Brighton and Hastings. Monday was back to drill as usual.

The following Sunday, however, he was paraded before a medical board and pronounced "unfit for further service." The diary tells us nothing about an accident and, in fact, until December 18 makes no mention of any symptoms that might have justified such a serious medical finding.

For two weeks following his disqualification Diefenbaker became almost a complete tourist, visiting Tunbridge Wells, back to London where he dropped in on the House of Commons, and then to Lewes. Finally, his commanding officer ordered that all men "unfit for service must report to every parade and then be dismissed."

Diefenbaker continued "lounging about," as he described it, waiting to be sent off to hospital in Brighton or Hastings. On Sunday, December 17, he spent the afternoon "taking an extended walk." The following day his diary entry reads: "Spent very sick day. Spat blood on and off and at night became very feverish." He stayed in bed Tuesday but was back to normal on Wednesday, noting cryptically that "the usual uniqueness pervades the atmosphere."

By Friday, apparently completely recovered, Diefenbaker was touring again. He went off to Seaford, back to London, over to Liverpool and then back to London for Christmas, not returning to camp until Saturday, December 30 for another medical examination. On New Year's Day he entered hospital where he appears to have spent most of January "being allowed out in afternoons and spend time at picture shows, etc."

On February 7, the November medical finding was finally confirmed. Lieutenant John G. Diefenbaker received the following order from the Director of Personnel Services, Canadian Expeditionary Services: "You are being returned to Canada, having been found permanently unfit for service." He was ordered to board S.S. *Grampian* sailing from Liverpool on February 13. He did, after another visit to London, and was back in Canada at the end of the month, his military career at an end.

The army's actual medical diagnosis will remain sealed among John Diefenbaker's personal military files until 1999, twenty years after his death. What seems clear on the basis of the facts exposed so far is that there was no accident, nor any external symptoms sufficient to support the disqualification without considerable description from Diefenbaker himself, particularly in view of the limited diagnostic tools then available. He was not so seriously invalided as to interfere with his travels about England and, whatever the problem, it seems to have disappeared as soon as he returned to Canada.

It appears, however, that the young officer might have been suffering from chest pains and discomfort, a condition that recurred occasionally in later years and defied diagnosis until finally identified as gastric ulcer, for which he underwent surgery in 1923.

When he graduated from law school two years after his return, the Saskatoon *Star* and *The Sheaf* both explained that Lieutenant Diefenbaker had been returned from overseas "on account of illness contracted in active service."

Back in Canada, and before going on to Saskatoon, Diefenbaker stopped a while in Toronto. As if he had reconsidered his position, he immediately set about trying to secure a posting that would take him back overseas. From Toronto, in March 1917, he applied to the officer commanding the Saskatchewan military district. Stuck with his medical file, he was unable to secure acceptance by any unit, including the Royal Flying Corps.

Diefenbaker returned to Saskatoon and dropped from sight until the spring of 1918. Continuing his attempt to get back into active military service, he tried a new tack and consulted a practising physician who gave him a note for the army: "This will introduce to you Lieut. Diefenbaker, invalided from France [*sic*]. Claims now to be O.K. and I think is. Wishes to go back at once. Does not like sticking out here. Can you do anything for him?"

Finally admitting defeat, Diefenbaker applied for a military pension. He failed again. In early April 1918, he was advised by the Board of Pension Commissioners: "This Commission has given full and careful consideration to the proceedings of the Medical Board which examined you prior to your retirement, and to the other documents and information on your file. Owing to the fact that you are suffering from no disability which was due to or was incurred during your military service it has been decided that you are not entitled to pension."

And that was it. John Diefenbaker, having come so close, missed the war and did not even get the recognition of a disability pension. He turned back to his legal training.

On April 6, 1918, the law student resumed his duties in the office of Russell Hartney. Perhaps perceiving that he could do better, in June he secured a position with Ferguson and MacDermid, a highly respected Saskatoon firm. Unfortunately, he lasted only three months. He was released, a shattering experience for an articling student.

Years later, Frederick MacDermid explained what happened: "We didn't get along too well. Any student I had, I wanted him in the office looking after business but he was always running around, into politics. So, we soon parted ways."

The dispossessed Diefenbaker was fortunate to land another position, with Lynd and Yule, another fine office, but one which did not pay much attention to its students.

In September 1918, John Diefenbaker re-enrolled in the College of Law and set about to take full advantage of the exemptions available to him because of his military service. The law classes he had taken during his undergraduate arts program gave him credit for nearly one of the three years of the law course. The university gave him another year for his time overseas so he had one to go and he buckled down.

The raging influenza epidemic of 1918 caused the authorities to delay opening university until nearly Christmas. This was a hardship to Diefenbaker, who was making up nine classes for his degree, but he applied himself and was successful in all his examinations, achieving three "A"s. One "A," prophetically, was in criminal law.

In May 1919, John Diefenbaker was awarded his Bachelor of Law degree which, together with his B.A. and M.A., made him the first graduate to receive three degrees from the University of Saskatchewan.

Shortly after Diefenbaker's graduation, in the summer of 1919, a long-simmering dispute among the faculty of the ten-year-old University of Saskatchewan boiled over. President W.C. Murray, supported by the Board of Governors, dismissed four professors. Since this was fifteen per cent of the total faculty, and three of those dismissed were department heads, the action was extremely drastic and created a sensation throughout the province. Protests and demands for an investigation came from all over Saskatchewan.

A group of graduates called a meeting of the university convocation, which consisted of the chancellor, the senate, and all graduates in the province. The meeting, on November 20, furiously debated a resolution calling for a Royal Commission to inquire into the dismissals. Royal Commissions were not then the panacea for troublesome issues they have since become, and the request itself was evidence of the depth of the public concern.

Diefenbaker involved himself in the debate before convocation on the side of the professors. The issue, brewing at the university since 1913, revolved around the rumour that President Murray had been guilty of misconduct. The young law graduate was apparently impressed with the gossip as he made an impassioned speech to convocation.

"We are at the parting of the ways," he said. "Unless a Royal Commission is appointed and the whole matter exposed to the light of day, the future of the university will be nil."

He had a diploma from the university, he went on, "but unless this fatal blemish on the university is wiped away that diploma will be but a scrap of paper."

"I know a few things that I can tell and will tell at the proper time," he concluded darkly.

They were strong words, and, as a later judicial inquiry determined, stronger than the evidence could support. President Murray was fully vindicated and the professors shown to be foolish and mistaken. But it was John Diefenbaker's first participation in a great public drama, and he did not make the mistake of allowing himself to go unnoticed.

All that, however, was in the future. In the summer of 1919 Diefenbaker's most pressing concern was to clear the bar examination of the Law Society and satisfy its requirements for three years under articles.

The previous fall, Diefenbaker had convinced the benchers of the Law Society that he had been convalescing for a year after his return from overseas and had provided some medical evidence to that effect. It is not known how he squared that with his determined effort to assure the military that he was fit for active duty. In any event, he filed with the Society his sworn affidavit stating: "I enlisted for overseas service on the 25th of August, 1916, and was discharged after service and convalescence on the 1st day of April, 1918."

The benchers accepted the law student's evidence and granted him two years exemption for military service. This meant that he was waived through his first and second intermediate bar exams, allowed to write his final bar in May 1919 following graduation, and relieved of the requirement to spend any more time under articles.

In May 1919, John Diefenbaker wrote his bar examination, achieving an average of 67.3 per cent which gave him a respectable ranking in the order of merit of seventh out of thirty-nine candidates. On June 30, 1919, he was enrolled as a barrister and solicitor, signing the official Roll of the Law Society as the 698th member since its commencement in 1886 as part of the North-West Territories. Now all he needed was a place to hang up his shingle. But, very much the young man in a hurry, he had already made all the arrangements while awaiting formal acceptance by the Law Society.

The very next week, the office of John G. Diefenbaker, M.A., Ll.B., in Wakaw, Saskatchewan, was open for business.

3

The Wakaw Years

A broad belt of parkland sweeps northwest across Saskatchewan, dividing the treeless prairie of the south from the spruce and poplar forest of the north. It is, to many eyes, the most beautiful sector of the province. A rolling contour, a good population of small lakes and streams, all interspersed with clumps of woodland, provide pleasant relief from the sameness of the province's north and south.

It was these woodlands that, in the early years of the 1900s, drew the wave of immigrants arriving from eastern Europe, attracted to the free homesteads in the Canadian West advertised by Sifton and Laurier. "Stalwart peasants in sheepskin coats," according to Sifton's specifications, they came from what is now Poland and the Ukraine but was then called Ruthenia and Galacia and Bukovina, from Hungary and from Germany. Taught by their tradition the value of wood, they ignored the more fertile, but treeless, plains to the south and settled into the parkland region. The smoke of thousands of primitive hearths began to fill the empty western sky. An agricultural empire was rising.

Forty miles south of Prince Albert lies one of the most attractive of the parkland lakes, Wakaw Lake. More than ten miles in length, it serves as the headwater of the Carrot River. Two miles south of the west end of the lake the Carlton Trail intersected with the Prince Albert trail winding north from Qu'Appelle. Only thirty-five miles east of the clearing house which the Canadian immigration service established in Rosthern, the woods and lands around Wakaw Lake attracted the earliest of the land-seekers.

The years 1901 to 1903 brought the first and largest influx of settlers to the Wakaw area, mostly Galacians and Hungarians with some Germans and French. As more land was freed up by release from reserved tracts, homesteading continued at a lesser pace for twenty more years.

To service the settlers, a fledgling town arose on the attractive shores of Wakaw Lake. Sadly, the Grand Trunk Pacific Railroad, when it built a branch line from the south in 1911, fixed the townsite a mile west of the lake, and the chance for a beautiful lakeside community was lost. That decision may have been due to the fact that the new location was owned by the Western Townsite Co. Ltd., a company formed by Liberal Senator Thomas Osborne Davis of Prince Albert. The Village of Wakaw was incorporated at the new site on December 26, 1911.

Builders quickly discovered two deficiencies in the new town: a supply of suitable drinking water could not be found, but water could not be kept out of their excavations. Senator Davis himself, when building a hotel for the community, had difficulty pumping the water quickly enough to pour his foundations. For many years the Davis name was damned in Wakaw.

Only one of a string of communities along the new branch line, Wakaw soon dominated its neighbours. A mission hospital and school, which had been established on Wakaw Lake in 1903, helped to give the community an advantage, as did a flour mill. By 1914 Wakaw was styling itself a "boom town" and, although that claim was far from unique in the new West, enough entrepreneurs believed it to help make it true. Forty business outlets located in Wakaw during its first two years of existence.

The early village councillors displayed confidence and courage. In 1914 they constructed a large two-storey town hall and an $8,000 two-room brick school, the latter over the objections of the Western Townsite Company. Pointing out that it "is the owner of practically the whole of the Townsite of Wakaw and pays easily three-quarters of the taxes," the developer insisted that a $3,000 building would be "amply sufficient." The facilities of the new town hall were later chosen as one of the judicial stops on the circuit of the District Court of Prince Albert.

In 1919, the newly graduated John Diefenbaker, seeking a community in which to launch his legal career, appraised the polyglot village of Wakaw and found much to commend it. Fulfilling much of its early boast, it was a bustling, busy mix of industrious peoples still confident of the future. The early settlers had been on their farms long enough to become established, their first years of privation and pain behind them, and were coming into a period of relative prosperity. Agriculture in Saskatchewan was enjoying the fruits of high production and prices, not a little due to the First World War, then just over. The war, said Provincial Treasurer Charles Dunning, "had been the economic salvation of Saskatchewan." The province and its people "were more prosperous now than ever before." This was particularly true in the Wakaw district.

Wakaw had some special advantages for a young lawyer. At the southern reach of the Judicial District of Prince Albert, which then extended to the Manitoba border on the east and Rosthern on the west, it was one of the seven centres outside Prince Albert itself where the District Court sat, twice a year. Good rail service had covered the forty miles to the court house in Prince Albert since the extension of the Grand Trunk Pacific in 1917. The Royal North-West Mounted Police had, in its day, maintained a detachment at Wakaw, and the Saskatchewan Provincial Police, formed in 1917, had re-established a police unit and cells in the village. That meant a certain centralization of activity in the criminal justice system, and police court practice was essential to a beginning barrister.

The population of Wakaw in 1919 was just over 350, but that was only a small portion of the number of potential clients in the village's service area. Sifton's sheepskin-clad peasants had left a land where they had eked out an existence from plots no larger than half a dozen or a dozen acres. To these homesteaders, 160 acres of virgin land was a boundless estate. They had no need for more and, with their large families, they filled the countryside to a density that seems impossible when one looks at the land today.

The 1921 census-takers found that, on average, nearly ten persons resided on each square mile throughout most of the parkland settlements. The western system of survey laid out the land in townships six miles square, creating in each thirty-six sections, one mile square. Some of these rural townships in the Wakaw district contained more residents than the town itself. Most held at least 250 to 300, adding up to a population of several thousand within the trading radius of roughly twenty miles. There would be clients enough, even though their need for legal services was minimal.

Another of Wakaw's features — its large population of German origin — was of particular interest to John Diefenbaker in 1919. He was sensitive about his German name and remained so for years. During his time in the army, Diefenbaker took the precaution of preparing and carrying a letter signed by several law professors and lawyers certifying him to be "a Canadian by birth." The war had made anti-German sentiment patriotic. Berlin, Ontario, where Diefenbaker's father attended school, changed its name to Kitchener in deference to that feeling, and attempts were made to de-Germanize even Humboldt, Saskatchewan, by removing the "d." In later years, when he became more concerned about his political career, Diefenbaker was convinced that his name would limit his success. On several occasions he attempted to adopt Dutch ancestry to disguise his German roots. But in Wakaw, with so many of its settlers from Germany and its Austrian-Hungarian ally, John Diefenbaker would meet as little anti-German prejudice as could be found anywhere in Saskatchewan.

Another consideration that attracted John Diefenbaker to Wakaw was its proximity to Saskatoon, where his parents lived. The lawyer was unusually close to and influenced by Mary Diefenbaker and remained so throughout her life. Approximately sixty miles distant, Saskatoon was close enough for weekend visits, given the transportation of the day, and later, with improved travel, visits could, and did, occur at almost any time.

And, finally, in the midst of the foreign cultures clustered in and around Wakaw was a church of John Diefenbaker's denomination. The onion dome of the Ukrainian church graced the village, but a mile east was a small Baptist church on the shore of Wakaw Lake which served for baptisms. More than fifty years later the church was to supply some of the obsolete lumber required to build a replica of the John Diefenbaker law office in Wakaw.

Wakaw was much in the news in June 1919 as John Diefenbaker was choosing a town in which to hang out his new shingle. It was just the sort of news to attract the attention of an aspiring criminal lawyer. For two weeks the public followed the evidence as it unfolded in the Prince Albert trial of one Mike Syroshka, charged in connection with a multiple murder that had taken place at Wakaw in April 1916. Five members of the Prokop Manchur family and their hired man had been shot, and their farm burned.

The shooting had been done with the hired man's rifle, and the coroner's jury had concluded that he had done the killing and then committed suicide. But when Detective Sergeant Harreck and Constable W. J. Sulaty of the provincial police detachment at Wakaw took the case over in 1917, they became convinced that Syroshka, an estranged son-in-law of the Manchurs, was the murderer and arsonist. While they could not prove the murder, they were sure they had the evidence to establish the arson.

So Syroshka, defended by Saskatoon's brilliant Hal Ebbels, was in effect on trial for murder, although actually charged with two counts of arson. The jury convicted him and added the interesting recommendation that, after his sentence expired, Syroshka be deported to his native Austria. The trial judge assessed a penalty of six years on each count and agreed with the jury's suggestion.

Syroshka's trial concluded on July 1. When the successful Harreck and Sulaty returned to Wakaw, they found that a new lawyer had taken up residence during their absence. They met him just a month later on the Chernyski case.

When John Diefenbaker arrived in Wakaw in the summer of 1919, he was not the first lawyer to try his luck there. He was the fourth, and the third was still in town.

In 1914 the Board of Trade had placed an impressive advertisement in the Wakaw *Recorder*: "Wakaw, Sask., 2 1/2 years old, population 400. Wanted: Brick plant, flour mill, boat-builder, bakery, lawyer, dentist." Perhaps in response to the ad, two lawyers, Robert O. Hargreaves and William D. Morse, had located in Wakaw and practised in opposition to each other until 1918, when they both vacated in favour of Arthur E. Stewart.

Stewart had secured the allegiance of Wakaw's business section. Diefenbaker claimed that this was so true that he was frozen out of all available office space and forced to build his own premises. And he did, running up in short order what was surely the country's smallest free-standing legal office building. A carpenter named Joe St. Pierre and $480.08 worth of materials secured on credit from the North American Lumber Company produced a twelve-by-sixteen-foot structure containing a modest office and an anteroom partially divided by a counter. The anteroom would accommodate two or three waiting clients, but certainly not a secretary. However, there was no secretary. Nor was there any plumbing and heating was by pot-bellied stove. The determined newcomer was in business.

Articling with Diefenbaker was Michael Stechishin, an immigrant from the Ukraine who had mastered English well enough to cope with Canadian university. He and John Diefenbaker were classmates during their final year of law school. Although the two had written their bar examinations together, Stechishin had no military service to his credit and was required to complete his period of service under articles. By special dispensation of the Law Society, Diefenbaker was permitted to take his classmate with him to Wakaw as an articling student, although the principal had no more experience than the student.

Stechishin's proficiency in the Ukrainian language made him a great asset in the establishment of the Diefenbaker practice among the immigrant community at Wakaw. He remained with Diefenbaker at Wakaw until 1921 when he was admitted to the bar and moved to Yorkton. There he practised until 1940 when he was appointed District Court Judge at Wynyard, Saskatchewan.

Diefenbaker's successful defence of John Chernyski in the fall of 1919, a few months after he had settled in Wakaw, led directly to a much more lucrative case, one that set him quickly on his feet. Fourteen Wakaw farmers, all of them immigrants from Stechishin's homeland, were charged with wholesale fraud and theft against the Progressive Farmers' Grain Company elevator at Wakaw. Four of the accused retained prominent lawyers from Saskatoon and Prince Albert, but ten chose the new local barrister.

The story was the western classic of corrupting the company's grain buyer and inducing him to issue cash tickets in excess of grain actually delivered. The amounts stolen were considerable for the day, ranging from $7,500 in the case of the main offender down to several hundred for the average. The offences took place over the winter of 1918-19. In March the elevator burned down — the police alleged arson in an attempt to destroy the evidence.

The trials ran for ten days in February 1920 before King's Bench Justice James McKay sitting with a jury at Prince Albert. Out of the fourteen accused, six were acquitted. John Diefenbaker secured five of those acquittals by convincing the juries that there was insufficient evidence. He was perhaps lucky in that his were the minor offenders, but only one other lawyer succeeded on his client's behalf.

The young lawyer collected fees totalling more than $3,000, enough to pull him out of debt and provide him with a fair measure of security. The case established John Diefenbaker in Wakaw. Now able to rent more suitable space, he converted his office building into bachelor quarters. He splurged on a new Maxwell touring car, which, at $1,760, was more than twice the cost of a more modest vehicle. Diefenbaker paid $700 down and financed the balance at $133 a month for eight months. On the credit application, he stated his monthly income to be $300, a bit optimistic as it turned out.

Now welcomed, John Diefenbaker moved quickly into the Wakaw community. In December 1920 he won a three-year term on the town council, defeating the oldest serving member in a close and hotly contested election; it would be twenty years before he won another election. He was active in Wakaw's social life, too. Although not at all athletically inclined, he became vice-president of both the Wakaw Tennis Club and Curling Club, and an honorary president of the Wakaw Athletic Association. He chaired the annual meeting of the Agricultural Society and posed for a photograph with the members of the local football team. Surely the pale and frail curly-headed intellectual in the second row did not go on the field with the burly men around him?

But all was not roses. In fact, the early professional success soon withered. Although Diefenbaker had captured most of the criminal defence work in and around Wakaw and a good portion of the civil litigation, by late 1920 he was having a difficult time of it financially. He cancelled his ad in *Turner's Weekly*, published in Saskatoon, frankly explaining that "financial conditions are such that I cannot keep same up." In 1921 he was unable to meet drafts drawn upon him by his office stationery suppliers and Edward S. Wilson, the lawyer at Humboldt who handled Diefenbaker's agency work at the court house, continually pressed for payment of his account.

Diefenbaker was not the only one having financial troubles. The prosperity of western agriculture provoked by the First World War was over. Average wheat prices in 1921 were half of the 1920 levels and less than a third of the high achieved in 1919. Seduced into single crop production by the high wheat prices, farmers paid the penalty of disappearing cash returns. Business was tight for everyone.

In the 1920s Saskatchewan lawyers did what they could to earn a living. In 1921, 575 lawyers served a population of 750,000 — compared to 1,200 serving 1,000,000 in 1988 — but the simpler society of those days had less need for legal services. Like his contemporaries, John Diefenbaker sold fire and hail insurance and arranged loans for mortgage companies. His professional card in the Wakaw *Recorder* was standard for the day.

JOHN G. DIEFENBAKER, M.A., LL.B.
Barrister, Solicitor
Notary Public
Loans and Insurance
Wakaw, Sask.

Some features of the insurance business might have been distasteful to the man who later introduced the Canadian Bill of Rights. Forwarding a fire insurance application to his company, Diefenbaker felt obligated to report that "about one year ago this risk was refused by the Canadian Indemnity Company for the reason that same was being occupied by a Hebrew, but as this party has now moved out I take it that there will be no objection to this risk."

Business and professional ethics were far below today's levels. In 1920 Diefenbaker received a letter from the manager of The Western Trust Company at Prince Albert drawing his attention to the newspaper account of a Wakaw farmer dragged to his death by his horses in a runaway. In a ghoulish solicitation, the manager thought the farmer's estate would be "a case in which a Trust Company should act, there being several minor children." He suggested that "in the event of the estate coming to us, we would of course retain you for the legal work." The lawyer was not offended, even though the family were not his clients. He replied: "I am writing a letter calling in the beneficiaries in order to take up the administration of the estate by yourselves with them, and in case I am successful in doing so, I shall advise you."

The court work that came to Wakaw's two lawyers, John Diefenbaker and Arthur E. Stewart, was handled at three levels: police court, as it was then very aptly called; District Court; and, for the more substantial civil and criminal cases, the Court of King's Bench, usually sitting with a jury. Police court — presided over by the local justice of the peace, an itinerant magistrate or two J.P.s sitting together — was the court of first instance in all criminal matters, and provided, as today, the final disposition in the great majority of cases. Appeals were heard by the District Court, usually by way of new trial. Serious criminal cases went to a King's Bench jury after a preliminary inquiry.

With their civil work, the lawyers were almost exclusively before the District Court judge, who handled not only his court's jurisdiction but a great deal of the King's Bench files as well. District Court sat twice a year at Wakaw, setting up a formal court in the town hall. In between sittings, and for the King's Bench sittings, the Wakaw lawyers had to travel the forty miles north to Prince Albert.

John Diefenbaker did a great deal of criminal defence work in police court. Occasionally he captured the business of all of the current defendants who were sufficiently affluent or frightened to engage a lawyer, and appeared in six or seven cases at the bi-monthly sitting of the court.

The most influential judicial presence in the Prince Albert judicial district was District Court Judge Algernon Edwin Doak who presided for more than thirty-three years, from 1913 to 1947. His continuous presence in the local judicial system, and the authority he exerted over so much of the legal work generated within his district, made him by far the dominant judicial figure with whom John Diefenbaker had to contend throughout his career. Doak's interpretation and application of the law, and his foibles and prejudices, were the rules that guided the young lawyer in his practice. He succeeded very well in Judge Doak's judicial world.

Doak was born in Couticook, Quebec. He took his law degree from McGill, then spent a year in post-graduate study in Paris.

He commenced practice in Prince Albert in 1903, and served as the part-time city solicitor. A man of unusual probity, Doak threw the departments of Justice and Finance in Ottawa into a quandary upon his appointment to the $3,000 per annum District Court position. He returned his first pay cheque, explaining that since he had not heard of his appointment for ten days after it had been made (a most unlikely happening today), he had continued to practise law and had not earned the stipend. The government finally accepted the return of the money, but concluded that the case was "of such an exceptional character" that no revision of policy was required to cover any similar occurrences in the future.

The year 1922 was the one in which Diefenbaker turned the corner in his Wakaw law practice. When he completed his books for 1921, he found that he had earned gross fees of $6,500 for the year, quite a respectable performance. But he had spent more than $4,000 running his office and on professional expenses, leaving him a net of only $2,400.

A monthly income of $200 was quite adequate for a single man in 1922, but a long way from affluence. Diefenbaker would have been stretched if the $133 monthly payment on his Maxwell had not been paid out.

Except for the big car, his lifestyle was simple and inexpensive. Neither a smoker nor a drinker, his personal wants were few and there is no evidence that he was yet much interested in the opposite sex. His relaxation was at nearby Wakaw Lake or visiting with his parents in Saskatoon. Although he loved to drive the Maxwell, and even took it as far as California, he lacked coordination and never developed into a skilful driver.

In 1922 Diefenbaker became involved in a unique case surrounding the conflict between the two official languages of Canada. It was a small chapter in a serious public debate which had been raging in Saskatchewan when the province was formed in 1905, and which surfaced periodically thereafter.

The trial was the climax of Diefenbaker's struggle against his entrenched competitor in Wakaw, A.E. Stewart, and brought him province-wide publicity. Ironically, he won the case on a technicality.

William Mackie was the only English-speaking Protestant ratepayer in the Ethier School District near Domremy, a French-settled community a few miles north of Wakaw. In January 1922, Mackie lost the last of his patience with the teaching of French and religion in the school. He had been complaining to Premier William Melville Martin since the previous summer but had been rebuffed. Martin, aware of the sensitivity of the matter of foreign language instruction in Saskatchewan schools, was convinced "that the only way that the question can be dealt with is by allowing some privilege to the French language."

Mackie consulted lawyer Stewart who took him before Wakaw Justice of the Peace Edward H. Firneisz. They formally charged two school trustees, Remi Ethier and Leger Boutin, under the School Act. The charge was that the teacher "within school hours used the French language as a language of instruction." The School Act provided that "English shall be the sole language of instruction in all schools."

Firneisz tried Boutin and Ethier on February 11. He convicted both trustees and fined them $30 and costs. Boutin and Ethier then retained John Diefenbaker and filed an appeal. The French community in Saskatchewan, concerned that the case would be a precedent with a prejudicial effect in other school districts where French was taught, stepped forward. The cause of the two convicted trustees was taken up by L'Association Catholique Franco-Canadienne de la Saskatchewan and its official organ, *Le Patriote de l'Ouest.*

The appeal was heard by way of a new trial on May 23 in Wakaw's town hall before Judge Doak. After hearing eleven witnesses, mostly pupils in the school, Doak concluded that Mackie's allegation that "the school was being conducted practically entirely in French is well founded." Some of the children who had been in the school for four years were unable to give their evidence in English and needed an interpreter.

But Diefenbaker also argued for a narrow interpretation of the section of the School Act under which Boutin and Ethier were charged. He contended that the trustees could not be convicted with respect to the conduct of the school. Judge Doak agreed: "While I have no doubt that there has been in this case a flagrant violation of the Act, I cannot uphold the conviction."

It was a narrow and technical victory that did little to solve the problem of teaching French in Saskatchewan schools, but the province's French community was elated. *Le Patriote* announced that the proceedings at Wakaw concerned the entire French Catholic element in Saskatchewan, and called for a subscription to pay Diefenbaker's fee of $262.

The case may have been the last straw for A.E. Stewart. A month after Judge Doak's decision came down he left Wakaw. Thomas Paterson, Stewart's successor, did not last long in competition with the rising reputation of John Diefenbaker.

That reputation got another boost at the King's Bench jury sittings at Humboldt in the fall of 1922.

Dora Hrynuik, a widow living on a Cudworth farm, had been receiving attention from Joseph Treschuk, a railroad section hand living near Regina. Although Treschuk was a married man, he persuaded Hrynuik to visit him in Regina. To enable her to attend the proposed rendezvous, he sent her his railroad pass, then a standard employee benefit.

Hrynuik met Treschuk in Regina, and they had been "friendly," as she later admitted to Diefenbaker in cross-examination. But something went wrong and the widow returned to Cudworth with Treschuk's pass, holding it against an alleged debt. An upset Treschuk wrote Hrynuik an unfortunate letter: "I am losing my job over this pass but don't you expect to get away with that...I will lose my job but you will lose your life also."

The dispute might have remained merely a very personal spat except for the circumstances that had caused Dora Hrynuik's widowhood. Her husband had been murdered four years earlier, shot on a lonely corner of their homestead, and the murder had not been solved. As she told the court in considerable understatement: "I thought of my husband's murder. It looked quite peculiar to me....The connection of this letter," she went on, "made me scared."

The police also found the matter peculiar, although there was no evidence to link Treschuk with the murder of the late Hrynuik. The sectionman was charged with "threatening to kill Dora Hrynuik." Treschuk engaged John Diefenbaker to defend him.

It was not a tough case and it was a natural for Diefenbaker's growing skills in cross-examination. Dora Hrynuik quickly admitted to the defence counsel that she never really believed Treschuk meant any threat to her and the jury saw the case the same way.

By today's standards, the trial would have set a speed record. Although both Hrynuik and Treschuk were Ruthenian and testified through an interpreter, and their correspondence required translation, the case ran only two hours, including twenty- five minutes for the jury to consider its verdict. John Diefenbaker avoided any inclination to grandstand, restricting his jury address to five minutes.

That same fall the young Wakaw defence counsel successfully defended a charge of horse theft before a Prince Albert jury by throwing into question the ownership of the horse. Except for the grain fraud case, which was in itself a triumph, he was batting 1,000 in front of juries.

The dutiful son spent the New Year's holidays in Saskatoon relaxing with his parents. While he was away, the worst fire in the short history of Wakaw destroyed a large section of its business district, including the building housing Diefenbaker's law office. The total loss of a modern law office with its files, records and documents would be a fatal disaster. But John Diefenbaker survived the destruction of his office, apparently without missing a beat in his practice, a fact that speaks volumes about the simple nature of his work. Ten days after the fire, he confidently announced that he was "contemplating the erection of a new office in the business section."

Although wheat prices in 1923 dropped to a low-point not to be equalled until the Depression, Wakaw, with its mixed farms and frontier economy, was prospering. So, too, was John Diefenbaker. Immigration to the region was strong, the population burgeoning, and seventy-cent wheat did not seriously slow the community's business expansion. Halliday and Davis, the Prince Albert law firm of Thomas Clayton Davis (who would soon become John Diefenbaker's political nemesis), considered Wakaw so affluent that they tried establishing a branch office there. The experiment did not succeed, but was the first shot in a struggle between Diefenbaker and Davis that would last for many years.

Wakaw's pre-eminent lawyer began to enjoy real success, in spite of a worsening of the mysterious medical condition that had afflicted him during the war. Prince Albert lawyers began to court his agency work in that city. In July he hired an associate, Alec Ehman, to assist him.

Diefenbaker needed help, even if only to cover for him during his more frequent and serious illnesses. He was absent for a total of two months during 1923. In March his condition put him in bed for several days. His mother came up from Saskatoon to nurse him, then took him home to Saskatoon for a further week's rest.

The symptoms defied diagnosis. In April, suspecting tuberculosis, Diefenbaker spent a week at the recently-built sanatorium near Fort Qu'Appelle. Finally, in November, he journeyed to the Mayo Clinic in Rochester, Minnesota, where he underwent surgery for a gastric ulcer.

The operation was a success and Diefenbaker very soon felt better than at any time during the previous two or three years. The condition remained with him for some years, however, and occasionally caused him great distress. Already abstemious, which accorded with his Baptist beliefs, he became more rigidly disciplined in his diet and habits.

His illness notwithstanding, Diefenbaker had finally cornered the legal market in Wakaw. Thomas Paterson, the successor to A.E. Stewart, closed his office and left town. Halliday and Davis turned their short-lived practice over to a newcomer, J.J. Krause.

As 1924 opened, John Diefenbaker had clearly conquered Wakaw and it was time to take his talents to a larger field of play. Diefenbaker was careful not to burn his bridge to Wakaw; it would be the mainstay of his practice for some years. He converted his firm to Diefenbaker and Ehman, announced he would be in weekly attendance, but took new offices in the Bank d'-Hochelaga building in Prince Albert. By May 1, 1924, he was open for business in the northern city.

The Man From Prince Albert had arrived.

4

The Davises of Prince Albert

John Diefenbaker had not known when he chose Wakaw to launch his career that he was encroaching upon the sphere of influence of the Davis family of Prince Albert. However, it was otherwise when, after five years in Wakaw, he moved into Prince Albert. Then he was fully aware that he was challenging the political, professional and business establishment of that city, led by the eldest son of the late Senator Thomas Osborne Davis. For fifteen years thereafter, John Diefenbaker's political ambitions were thwarted by Thomas Clayton Davis and the Liberal organization of Prince Albert he headed.

Thomas Osborne Davis was born in Quebec of Irish parents. His father, a brother of the Thomas Osborne Davis of the Young Ireland movement, was a graduate of Dublin's Trinity College. The young Davis was tutored at home, but the results were rough since he ran off in his early teens. Yet he fitted in quickly when he arrived in the North-West Territories in 1880 at the age of twenty-four. Two years later he was in business with the Woodbine Billiard Parlour, the Palace Saloon of the Northwest and, later, the Horseshoe Store. He was soon successful, due largely to such innovative and entertaining advertising as: "Come where the woodbine twineth, and the Whangdoodle mourneth for her young."

The Qu'Appelle-Long Lake and Saskatchewan rail connection did not reach Prince Albert until 1990 and "T.O." or "Tommy" Davis freighted his own goods from Winnipeg by Red River cart along the trail from Qu'Appelle. On one such trip, in

1885, his supplies were commandeered by the troops of General Middleton on their way to engage Louis Riel at Batoche. On another trip, he discovered among his cargo his brother's fiancée, an Irish colleen on her way to her wedding. The engaging Tommy convinced Rebecca Jennings to transfer her affections to him and she arrived in Prince Albert a different Mrs. Davis than first intended. Perhaps for this reason the brothers were implacable foes, even sometimes in politics.

Davis was naturally attracted to politics and achieved success in spite of an abrasive personality. Brash, hot-headed and intensely ambitious, he was not universally popular among his fellow Liberals in Prince Albert, although he was well-liked in the rural areas. Cast in the Tammany Hall mould, Davis was skilled in all methods of electoral organization and did not make a fine distinction between the legal and the illegal.

In 1894 and 1895 Davis was mayor of Prince Albert and president of the local Liberal organization. Thus, he was well positioned to strike at the political opportunity that arose following the 1896 federal election that made Sir Wilfrid Laurier prime minister. Laurier had been elected both in his home riding of Quebec East and in the District of Saskatchewan, which included Prince Albert, the first of three prime ministers to represent the community. Laurier preferred Quebec East and let his western riding go.

Serious strife immediately broke out in the Liberal organization between Davis and his supporters and those who were determined to prevent him from succeeding to the Liberal nomination. Clifford Sifton, Laurier's minister of the interior, fearful that the Liberals would lose the seat, commissioned his brother Arthur to act as mediator.

Arthur Sifton, then a lawyer in Calgary, had earlier practised in Prince Albert and was later to serve as premier of Alberta. He did not hold a high opinion of T.O. Davis, even after Davis succeeded in winning the nomination. "It will be an awful...job to elect Davis if there is opposition," Sifton reported. "There is hardly a respectable grit in the District supporting him with any enthusiasm, and he is depending largely on the efforts of [half-]breeds and purchasable Tories." But Davis did win the election, humbly attributing his victory to "my personal popularity." A group of unhappy Liberals began proceedings to disqualify him for having "bought his seat," and Laurier had to intercede to save his new MP.

Once elected, Davis skilfully consolidated his position and took under his wing all patronage in the region. Under his direction the Liberal organization in Prince Albert became a powerhouse. "A machine," said his opponents. He was easily re-elected in 1900 and appointed to the Senate in 1904. He was in full control of Prince Albert until his death in 1917.

The senator had been dead two years when John Diefenbaker arrived in Wakaw in 1919, but his Western Townsite Company and other business and political interests were still active, now under the direction of Thomas Clayton Davis. "T.C.," like his father also known as "Tommy," was six years older than John Diefenbaker, was a graduate of Osgoode Hall, and had been practising law in Prince Albert since 1914. A younger son, whose name, Clifford Sifton Davis, bespoke his father's deft political touch was just beginning his legal training.

Tall, broad-shouldered, spectacled but ruggedly handsome, T.C. Davis inherited none of his father's harsh personality but all of his acumen and political dexterity. A man of charm and ability, he succeeded easily to his legacy. Following a route similar to the senator's, the younger Davis served his apprenticeship as an alderman and had been mayor of Prince Albert since 1921 when John Diefenbaker arrived in the spring of 1924. Until 1939, when he left the political arena for the judiciary and, later, the Canadian foreign service, this Davis scion enjoyed the political success and prominence that Diefenbaker coveted.

The Prince Albert that T.C. Davis presided over in the early 1920s was just coming out of a ten-year period of economic misery and about to enjoy a few years of relative prosperity. But, in that spring of 1924, any imminent relief from their economic distress was not apparent to the citizens. The city was in serious financial bondage, the result of a failed hydro-electric scheme, and had just imposed yet another in a long series of civic belt-tightening economies. This last one had closed a school, dismissed half of the six-man police force and the city magistrate, closed the police station, and, in a desperate search for revenue, instituted a tax even on privies. Already woefully short of services, the northern city did not hold much promise when John Diefenbaker chose it for his future.

Once, it had been different. Prince Albert had been settled in 1866 as a Presbyterian mission and, until the First World War, seemed to have an obvious future as a thriving metropolis. Situated on the North Saskatchewan River a few miles west of its junction with the South Saskatchewan, it was well positioned to serve both the agricultural settlement in the south and the fur, fish, lumber and mineral economy of the north. The frontier town had as colourful a beginning as any in the new land and was known as "The Roughest Town in the Northwest" when it was incorporated in 1885.

For all its promise, Prince Albert's progress was only modest before 1900, when its population was still under two thousand. Then the wave of homesteading and the development of the northern hinterland produced real growth and prosperity. By 1910 the population had swelled to nine thousand and the boom was on. Certain that its time had come, Prince Albert extended its boundaries so that in 1912 it encompassed only two hundred fewer acres than Toronto with its population of a third of a million.

In its orgy of optimism the city embarked upon a grand project that resulted only in a case of fiscal strangulation that lasted fifty years. Local visionaries saw in La Colle Falls, some twenty miles downstream on the Saskatchewan, a hydro-electric bonanza suitable for the metropolis Prince Albert was to become. One of several prominent promoters to give the scheme respectability was A. E. Doak, not yet appointed to the District Court.

Negligent feasibility studies, naiveté and excessive enthusiasm disguised until too late the fact that the flow of the Saskatchewan River in winter was inadequate to operate the generators. When the onset of the First World War mercifully killed the venture, it had consumed more than one and a quarter million dollars. Worse, other civic needs, such as street paving, water and sewer projects, hospital and fire services, had been sacrificed for the great project. Central Avenue, the main street, remained unpaved until 1930.

The economic tragedy deepened as the war brought business in the community to a standstill. By 1916 the population, which had reached a high of nearly 14,000, had dropped to less than 6,500. The city's debt then stood at almost $4 million. By September 1918, the city was out of credit and was able to open its schools only when the mayor pledged his personal assets.

The end of the war brought some relief as business re-established itself, but by then extensive logging had killed Prince Albert's lumber industry, once its biggest employer. It was a slow struggle back to solvency as the city's bondholders held it in a tight noose. Not until 1966 were the last of the La Colle Falls debentures retired.

Apart from Davis, there were a dozen other lawyers in Prince Albert when Diefenbaker arrived there. Still, the newcomer's prospects were good. By 1924 he had become a busy barrister. His civil practice had developed quickly on top of his ongoing criminal defence work, and he was a regular at the sittings of the District Court at Wakaw, Humboldt and Prince Albert. He snared several civil cases before the King's Bench at both Humboldt and Prince Albert. Only five years at the bar, he was a sought-after counsel, even if most of his work still emanated from Wakaw and district.

A cornerstone in Prince Albert's economy, the federal penitentiary, built in 1909, was joined by a provincial jail in 1923. Together, the penal institutions provided something of a guaranteed client population for the local criminal defence bar, which, after 1924, included John Diefenbaker.

The cases which came to Diefenbaker were a potpourri of disputes from a very fractious society. Most, of course, involved money, but the amounts were often so small, even for the day, as to suggest that the parties were more interested in litigation than economics. Matters of principle and honour, then as now, are grist for the lawyer's mill.

Allegations of assault and theft between neighbours were common. The cases seldom taxed the legal knowledge of either counsel or court; the difficulty lay in determining where the truth was. The conflict in testimony between plaintiff and defendant was extreme and often frustrating to the judges.

Some of the judges attributed the problem to the difficulty so many of the recent immigrants faced in adjusting to the Canadian judicial system, which, of course, was the British system. Others were more blunt. King's Bench Justice Henry V. Bigelow, speaking from the bench at Humboldt in 1925, told an accused just convicted of assault by a jury:

"It is a matter of regret to me, and to other people who are engaged in the enforcement of the law in this province, that the people of your nationality, Ruthenians, Galacians, or whatever you call yourselves, are getting a very unenviable reputation in this province, both as to keeping the laws or not keeping them, whichever way you want to put it, and, further, of coming into our courts and perjuring themselves.

"There are certain communities in this province where most of the criminal work is taken up with people of your nationality, not only in the commission of crimes, but coming into the courts and swearing whatever you like, and thinking you can deceive the courts all the time.

"I do not know why it pertains to people of your nationality, but it is a recognized fact. Now, Canada wants settlers, but not so badly that settlers of your class are to be tolerated, unless they observe the laws."

Such comment by a jurist today would guarantee a rebuke by the Canadian Judicial Council.

The year before, Judge Doak, a patient and tolerant jurist, had also spoken out when sentencing a Wakaw farmer to two years for theft of his neighbour's grain: "This business of stealing in Wakaw and St. Julien districts has got to stop. For the last few years the district has been the scene of crimes from murder to theft and I am not going to show a leniency to anyone from that district."

In 1924, an unladylike expression used at a Wakaw dance gave Diefenbaker a well publicized slander case in Prince Albert King's Bench and a chance to display some knowledge of the Ruthenian or Ukrainian language. An angry Mrs. Gawliuk had called Mrs. Kuneruk "*masch ty publica*," which, the offended plaintiff complained, implied that she was "of unchaste character." W.J. Mushinski, a local lawyer fluent in the language, testified for the defendant and stated that the words meant only a troublemaker. Under cross-examination, however, he agreed that the words could have the meaning complained of and Diefenbaker carried off victory with a judgment for one dollar and the costs of the action.

By the time he had moved to Prince Albert, John Diefenbaker had learned the value of publicity to an ambitious lawyer. Court proceedings, including the names of counsel, were reported assiduously by local newspapers and watched jealously by lawyers. More interesting cases, such as the slander action, might be fed to the dailies in Saskatoon and Regina. The weekly Wakaw *Recorder* was the first newspaper important to John Diefenbaker's career. In Prince Albert, it was the *Daily Herald*.

Not content with the excellent coverage he received in the *Herald*'s legal columns, Diefenbaker invented a public relations strategy to ensure that Prince Albert knew he was in town. He acquired a large "five gallon" black hat that caused passers-by to turn and inquire, "*Who* is that?"

"That," would be the reply, "is John Diefenbaker."

As John Diefenbaker looked around Prince Albert a year after his arrival, he saw himself frozen out of much of its establishment, particularly the political one where his real ambition lay. The Liberal Party, in power since the formation of the province in 1905, was again returned to office on June 2, 1925, under Premier Charles Dunning. In that election, T. C. Davis succeeded to the Prince Albert seat in the legislature, and all government patronage, federal and provincial, was firmly in his hands. Another lawyer, Samuel J. Branion, known as "Ban the Bar Branion" because of his strong prohibitionist views, followed Davis as mayor.

In the early 1920s, Saskatchewan was almost a one-party province. The Liberal political organization was so effective that it became the subject of essays by political scientists. Agrarian unrest brought United Farmer governments to power in Ontario, Manitoba and Alberta, but not in Saskatchewan where the Liberals co-opted the rural dissidents and maintained power. After 1926, when James G. Gardiner succeeded Dunning in the premier's office, the Liberal Party became known as "the Gardiner machine."

In contrast, the Conservative Party was particularly weak in Saskatchewan. It won only three legislative seats in the 1925 election and was in third place federally, behind the Progressives, an agrarian group. A Progressive, Andrew Knox, held the Prince Albert federal constituency. Charles McDonald, the former MLA, was the Liberals' choice to run against Knox. Although he was retired and living in Vancouver, McDonald still had business interests in Prince Albert and was popular.

This was the dim political scene that existed in the summer of 1925 as expectations of a fall federal election increased. It held little apparent opportunity for John Diefenbaker. Although his political leaning was to the Liberal Party, Diefenbaker could see no room for himself as a candidate in the Liberal organization of Prince Albert. The positions were filled and looked to remain that way for years to come. His political ambitions would have to find an outlet under a different label.

Diefenbaker was born and raised a Liberal in an age when that was the accepted and customary way to come by one's political beliefs. He later stated that he became a Conservative in university, but the mock parliament in which he served as party leader was non-partisan. He said, also, that he supported the Union government, a Conservative-Liberal coalition formed by Prime Minister Robert Borden, in the federal election of 1917. As a returned soldier, it was natural that his sympathy would lie with that wartime government's conscription policy, and many Liberals, particularly in the West, felt the same. In that 1917 election, the Liberals had not run a candidate in Saskatoon, where Diefenbaker then lived. During his years at Wakaw, John Diefenbaker did not take part in any election campaign, federal or provincial.

Prior to 1925 John Diefenbaker had not declared his political colours openly and beyond question, but he was viewed as a Liberal by his contemporaries. In March of that year, after he had moved to Prince Albert, the Wakaw Liberal Association debated at length a motion to support him as Liberal candidate for the provincial riding of Kinistino. Diefenbaker's law partner, Alexis Etienne Philion, was at the meeting, one of several who surely would have known if they were putting their man into the right pew but the wrong church. In any event, the motion was defeated. Joseph Mohler of Wakaw later insisted in letters to the editors of several Saskatchewan papers that Diefenbaker spoke on behalf of Liberal candidate T.C. Davis in the 1925 provincial election. Davis himself confirmed that Diefenbaker was one of his supporters in that election.

For years the story persisted that Diefenbaker had served as the secretary of the Wakaw Liberal Association, and he took pains to refute it, saying he had been elected in absentia without his permission.

Conservative or Liberal, John Diefenbaker still had his political options open when he arrived in Prince Albert. He made his choice on August 6, 1925, when he accepted the Conservative nomination for the federal election of October 29. T.C. Davis explained what happened: "In a matter of one day he turned Tory when there were no issues and no election. He changed because a prominent friend of mine, a good Tory, told him that he had better switch as I would always be in his road in the Liberal Party."

The "prominent friend" was Sam Donaldson, the elder statesman of the Conservative Party in Prince Albert. Donaldson, a liveryman, was an old political foe of Senator T.O. Davis. He succeeded Davis as mayor in 1895, was twice elected to the legislature, then promoted to Parliament in a 1915 by-election where he served two years. Donaldson took the newly arrived and ambitious John Diefenbaker under his wing and became his political advisor. For a time, Diefenbaker boarded in the Donaldson home.

Diefenbaker's political conversion might not have been "a matter of one day," as Davis claimed, but it was sudden. It occurred less than three weeks after his participation with the Liberals in the provincial election on June 2. On June 19, the Prince Albert Conservatives held an organizing meeting in anticipation of the upcoming federal campaign. The main speaker was John Diefenbaker.

The recent arrival from Wakaw spoke eloquently and idealistically of the day when immigrants of all races and creeds would be united as Canadians, and even the conflict between East and West would be at an end. It was strong philosophy for factional Prince Albert, and it must have made an impression on the three dozen faithful in attendance. They called a nominating meeting for August 6 and, since there was no other prospect in sight, the party members must have settled on Diefenbaker as their candidate.

It was a marriage of mutual convenience. The prospects of the disorganized Conservatives were not such as to attract candidates of substance, but a candidate was needed. Who better than the young, attractive and articulate lawyer, the newcomer without barnacles? For his part, Diefenbaker craved the publicity the nomination would bring and the opportunity to improve his stature in the community.

Sam Donaldson enlisted Mayor Branion, another prominent Conservative, to assist in Diefenbaker's acceptance by the Prince Albert party. Branion placed the candidate's name in nomination before eighty Conservatives gathered in Prince Albert's Memorial Hall on the afternoon of August 6. A. Ostrovsky of Wakaw seconded the nomination, and that was it. There was no one else. The meeting, however, was enthusiastic about its "adopted candidate," as the *Herald* described the event, and the party's delight with Diefenbaker grew as the campaign developed.

Diefenbaker immediately displayed a grasp of political issues and a talent for public speaking that gave him the appearance of a seasoned candidate. At least two of the issues he seized had such enduring qualities they were still current half a century later. He promised that, if elected, he would have the Hudson Bay Railway built within two years, or resign. Also, in a theme that he would maintain all his life, he spoke of the need for union of creeds and nationalities if a Canadian nation was to be built: "The word 'New-Canadian' has got to be eliminated and a united nationality developed instead of the hybrid variety as it exists today."

Perhaps partly motivated by anger, the Liberals ignored the sitting member, Progressive Andrew Knox, and went after Diefenbaker as if he was the real threat. The Liberal official agent publicly called the new Conservative "a stray lawyer from Wakaw" and "a goat for the older men of the party."

Diefenbaker seemed to enjoy the attention and largely ignored the attacks upon him. But he was stung when T. C. Davis entered the campaign and referred to him as a fallen-away Liberal. Davis went on to say that Diefenbaker should "start at the bottom of the political ladder and prove his political worth before seeking the highest election honour in the gift of the people."

"I have nothing against him," Davis concluded patronizingly, "he is a young man of seeming ability."

"Davis seems to think the fact I was once a Liberal is an offence," Diefenbaker promptly retorted. "I was a Liberal, but I could not help but see the failures of the Liberal government in carrying out their promises." He denied that he had sought the provincial Liberal nomination in Kinistino the previous year, "although it is true certain persons wanted me to accept."

The Progressives also took note of John Diefenbaker, one speaker describing him in this way: "He takes himself very seriously and you will all do well to take him the same way. He has any amount of ability and has distinguished himself in his profession by his hobby of taking tough cases. He can take an out and out rascal and describe him with such wonderful oratory that one may almost see a halo around the rogue's head."

A quarrel broke out in Wakaw, part of the Prince Albert federal riding. Several Conservative businessmen threatened to pull their advertising from the *Recorder* unless it supported their candidate editorially. The *Recorder* editor had been giving weighted coverage to the Liberals, and knew where his bread was buttered. In a prominent editorial, set in large type, he stated that the *Recorder* was "too conscientious to sell our conviction, neither for the support of a few advertisers, nor for any price." He went on to declare his support for the Liberals. Conservative election ads disappeared from the paper.

Diefenbaker ran a thorough campaign, speaking throughout the rural area of the seat (although, curiously, not Wakaw) as well as the city. He drew good crowds and they responded well to him. His advertisements covered all the issues. One ran in French, a novel idea then, and one carried an old photograph of the candidate in uniform.

But it was all for nought. The Liberal McDonald won, taking the Progressive and Conservative deposits. In fact, Diefenbaker harvested five fewer votes than the Conservatives had polled in 1921, although his percentage improved due to a lower voter turnout. Even Wakaw was a disappointment, giving the Liberals 105 votes to 32 for the favourite son and 20 for the Progressives.

Nevertheless, his election campaign accomplished much for Diefenbaker as a lawyer, perhaps all he had hoped for. He gained the attention of the stalwarts in the Conservative Party, enhanced his reputation in and around Prince Albert, and acquired experience and maturity as a politician and orator.

The *Daily Herald* commented favourably: "The Conservative candidate, John G. Diefenbaker, is young and energetic. He has no reason to feel discouraged by the result of this, his first excursion into federal politics. There are many today ready to prophesy that the last has not yet been heard of him in the political life of this country."

The Prince Albert Conservatives were thrilled by the performance of their candidate. Six weeks after the election, 250 supporters from all parts of the riding attended a complimentary banquet in honour of their defeated champion. In proposing the toast to the guest of honour, Reverend R.F. Macdougall said, to loud cheers, "No community can defeat such a man as J.G. Diefenbaker." It was a glorious loss. It was soon to become more so as fate and circumstance combined to bring the constituency of Prince Albert, and John Diefenbaker, into the national spotlight.

Few anticipated that Mackenzie King's Liberal government would face much difficulty in securing a continued mandate in the 1925 election, but the voters registered a surprise verdict. King fell short of a majority; in fact, he garnered only 101 seats to 116 for Arthur Meighen's Conservatives. The wily King continued to govern by relying upon the support of the 28 Progressives and Independents who survived the election.

King lost his own riding of North York in the 1925 election and needed a seat. He settled on Prince Albert, where Charles McDonald was happy to step aside for the prime minister. A by-election was called for February 2, 1926, the first event in a busy political month for John Diefenbaker and Prince Albert.

Few lasting political careers are built running against prime ministers, and such by-elections are suicide. Diefenbaker and the Conservatives wisely declined the contest. A token Independent candidate was put up and King was elected in Prince Albert by a margin of almost four to one. Prince Albert was now represented by its second prime minister.

King's assumption of the Prince Albert riding was of special interest to John Diefenbaker for two reasons. First, if he wanted to enter the field again, and he did, his Liberal opponent was already in place, and he was formidable indeed. Second, and perhaps more galling, King, busy running his government, turned the care and keeping of his new constituency over to T.C. Davis as his local lieutenant. Diefenbaker's major competitor grew in influence and power.

No sooner was King elected than John Diefenbaker and the Conservatives, undaunted, held a nominating convention. Two weeks after the by-election, on February 16, three hundred party members unanimously endorsed their 1925 candidate for another campaign. Because of the uncertain situation in the House of Commons, the election was expected in June.

Then, to complete the month's activities, Liberal Premier Charles Dunning left Regina to join King's Cabinet in Ottawa. He was succeeded by James G. Gardiner who, on February 26, took T.C. Davis into his Cabinet as minister of municipal affairs. This was the beginning of a unique bond between Gardiner and Davis that was to last thirty years. For just as long, John Diefenbaker looked upon both of them as his special foes.

The Conservative candidate continued to be busy in his law practice, but his cases were mostly run-of-the-mill. He successfully defended the proprietors of two notorious gambling and bootlegging dens in Prince Albert's River Street district, polishing his criminal defence reputation. The big case, however, still had not come his way.

The Prince Albert end of Diefenbaker's practice had developed well enough to justify the addition of a junior partner, and Frank C. Cousins joined the office upon his admission to the bar early in 1926. But things had not been stable in the Wakaw office. Alexander A. Ehman stayed only six months after the opening of the Prince Albert office, and shortly after joined the opposition. Diefenbaker acquired Alexis Etienne Philion in

January 1925, but that arrangement also fell apart before long, and Richmond B. Godfrey took over. When Cousins arrived, the firm became Diefenbaker, Cousins and Godfrey. That put the senior partner in a better position to participate in the 1926 election.

That summer, as a result of a scandal involving corruption in the Customs Department, Mackenzie King lost his grip on power. Refused dissolution and an election by Governor-General Byng, King turned the seals of office over to Arthur Meighen and the Conservatives. Then Meighen, too, saw power slip from him and the country was thrown into an election. Voting day was September 14.

The 1925 election was a placid affair compared to the struggle a year later, and John Diefenbaker's campaigns reflect the difference. As a new candidate in 1925, he had stayed with his issues and avoided provocative rhetoric. In 1926, he gave as good as he got on all fronts. Once again he faced personal attack. This time, he had to defend himself against campaign rumours about his nationality, that he "was a German." His only German ancestor, he pointed out, was his great-grandfather. "And suppose I was a German, does it make for a united Canada to knock settlers?"

Personal attacks were more general than usual in the 1926 campaign, but, in the neighbouring riding of Mackenzie, the Progressive MP, Milton Neil Campbell, went a little too far. He made the titillating charge that the Honourable Jacques Bureau, a minister in the King government, operated a house of prostitution on the premises of the House of Commons. According to Campbell, Bureau's real purpose was to compromise Opposition members. The accusation naturally provoked a healthy lawsuit, but Campbell won the election.

Prince Albert was a two-way contest between King and Diefenbaker, but the prime minister campaigned across Canada and only the challenger was in the riding. The local debate was not elevated when Colonel T. H. Lennox, who had defeated King in North York, derided him for leaving "to run near the North

Pole, among foreigners who can't speak English, up north among the Eskimos." Forced to defend the slur on Prince Albert, Diefenbaker was furious with his eastern colleague. Yet he, too, was not above making inflammatory accusations. King supporters, he said, were threatening the foreign-born voters of Prince Albert that "they would be deported one by one without trial if they voted Conservative." Diefenbaker ignored a public challenge from the esteemed Dr. Robert G. Scott of Wakaw to prove his allegation.

In his second campaign, John Diefenbaker, no longer quite so serious and high-minded, charged directly at King himself. King, he said, was a parachute candidate: "He entered the constituency, jumped to Marcelin, jumped to Prince Albert, jumped to Wakaw, jumped to Rosthern, then jumped right out of the constituency." In a reference to King's attempt to maintain power with only a minority, Diefenbaker declared: "The Liberal party is noted for its bulldog determination. Well, a bulldog is noted for its determination to hang on, but not for its intelligence."

Diefenbaker did not overlook the customs scandal, a prime issue in the campaign: "If you are a cut-throat or a thug, you are sent to the penitentiary, but the penalty for one who debauched the customs was imprisonment for life in the Senate."

On King's several promises of Senate reform: "Now, if a member of the community tells you an untruth once, you would probably say that he exaggerated. If he tells you an untruth twice, you might say he was following that line more often than he ought. But, if he tells you an untruth three times, what would you call him?"

"A liar," his audience dutifully responded.

The Prince Albert Conservative was no free trader. "The one salvation in the west is protection," he claimed. "It saves American farmers. Why won't it work both ways?"

"I want you to create a record for Mr. King," Diefenbaker requested. "He has never yet been elected twice in the same riding. Let him be elected and defeated in the same riding in the same year."

Prince Albert ignored the suggestion. King was returned to office in Prince Albert and in Canada. The tantalizing taste of power that had so briefly come to Meighen and the Conservatives was snatched away.

The restored prime minister overwhelmed John Diefenbaker by more than four thousand votes. But, in the city of Prince Albert, only 135 votes separated the two, and the young challenger had won or tied in fully one-quarter of the polls. King's majority had come from the ethnic polls, including Wakaw, which again gave Diefenbaker a drubbing.

A month later, John Diefenbaker attended an Ottawa caucus of Conservative candidates — elected and defeated — and the Conservative senators. Arthur Meighen resigned as party leader and was succeeded by Hugh Guthrie of Guelph.

The candidate from Prince Albert was not cowed by his distinguished company, nor by the presence of Colonel Lennox of North York. Diefenbaker openly criticized Lennox for his offensive comments about Prince Albert during the campaign. The published summary of the meeting described his comments respecting "the handicap under which certain candidates were placed as a result of indiscretions and unsound judgement of individuals whose verbosity had been detrimental to the interests of the Conservative Party." With that off his chest, John Diefenbaker returned to his Prince Albert law practice. With Liberal governments solidly entrenched in both Ottawa and Regina, there was nothing else for him to do.

But he could wait. After all, he had just turned thirty-one years of age.

5

The Good Years

Anthime Bourdon was an unlikely man to be accused of murder. Seventy years old, he had never before been in trouble with the law. A long-time settler in the French district of Domremy, a few miles north of Wakaw, he had put together a very successful farm — nine quarter-sections in all — and raised a fine family.

It would have been understandable if Peter Champagne had been charged with murder. Forty-six years old, the tall and powerful farm labourer had terrified many of the district residents with his violent, drunken rages. The previous year, William Jobin had fired a rifle at Champagne to drive him away when the enraged man had threatened him with an axe.

But it was Peter Champagne who was dead, and it was Anthime Bourdon who was charged with murdering him.

It had been a long day of drinking, a rainy Sunday in August, 1927, when little work could be done anyway. Bourdon's wife was visiting in Montreal and he was alone. He and Champagne took the buggy out, but lost control of the horse and suffered a bad spill. Bill Jobin found the elderly farmer lying at the edge of the road, alone and in the rain. He was covered with a robe. He explained that he was "waiting for my man." Later, after Champagne's death, that statement took on an ominous double meaning.

As Bourdon was picked up, Champagne reappeared and the two were delivered back to Bourdon's farm. There Champagne produced a jug of wine and insisted on sharing a drink with their rescuers. He himself drank so deeply that he had to be stopped. The two were left alone. They seemed to be happy.

An hour later, a shoeless Anthime Bourdon ran across the muddy fields to a neighbouring farm where he excitedly asked for help. He wanted to go back to see if Peter Champagne was dead. He had shot Champagne, he said, but did not think it had been fatal. Bourdon was frightened that, if he returned alone, the younger man would kill him.

Peter Champagne was certainly dead. He had been shot in the chest at close range with Bourdon's twelve-gauge shotgun, and was lying just beyond the kitchen steps. Near him was an axe.

When Constable Flanagan of the provincial police arrived well after midnight the situation seemed clear to him. A groggy Anthime Bourdon, speaking through an interpreter, retold the story he had given the neighbours.

Champagne had demanded more drink. When Bourdon refused, Champagne attacked him, choking the older man, but Bourdon finally escaped. "If I can't get the best of you this way," Champagne had said, "then I'll get your gun." He went into the bedroom where he knew the gun was kept. When Champagne came back into the kitchen, Bourdon seized the gun. As they wrestled, the gun discharged and Champagne lurched out the kitchen door. Bourdon, not looking back, ran out another door for help.

Flanagan had given Bourdon the standard police warning — his statement was voluntary. The policeman did not believe that the elderly Bourdon had twice physically bested the younger and more powerful Champagne. He placed Bourdon under arrest, made a cursory sketch of the premises, and left. Flanagan did not notice a hole in the kitchen screen door, or the fact that it had been hooked.

Bourdon retained Prince Albert lawyer Joseph Emile Lussier, who promptly called in John Diefenbaker with his greater trial experience and better knowledge of the district. There was no time to lose. The shooting had taken place on Sunday, August

14, and the inquest and the preliminary inquiry were both set for the following Saturday, April 20.

Lussier and Diefenbaker had a problem. In his statement to Flanagan, Bourdon had described a killing in self-defence. That version was not only somewhat unbelievable, it was contradicted by some hard facts.

The police had gone back to Bourdon's house for a closer look. There was no evidence of a struggle in the kitchen, the gun had been found carefully stowed in the pantry, and, most important, they had spotted a hole in the screen of the kitchen door. Examination showed that the hole had been caused by a shotgun fired at close range from inside the door. The hole was chest high on a man.

Bourdon amended his story. He had, he insisted, struggled with Champagne for the gun and won. He then ordered the other from his house and Champagne left, seizing the axe from the kitchen wood box as he went out.

Champagne, axe in hand, approached the screen door. Bourdon managed to hook the door and held it with one hand while the gun was under his other arm. The gun went off and the frightened Bourdon ran, not remembering where he had left the shotgun.

Bourdon's revised version of the killing caused Diefenbaker and Lussier more difficulty than the original. Their client retained all the improbable features of his story and added the dimension of an accidental shooting.

One element supported Bourdon's description of the event. The gunshot hole in the screen was chest high. That was consistent with the single-barrelled gun having been tucked under Bourdon's arm and not raised to his shoulder in a deliberate, aimed shot. Also, although it was his gun, Bourdon would testify that he had never used it and was unfamiliar with firearms.

At the preliminary inquiry, John Diefenbaker cross-examined Constable Flanagan on the thoroughness and accuracy of his investigation. Handing the policeman the sketch he had made of the Bourdon house, the defence lawyer began in a curious way:

"Now, constable, did you use a compass when you went out there and made this sketch?"

"No, I did not."

"My information from the accused is that what you have as north is, in fact, east. Is it possible you made a little error when you went out there?"

"Yes, it is possible, as I did not have a compass with me."

"That was done at night and you say it is just possible you got yourself turned around?"

"Yes, it is just possible."

No conclusions turned on establishing whether the directions were correctly displayed on Flanagan's sketch, but Diefenbaker had what he wanted. His witness was a little off-balance and un-sure of himself. The lawyer continued, bringing out the fact that Flanagan had not made a note of the fact that the screen door had been latched and had overlooked the hole in the screen.

Diefenbaker was also very interested in the position of Champagne's body and its juxtaposition to the axe.

"You do not recall the position of the fingers?"

"No."

"Do you know whether the fists were open or closed?"

"I could not tell that."

"You do not know if the fingers were extended to the side or not?"

"No."

"What was the position of the left hand?"

"I believe the left hand was partly clenched. I would not state that definitely." Flanagan came part way to Diefenbaker, who was trying to establish evidence of a pugilistic Champagne.

The defence set the testimony up nicely for the trial. They were able to expose the police investigation as lacking in thorough-ness. More important, that investigation disclosed no serious evidence that was in conflict with Anthime Bourdon's version of the killing.

When they got to the trial, Diefenbaker found some more help in the testimony of Henry Guignon, the neighbour who had accompanied Bourdon back to his farm to check on Champagne.

"Did the accused say the deceased had threatened to chop him up with the axe?"

"Yes."

"Who asked you to notify the police?"

"Bourdon."

"What state was Bourdon in when you first saw him?"

"He was excited."

"Did you notice his shirt?"

"Yes, it was open."

"And you saw his neck?"

"Yes, it was all red."

"He told you the deceased had tried to choke him?"

"Yes."

"Were the marks on his neck wide or narrow?"

"They were wide."

Anthime Bourdon testified in his own defence. James Hawkins Lindsay, K.C., of Prince Albert, the prosecutor, was kind in cross-examination. But he brought out the confusion in Bourdon's versions of the shooting. He asked the accused about his statement to the police when they first arrived:

"There is nothing to it. I shot the man in self-defence." That was inconsistent with an accidental shooting.

"Would you remember the shooting better on the day it happened than you do now?"

"There were three or four days when I could remember nothing."

"Do you remember it all now?"

"Yes."

The Bourdon neighbours all supported Diefenbaker's portrayal of Peter Champagne as a wild and dangerous man. The women of the district were terrified of him.

Since it was Lussier's case, he claimed the privilege of addressing the jury. In his opening, the senior defence counsel paid tribute to the absolute fairness of the Crown in its presentation of the evidence. As he listened, John Diefenbaker must have winced. That was not his style. In his cross-examinations at the preliminary Diefenbaker had set the stage for allegations of inadequate, near-incompetent police investigation that might well have been more effective before the jury. Lussier ignored all that groundwork in favour of a positive appeal stressing those aspects of the evidence that supported Bourdon.

Lussier's approach worked, but the jury took nearly four hours to agree on an acquittal. Mr. Justice John Fletcher Leopold Embury, on thanking them, told the jury members that he agreed entirely with their verdict.

It was John Diefenbaker's first murder trial, and a lawyer could not hope for a nicer, cleaner, more easily defended case. Also, the client could afford the fee. But Diefenbaker never again acted as junior counsel in a criminal trial. In the future, his cases would be conducted in his style, and his style only.

John Diefenbaker was practising alone again. Early in June, 1927, his junior partner, Frank Cousins, died of a heart attack at the age of thirty-four. The death was attributed to wounds suffered overseas ten years before. Diefenbaker's prominence already was such that he was approached by several young lawyers hoping to fill the vacancy, but he took no one in for the next two years. The Wakaw branch continued to operate under R.B. Godfrey until it was closed in 1929. The Prince Albert office reverted to Diefenbaker and Company.

The bachelor lawyer had been living in the Avenue Hotel since arriving in Prince Albert, but now he moved into Sam Donaldson's home. He was joined there by his younger brother Elmer. Elmer had qualified as a teacher and taught school in the Prince Albert district, but soon gave that up in favour of a career as a local insurance agent. Easygoing and affable, a good mixer, musical — all qualities that John lacked — Elmer nevertheless achieved little success. All the spark and talent in the Diefenbaker family seems to have gone to John, who frequently had to come to Elmer's assistance.

It was a quiet time politically for John Diefenbaker, but he continued to maintain his contacts within the Conservative Party. In the fall of 1927 he attended its national convention in Winnipeg where R.B. Bennett was chosen leader in succession to Arthur Meighen. What thoughts were with him as he returned to Prince Albert? Bennett, after all, had begun as a lawyer in Calgary.

The previous year, Diefenbaker had accepted an invitation to address the British Columbia Conservatives in convention at Kamloops. There he was observed and described, perhaps too vividly, by Bruce Hutchison, Canada's veteran political reporter: "He was tall, lean, almost skeletal, his bodily motions jerky and spasmodic, his face pinched and white, his pallor emphasized by metallic black curls and sunken, hypnotic eyes. But from this frail, wraithlike person, so deceptive in his look of physical infirmity, a voice of vehement power and rude health blared like a trombone."

Eclectic clubs — young men's service organizations that merged into the Kinsmen Clubs in 1928 — were active during this period and John Diefenbaker became a prominent director of the Saskatchewan group. Unlike many of the clubs and fraternal lodges he joined later, he had a sincere interest in this activity.

During the last half of the 1920s prosperity returned to Saskatchewan and, finally, to Prince Albert. Wheat prices recovered, although not to their end-of-war peak, and crops were generally good. Improved farming methods and mechanization contributed to increased farm income. Horse-drawn implements began to disappear.

John Diefenbaker, tall, stiff, formally dressed even by the standards of Prince Albert's business and professional group, was an anachronism as he strode to his office on Central Avenue. The sidewalks on either side of the unpaved street were filled with men of the outdoors. The lawyer passed trappers outfitting for their fall migration into the North, bush pilots and policemen, farmers and fishermen. Cree Indians, some lumbermen still, prospectors, railwaymen, gold-miners dredging the alluvial deposits of the Saskatchewan River and its tributaries, prison guards, sportsmen drawn by the fish and game of the North — all passed the doors of the Bank d'Hochelaga building. The stairs up to the second floor led to the law offices of Diefenbaker & Company.

The proprietor's 1927 Chrysler sedan, parked on Central Avenue when an out-of-town trial was due, was impressive, but not overly so. It kept company with a random collection of vehicles ranging from the ubiquitous Model T to luxurious Studebakers. Some horse-drawn buggies and wagons could still be seen on Central Avenue, but most stopped short of the business section.

Saskatchewan's automobile population doubled during the 1920s, reaching almost the highest number of vehicles per capita in Canada. Highways, of a sort, came into being. Horse-drawn buckets and scrapers improved and straightened the dirt road allowances of the western township survey. Tire chains remained an essential accessory, but Highway Number Twelve slowly cut back the four hours needed to navigate from Prince Albert to Saskatoon. Winter driving, however, was still for the intrepid only, and the family car stayed on blocks during the cold weather. Railways were the reliable method of winter transportation.

Prince Albert enjoyed reasonable rail service; five lines focused on the city. Still, the twice-daily run to and from Saskatoon required three hours, and the 250 miles to Regina was an overnight journey of eleven hours. An appearance before the Court of Appeal in Regina, an event that was becoming more common in John Diefenbaker's practice, required two nights on the train. Sleeper cars were standard and Regina passengers could stay on board until nine in the morning, eliminating the need for a hotel.

"Bush flying" developed as a means of servicing the North, and the business was centered in Prince Albert. The river adjacent to the downtown district was a natural runway. The thunder of pontoon and ski-equipped aircraft on takeoff was, until very recently, a common sound in the city. Mineral finds in 1928 sparked a rush of prospecting, and the next year three air service companies were in business.

Great winter caravans of sleighs, drawn first by horses and later by crawler tractors, hauled supplies into the remote camps and communities of the North; fish and fur came back for sale and forwarding. As late as 1928, the twenty-four-member detachment of the provincial police logged more than twenty thousand miles by dog-team and canoe. Even the Post Office depended upon dog mushers and boatmen to deliver the mail into many northern outposts.

Diefenbaker remained impervious to the romance and adventure all about him. He enjoyed a fishing trip into the new Prince Albert national park, but otherwise the North held little attraction for him. Opportunity abounded, but he was not seduced by any of the prospectors or mining promoters with their lure of gold and other mineral finds. Although the 1920s roared as wildly in Prince Albert as anywhere, John Diefenbaker remained a lawyer whose only vice was politics. He avoided entanglement in any of the city's business ventures or civic undertakings. Single-minded and determined, economic success was not among his dreams.

As his prominence and prospects continued to grow, John Diefenbaker thought more seriously of marriage. It was not unusual, even standard, for men to avoid matrimony until they were established, but when Diefenbaker turned thirty-two in 1927, his political ambitions required a wife at his side.

Diefenbaker enjoyed the company of women, but was socially inept. Although he was a born raconteur and could perform well when he was the centre of attention, he found small talk difficult. A lack of coordination and rhythm made Diefenbaker an uncomfortable dancer and, in the 1920s, dancing was the major social interaction between unmarrieds.

Shortly after he moved to Wakaw, Diefenbaker had been close to marriage. But his fiancée, Beth Newell of Saskatoon, was stricken with tuberculosis and the romance foundered. Beth died in May 1924, the month Diefenbaker moved to Prince Albert.

George Will was the pre-eminent realtor in Prince Albert. Will's daughter, Emily, was perhaps the most socially desirable young·woman in Prince Albert. John Diefenbaker began to court the tall and slim Emily. The two made a handsome couple, and many assumed the ambitious lawyer had made an outstanding choice for a wife.

However, sometime in 1927 Diefenbaker became attracted to a vivacious school teacher, Edna May Brower, who lived in Saskatoon. The Brower family had little to offer a prospective son-in-law, but Edna's brother, George, was a successful and well-connected lawyer in Toronto. Diefenbaker began to lose interest in Emily Will.

Edna Brower's background was strikingly similar to John Diefenbaker's. Four years younger than John, she was born in Manitoba, then moved with her family to a homestead west of Saskatoon. Like John, Edna attended high school in Saskatoon. She then went on to Normal School and qualified as a teacher. When she and John met, Edna was teaching in Saskatoon. Outgoing and widely-liked, Edna Brower was a sought-after young lady when she began to return John Diefenbaker's interest. But she would have to pass muster by her prospective mother-in-law, a serious ordeal.

In the summer of 1928, John and Edna drove to California on holiday. Chaperoning, an essential in those days, was provided by his parents. A photograph survives, taken by William. John and Edna, with Mary Diefenbaker dourly looking on, are pictured standing in front of an amusement park.

John Diefenbaker was very much in love with Edna, and Mary granted her approval. Yet Edna would later learn that her acceptance was only conditional and partial. Mary Diefenbaker had no intention of permitting her son's wife to replace her in his affections.

John and Edna began to plan a wedding, scheduled for June of 1929 in Toronto, where her brother Edward lived. But before the wedding took place, major events occurred to shape Diefenbaker's professional and political life.

"Justice delayed is justice denied," according to an old legal maxim, and there could have been little complaint of that sort with the judicial system of sixty years ago, at least in Saskatchewan. Its speed was remarkable, judged against the clogged and ponderous machinery of today. But, on viewing many of the cases in retrospect, one cannot help but wonder if that speed resulted in justice being served.

Diefenbaker's political and professional crony, H.E. (Bert) Keown of Melfort, was thrown into a situation terrifying to a conscientious lawyer. On the morning of October 30, 1928, he was called down to the court house on behalf of one Ernest Olson, a man he had never met. Olson, Keown discovered, was charged with murder and his trial was about to begin. The first question to be determined was whether Olson, because of insanity, was unfit to stand trial.

Keown went into the cells to interview Olson and did the best he could to find out something about the case. The presence of two other prisoners and several policemen made that somewhat difficult. Keown was unable to get any lucid answers from Olson and formed the opinion that the accused was subnormal and unable to instruct a lawyer.

A jury was sworn to decide the sanity issue. The best medical evidence called by the Crown supported Keown's opinion. Dr. L. McNeill, superintendent of the Battleford Mental Hospital, had examined Olson. He found the accused to have the mental age of a boy of eight or nine years, due to "congenital mental defects." McNeill's opinion was that Olson was "feeble-minded" and would be unable to understand his trial.

Dr. H.R. King of the Provincial Gaol at Prince Albert, where Olson awaited his trial, had a different view. King's professional qualifications were minimal, but that seldom deterred him from expressing an opinion. Olson was "normal and capable of understanding," said King. The jury agreed with Dr. King. In just fifteen minutes they were back with their verdict: "Sane."

That formality was dispensed with by noon, and Mr. Justice MacDonald adjourned until two o'clock for the commencement of Olson's trial for murder. Keown was frantic. He still knew nothing about the case.

Olson was charged with the murder of William Robson, a farmer for whom he had once worked. When Olson left Robson's employ some two years earlier, Mrs. Robson followed. She lived with Olson until six weeks before the murder; when she left him, she did not return to her husband.

Then someone burned down Robson's house with Robson and his housekeeper inside. The farmer's carelessness with kerosene lanterns was first thought to have caused the tragedy. No one had seen Olson anywhere in the neighbourhood the night of the fire.

Five days later, Mrs. Robson came forward with a story. Olson had visited her at the farm home where she was employed. Her former lover, she said, told her that he had murdered Robson and the housekeeper with an axe and then torched the house. Mrs. Robson had not immediately revealed this information to anyone. She went back into the house and said nothing. Not unnaturally, Keown found that circumstance suspicious. He went after Mrs. Robson.

"You knew a man had confessed to you he had killed your husband, yet you went into the house and did not tell? You mean us to believe that?"

"She is telling the truth." The interjection came from Mr. Justice MacDonald, and rang in the courtroom like the voice of doom. That judicial verification of Mrs. Robson's veracity all but finished the defence. But Keown soldiered on.

He did the best he could with the jury. Keown pointed out that Olson had no motive at all to kill Robson. Mrs. Robson, on the other hand, had plenty of motive. She was intimate with her new employer; she had left Robson because of his beatings; and it would be very convenient for her to have her husband out of the way. And Mrs. Robson, Keown emphasized, was the only direct evidence linking Olson to the crime. Her evidence should be viewed with great suspicion.

The jury disagreed. It took them only two hours to reach their verdict: "Guilty." Mr. Justice MacDonald rendered the automatic and traditional sentence upon Olson: "That you be taken hence to Prince Albert Gaol until February 5th, 1929, then you are to be hanged by the neck until you are dead and may God have mercy upon your soul."

Keown announced that he intended to appeal the finding of sanity by the first jury. He took the case to John Diefenbaker in Prince Albert.

Diefenbaker was appalled. Even in an era of rough justice, the Olson case stood out. The accused, mentally capable or not, did not have with him a properly prepared lawyer. Keown had no chance to search out any background on the case that might have enabled him to seriously question Mrs. Robson's story, or even to learn if his client had an alibi. The whole proceeding smacked of frontier justice.

But, Diefenbaker pointed out to Keown, there was nothing they could do with the first jury finding that Olson was sane enough to stand trial. There was no error in the trial on that issue. The jury had chosen to disregard the superior evidence of Dr. McNeill and had gone with Dr. King. That, Diefenbaker reluctantly said, was that. It was a different matter with the main trial. Surely an appeal court would agree that Mr. Justice MacDonald's intervention during Mrs. Robson's cross-examination had so prejudiced the defence as to justify a new trial.

Diefenbaker and Keown headed to the Court of Appeal. There John Diefenbaker presented a strong argument. He tried to convince the appeal judges that the trial judge's remark, at such a critical moment in the cross-examination of such a key witness, "improperly imparted to her an unmerited sense of confidence and gave the jury an unwarranted assurance of her credibility."

Diefenbaker went on to demonstrate weak points in Mrs. Robson's testimony. He suggested that she herself might have been responsible for the crime, and had fabricated Olson's confession for the purpose of directing blame upon another. Olson's conviction, Diefenbaker contended, was based upon a miscarriage of justice that could only be cured by a new trial.

The Court of Appeal agreed that MacDonald's comment was "unfortunate." However, on looking at his charge to the jury, when he told them they were the sole judges of whether or not Mrs. Robson was telling the truth, the court did not consider that a miscarriage of justice had occurred. Ernest Olson's murder conviction was confirmed.

But the appeal judges questioned the first jury's verdict on Olson's sanity, and its disregard of Dr. McNeill's testimony. They recommended that the medical evidence be brought to the attention of the minister of justice. John Diefenbaker did just that and, on February 1, 1929, the federal Cabinet commuted Olson's death sentence, leaving him to serve life in the Prince Albert penitentiary.

It was Diefenbaker's second involvement with a murder trial. Again, he regretted not having been in charge of the whole case.

Zealous police and prosecutors brought some bizarre cases before the courts. Shortly after Olson's commutation, Diefenbaker was engaged to defend a client charged with "abduction of an heiress." The offence, which no longer exists, consisted of fraudulently inducing a woman under twenty-one years who was possessed of property to leave her parents against their will, all with the intention of marrying her.

Diefenbaker's client certainly had persuaded the girl to leave her unconsenting mother, and did hope to marry her, in spite of the fact that she did not rate very highly as an heiress. The intended bride owned a one-third interest in a heavily mortgaged quarter-section of land and was worth all of $100.

The defence counsel pointed out the complete absence of any element of fraud, the trial judge agreed and took the case away from the jury. The accused was free to carry on with his plans for marriage, if he could still afford them.

Then there was the case of the trapper Verner Johnson. In an early version of what later came to be known as "mercy flights" when performed by air, Johnson, of remote Dore Lake, became famous throughout the North. Mushing his dog-team more than fifty miles through a blinding January blizzard, Johnson carried a young woman stricken with appendicitis safely to medical help. A year later, however, Johnson stood before a jury charged with perjury and John Diefenbaker defended him. The facts were strange.

Johnson had divorced his wife after finding her in bed with another man. At the divorce trial, he testified that he had left town, by dog-team, the morning after the discovery. Now his ex-wife was testifying against Johnson, saying that he had done no such thing but had stayed around town more than a week.

Perjury requires, in addition to false evidence, an intent to mislead, and it is hard to conceive what difference it would have made to the divorce action if Johnson left town when he said he did; his ex-wife freely admitted her adultery.

Diefenbaker established, by re-creating Johnson's journey from known points and calculations of the speed of dog-teams, that he must have left Dore Lake when he said he had. Johnson was acquitted in a blaze of publicity.

Soon afterwards, as the relative peace which had followed the one provincial and two federal elections in 1925 and 1926 began to evaporate, Diefenbaker was drawn back into the political arena. Two more contests — the 1929 provincial and the 1930 federal — were approaching, and the Conservative Party, to its later sorrow, would win both.

In the last half of the "Roaring Twenties" the political and social climate of Saskatchewan shifted. As prosperity was finally achieved, the frontier spirit of acceptance, equality and co-operation was displaced by an upsurge of racial and religious antagonism. The Anglo-Scandinavian and Protestant majority began to indulge in increasing intolerance towards the immigrants from eastern Europe, Catholics, Jews and, particularly, the French-speaking community.

Bigotry roared through the province and soon pervaded its politics. Diefenbaker was drawn into the maelstrom, as were almost all the political activists of the day. For years to come his career would be tainted by allegations arising out of two furious election campaigns, one a by-election and one a provincial general election.

The fires of prejudice were fanned by two organizations, usually peripheral to politics, but so immersed in the issues that dominated both elections as to be barely distinguishable from the Conservative Party. It, too, was singed when it came too close to the fires of prejudice and these two groups that served as spear-carriers.

The Loyal Order of Orange, a protestant fraternal society which originated in Northern Ireland, had a one-hundred-year tradition in Canada, and its lodges were common throughout western communities. In the 1920s it became an active antagonist in a campaign against the French language and Catholic influence in Saskatchewan schools. *The Sentinel*, the official organ of the order, was virulent in its attacks against what it saw as the "Rome-ruled Department of Education."

But the Orange Lodge was not alone. Into the fertile conditions Saskatchewan offered came another society, one with a history both extremist and violent. In 1926 the Ku Klux Klan arrived from the southern United States, via Ontario.

The Klan organizers were immediately successful: by 1927 their $13 membership fee had netted more than $100,000, with which the promoters promptly absconded. The Klan survived that setback and its affairs were taken over by J.J. Maloney, an emissary from Ontario first sent into Saskatchewan to help David L. Burgess, the contender against Mackenzie King in the 1926 Prince Albert by-election.

Under Maloney, who claimed to be a fallen-away Catholic theologian, the Klan became a raging success and a powerful political influence. Its product of Anglo-Scandinavian supremacy, anti-Catholicism, anti-Semitism and anti-French sold well. Local Klan chapters sprang up throughout the province, and many communities witnessed monster Klan rallies, with crowds in the thousands, hooded Klansmen and burning crosses. By 1928 Maloney was claiming seventy thousand members. That number, almost 10 per cent of the province's population, was a gross exaggeration. Better estimates put the total at between fifteen and forty thousand, but no one can guess at the number of fellow-travellers the Klan attracted.

The Ku Klux Klan in Canada, and more so in Saskatchewan where it became autonomous in 1928, was modelled on the American Klan, but adapted to the local climate. No night-riding vigilantes were seen in the West, and, with only one or two exceptions, no violence attended Klan rallies. The Klan constitution, stated in the Ku Klux Kreed, declared it to be "devoted to the sublime principles of a pure patriotism and valiant in the defense of its ideals and institutions." Those fine words, and more, encompassed the Klan's righteous discrimination against all who were not white, Protestant, Gentile and English-speaking.

A colourful description of the Klan was penned by the editor of a rural Saskatchewan paper, the *Maple Creek News*, in 1927, after attending a Klan rally:

"Having no private source of information, The News, in common with the average man in the street, believed that the pet aversion of the K.K.K. was Niggers, Chinks, Jews and Catholics. After hearing the Klan speaker in The Grand last Thursday night, we now know that we must add Germans, Russians, Austrians, Frenchmen, Spaniards, Italians and Liberals.

"S'death, the list grows more respectable."

The particular target of both the Ku Klux Klan and the Orange Order was the presence, however minimal, in the Saskatchewan school system of the Roman Catholic Church and the French language. The emotional barrage was extended to include the Gardiner Liberal government, viewed as the beneficiary of the political support of the minorities under attack. Because of their common enemy, the Klan and the Orange Order became political bedfellows of the Conservative Party in Saskatchewan.

Dr. James Thomas Milton Anderson, a prominent educator and a Saskatoon MLA, had been elected leader of the Saskatchewan Conservatives in 1924, but gave up the position after the party took only three seats in the 1925 general election. In March 1928 he resumed the leadership at a Saskatoon convention where the Conservatives organized to unseat the Gardiner government. The convention was well-attended by representatives of both the Klan and the Orange Order. In fact, Klansmen openly handed out their brochures to the arriving delegates until stopped, late in the morning, by an astute convention organizer.

An attempt by federal Conservative leader R.B. Bennett and others to establish a rapprochement between the Catholic community and the Conservative Party was squelched by the Saskatchewan Conservatives. Bennett's selected convention speakers, one a Catholic MP, were rejected. Only three of the more than three hundred delegates were Catholics, and a difficulty arose over granting any of the three recognition by appointment to the fifty-seven-member provincial executive. A powerful faction in the party strongly resisted any concession to Catholics.

After serious backroom debate, the nominating committee finally included two Catholics on lists to be submitted to the delegates. The first was defeated, and the second disappeared from the list in circumstances so suspicious that they were reported to R.B. Bennett. The amended list, it developed, had been typed by John Diefenbaker running one of the convention typewriters.

The result of having no Catholics at all upon the Conservative provincial executive caused some acrimony and concern, but was quite satisfactory to the party establishment, which seemed to include Diefenbaker. Anderson himself explained that the situation was "unavoidable as well as in some ways regrettable." The Klan and Orange influence had had its way.

Among the resolutions adopted at the convention was one calling for the prohibition of "the use of any religious emblems in the public schools of Saskatchewan...." The Conservative Party had put its finger on the single most controversial issue of the coming campaigns.

Several prominent Saskatchewan Conservatives wrote R.B. Bennett expressing their concerns about the party's attachment to the Klan and the Orange Lodge, and about its assumption of an anti-Catholic posture. John Alexander Macdonald Patrick, a highly-regarded Yorkton lawyer, stated, "I am afraid we have fallen far short of the traditions of the old Conservative party." Bennett enlisted Murdoch A. MacPherson, a prominent Regina lawyer and a leading Conservative, to give him an objective assessment of the situation. MacPherson reported that there had been manipulation at the convention, and that the new party vitality was "purely Protestant and anti-Catholic."

The leading spokesman of the extremist wing of the Saskatchewan Conservatives was James Fraser Bryant, another Regina lawyer. Bryant represented the Klan and its officers on several occasions when they had run afoul of the law. Also prominent was Dr. Walter Davy Cowan, the Unionist MP for Regina from 1917 to 1921, and soon to be the Conservative MP for Long Lake. Cowan was the Saskatchewan treasurer of the Klan.

Bryant was pleased with the outcome of the Conservative convention. He reported to R.B. Bennett, in a letter he requested be destroyed: "We were extremely careful in connection with our handling of the church problem and handling of the language question. The K.K.K. were very active indeed at the convention, as were also the Orangemen. The head officers of both organizations were present and the organizers of the Klan being very evident throughout the hall. We had some difficulty in keeping them in the background, but succeeded in doing so without any incident whatever...."

Premier Gardiner threw the gauntlet at the Klan, beginning in early January, 1928. He attacked its appeal to racial and religious differences, and accused both the Conservative and Progressive Parties of having links to the Klan. Hoping to defeat the Klan in head-on confrontation, Gardiner called a by-election for October 1928 in Arm River, a rural riding midway between Saskatoon and Regina.

The Conservatives were ready. So was the Klan. So was the Orange Order. The Conservative candidate, Stewart Adrain, another Regina lawyer, was the Grand Secretary of the Orange Lodge. Mrs. Adrain was the Grand Mistress for British North America of the Ladies' Orange Benevolent Association. Adrain had publicly declared his opposition to separate schools and bilingualism.

The Arm River by-election to this day holds the record as the most vicious in Saskatchewan's history. The school and language questions and the Klan were not the only issues. The Conservatives, led by Bryant, also attacked the Gardiner Liberals on patronage and corruption, and made many of their charges stick.

One of these charges involved the illegal trade in alcohol. The prohibition experiment, whatever else it accomplished, created an entirely new cottage industry in the making, selling and exportation of liquor. In 1923, the RCMP estimated that there were "more illicit stills in Saskatchewan, with a population of 760,000, than there are in the rest of Canada." By the time the experiment ended in Saskatchewan in 1925, two enterprising brothers, Harry and Sam Bronfman, founders of the Bronfman dynasty, had achieved pre-eminence in the industry. Early in 1928, a federally-established Royal Commission investigating customs abuses recommended the immediate prosecution of Harry Bronfman for attempted bribery of a customs official. Since the chairman of the commission was Chief Justice J.T. Brown of the Saskatchewan Court of King's Bench, the recommendation was seriously received in that province.

Attorney General T.C. Davis seemed reluctant to take action, suggesting lamely that it was a federal matter. The prosecution of Harry Bronfman became a hot campaign issue, and fitted in with the anti-Semitic prejudice of the day. No less a personage than G.E. Lloyd, Anglican bishop of Prince Albert, publicly warned that "Jews defile the country by engaging in disreputable pursuits."

During the Arm River campaign, J.F. Bryant charged that the Liberal Party was in league with the liquor interests and had turned Saskatchewan "into a bootleggers paradise." Harry Bronfman, "the king of the bootleggers," had paid the Liberal Party for immunity from prosecution. Feeling the once-solid Liberal seat slipping away, T.C. Davis promised that he would personally guarantee that Harry Bronfman was prosecuted.

Bryant's charges of corruption were as nothing compared to his wild accusations on the religion and language front. He saw a conspiracy between the Liberals and the Catholic Church to quietly seize political control in Saskatchewan. "Within five years, or ten at the most, under present political conditions, Roman Catholics will be the majority in Saskatchewan, and the French will control the political destinies of Quebec, Saskatchewan and all of Canada," Bryant claimed from one Arm River platform. From another, the Conservative spokesman revealed the first details of a plot he had uncovered to bring five hundred thousand Catholic immigrants into Saskatchewan. The story, he said, had been suppressed by the Liberal press.

Bryant was openly sympathetic to the Ku Klux Klan, which was "sweeping Saskatchewan like a prairie fire." The Klan, he claimed, was "an expression of the fact that thousands of Protestants in this province, who have a clear idea of the situation in Saskatchewan, are eagerly enrolling themselves under the banner of that order in the hope that, by a concerted effort wisely directed, they may yet save the day."

Bryant made no effort to conceal his religious bigotry. According to him, the Pope had recently stated, "What a vast and magnificently Catholic country is Canada." Bryant continued: "To make Canada a more magnificently Catholic country, the immigration policy of the Federal Government, directed by the French Catholic Bishops of Quebec, is endeavoring to fill Canada with Catholic immigrants."

Embarrassed by Bryant's virulence, several of the more traditional Conservative leaders discreetly declined to engage in the Arm River campaign. Party leader Anderson followed Bryant's lead, but somewhat more discreetly.

John Diefenbaker came down from Prince Albert to participate in the last few days of the by-election. Sharing several platforms with Bryant, he perhaps drew upon his experience six years earlier in Boutin v. Mackie as he spoke of public schools in his area where religious emblems and French language instruction had become inescapable. But his views had changed — he was no longer a champion of minority rights.

On the last Saturday of the campaign, Diefenbaker invaded a Liberal meeting organized for Premier Gardiner. It was a rash act, for Gardiner was known to be deadly in debate, but the Liberal leader invited the Conservative onto his platform.

"As it appears to be the custom for speakers in this campaign to indicate their religious beliefs," Diefenbaker opened, "I hereby state that I am a Baptist and I am not a member of the Ku Klux Klan."

He had come, Diefenbaker continued, to ask the premier "some questions in connection with education."

"I want to ascertain this evening the stand of the premier in respect to sectarian influences which we in the northern part of the province find pervading the entire education system." In Wakaw, Diefenbaker claimed, "nuns in religious garb teach in what is a public school and the crucifix is hung on the wall."

Then, as if he had been too long with Bryant, Diefenbaker referred to Gardiner's recent trip to eastern Canada.

"Do you know also where he went?" he asked darkly, before answering his own question.

"He went into Quebec province," Diefenbaker announced, reading an extract from a French paper in proof.

When Gardiner responded to Diefenbaker's concern about the Wakaw school, he asked the journalists present not to report his remarks. He was, he said, "more interested in getting peace and harmony and a solution in Wakaw than in winning votes in Arm River."

That went down well with the Arm River audience, but not with John Diefenbaker. Speaking in North Battleford after the Arm River election, the Prince Albert Conservative turned Gardiner's pious comment into a parody.

"The other night I had an opportunity on the platform with Premier Gardiner to ask him some questions. Nearly every answer, he instructed the reporter, 'Don't put that down.'

"He admitted the trouble in Wakaw school arose 'because we have a very bigoted priest there,' and then added, 'Don't put that down.'

"When I asked him, 'Mr. Gardiner, do you believe in teachers in public schools wearing clerical garb or lodge regalia during school hours?' he answered, 'I have no time to answer that, don't put that down, Mr. Reporter.' Then he spoke for two hours after." Diefenbaker's audience broke up in laughter.

The Arm River result was a harbinger of the provincial election to come. The Liberals kept the seat, but their majority was shaved to fifty-nine votes. Gardiner complained to Mackenzie King of the Ku Klux Klan activities in the campaign. On voting day, he said, they placed men dressed as priests near several polling stations to give the impression the Catholic Church was running the election for the Liberals.

The Regina *Daily Star* expressed the Conservative sentiments in an editorial: "By a small majority, the electors of Arm River have decided to sustain a Government which stands convicted of diverting public money to its own party's coffers, of debasing the public service, of rewarding men charged with penal offences with government positions, of neglecting the enforcement of law and order, of prostituting British Courts of Justice, of promoting policies for the purpose of securing votes, of shielding bootleggers, of raising religious differences for party purposes, of manipulating contracts to obtain support."

The Arm River election was over, but the campaign continued as the entire province heated up for the provincial election expected the following summer.

Bryant grew more specific with his charge that the Liberals and the Catholic Church were conspiring to quietly infiltrate the province with hundreds of thousands of Quebec settlers. His fantastic claim was taken up by the *Daily Star* and the Orange Lodge through *The Sentinel*. They saw Saskatchewan becoming a second Quebec. The Gardiner Liberals, those publications predicted, would be perpetuated in office by the new voters.

The school question continued as a burning issue. On the North Battleford platform, John Diefenbaker stated: "I do not believe in bigotry. I would not like to see the Conservative Party go into power on a religious question. I do not wish to hurt the religious feelings of any, but in the face of danger it is necessary to speak frankly."

Diefenbaker described a school where, he said, the "teachers were put out and nuns brought in and the crucifix erected in the school. An altar and crucifix were installed in every room. Protestants were forced to send their children there.

"Ask any Catholic, is that fair? Would you wish to send your child to a school presided over by an Orangeman in regalia or a Klansman in a nightshirt?"

In January 1929, the Prince Albert Orange Lodge, of which John Diefenbaker was a member, unanimously passed a resolution stating that it was "on record as being most vigorously opposed to the Papal Delegate receiving recognition by the Parliament of this country, and further that we stand opposed to any Ecclesiastical recognition by the government of this Dominion." The resolution was forwarded, not to the Prince Albert MP, Prime Minister Mackenzie King, but to Conservative leader R.B. Bennett.

In the spring of 1929, the Conservatives in Prince Albert organized to defeat Attorney General T.C. Davis, by then one of the stars of the Gardiner government, in his own riding. Samuel J. Branion had succeeded Davis as mayor four years earlier, and had earned respect in the office, proving himself in successive elections. The Conservative tide was rising, and Branion was ready to take on Davis.

But Branion, who had much to do with John Diefenbaker becoming the federal Conservative candidate in 1925, was chagrined by the actions of his protegé. Two hours before the nominating meeting, held on April 26, Diefenbaker, who had earlier declined entreaties to run, decided that he would, after all, be the candidate. Branion was overwhelmed by Diefenbaker, still popular from his 1925 and 1926 campaigns.

The late entrant posed as a reluctant draftee. "I have no ambition to become a member of the Legislature," he told the convention called to choose just that, "but I am willing to assist the Conservative cause." Diefenbaker did pay tribute to Mayor Branion, and spoke highly of the assistance he had received from him in his previous elections.

That evening the successful nominee shared a public platform with party leader Anderson. Diefenbaker received a loud and prolonged cheer when he rose. He spoke again on the school question, and the charge that the Conservatives were intolerant. "I want to say this is false. It would be presumptive of me to say anything against my good friends the Catholics, of whom I have many, or their great church."

During the election, the Prince Albert Conservative campaign literature included a brochure on the school question. It concluded: "When casting your franchise, be not led astray by various last minute stories which are being circulated by Gardiner supporters. Vote for the Conservative candidate, J. G. Diefenbaker, if you believe in A PUBLIC SCHOOL FREE FROM SECTARIAN INFLUENCES.

"BY YOUR VOTE YOU WILL DETERMINE THE FUTURE OF SASKATCHEWAN'S PUBLIC SCHOOLS."

The campaign across the province for the June 6 election was vicious, and it was no less so in Prince Albert. In spite of his Arm River commitment, T.C. Davis had not ordered prosecution of Harry Bronfman. Diefenbaker and the Conservatives hammered

Davis on this issue, and accused him of having a conflict of interest in the awarding of legal patronage in the city.

Clifford Sifton Davis, younger brother and law partner of the attorney general, charged in turn that the Conservative candidate was associated with the Ku Klux Klan: "Mr. Diefenbaker is hand in hand with the Ku Klux Klan, and if elected he would be directly answerable to it." Davis claimed to have a list of the Klan membership, "and it is only necessary to go into Mr. Diefenbaker's committee rooms and you will find the heads among them there." Diefenbaker, usually quick to respond to personal attacks upon him, made no answer to Davis's allegations. The charge of association with the Ku Klux Klan would stay with him for twenty years.

The Gardiner Liberals reeled under the Conservative charges of corruption, influence peddling, and, worst of all, political interference with the administration of justice, Davis's portfolio. Harry Bronfman's apparent immunity under the Liberals was the centrepiece of the Tory onslaught, but other specific accusations came forward. J.F. Bryant, running successfully for the Conservatives in Lumsden, produced affidavits from Liberal defectors swearing to instances of the use of the provincial police for political purposes.

When the ballots were counted on June 6, 1929, the Liberals had dropped 6 per cent in the popular vote and twenty-two members; the Conservatives had picked up 13 per cent and twenty-one members. Gardiner had retained twenty-six seats (two more came later in deferred elections) to Anderson's twenty-four, but he had no majority in the sixty-three-seat legislature. Six Independents and five Progressives carried the balance of power.

In Prince Albert, T.C. Davis held firm with a 415 vote edge over John Diefenbaker. It was a Conservative year, but not for the aspiring Diefenbaker, to whom it would not be apparent for several years how fortunate he had been to lose the 1929 election. The wormwood he suffered in his defeat by his arch-rival was tempered by the knowledge that Davis and the Gardiner Liberals would soon be out of office.

In the Arm River and Saskatchewan elections of 1928 and 1929, John Diefenbaker came perilously close to poisoning his future political career. Only a few 1929 Conservative candidates escaped the taint that came to be attached to that campaign. The Ku Klux Klan soon disappeared from the Saskatchewan scene, but its mark remained for years.

Because the political interests of the Klan and the Anderson Conservatives were identical, it was not possible to separate fully their activities, even without the unofficial arrangements worked out by Bryant and Dr. W.D. Cowan. No Conservative campaigner in Arm River could fail to meet a Klansman on a similar errand.

C.S. Davis was probably right when he claimed that Klan members were in Diefenbaker's committee rooms. Prince Albert had a large Klan, as politically active as any other; its membership was supposedly secret, and politicians are reluctant to reject campaign assistance. The Klan had wide appeal and, until Gardiner declared war upon the movement, at least some Liberals had been attracted to its cause.

Many Conservatives had been saved from too close an association with the Klan by a similar stricture issued by R.B. Bennett. The federal leader was disturbed when Saskatchewan leader Anderson was implicated in court affidavits filed by former Klan organizers prosecuted for absconding with Klan funds. "Indiscreet," Bryant called Anderson.

Battle-scarred Arm River, barely held by the Liberals in the by-election, fell to the Conservatives in the general election by nearly seven hundred votes. The Klan influence lingered longer in that constituency than any other area of the province. It later became the foundation of John Diefenbaker's political career.

Although the Liberals lost their majority, Gardiner still held the largest group of seats and had a legitimate claim to stay in office. This he did, against the advice of many prominent members of the Liberal Party who knew that the mood of the province for change had been but partially registered at the polls. Final defeat awaited only the calling of the legislature. That would come in early September.

The political situation in Saskatchewan was so tender during the summer of 1929 that it is a wonder that Diefenbaker was able to tear himself away, even for marriage. But he did, and met the pretty and charming Edna Brower in Toronto on June 29 for a wedding hosted by her brother, Edward. He was without family for his marriage; his parents and brother Elmer remained in Saskatoon and Prince Albert. That decision was perhaps dictated by economy, the groom deciding that the expense of bringing the three to the East was unwarranted.

His marriage did not keep John Diefenbaker away from Saskatchewan for long; the honeymoon was brief and consisted of the westward trip from Toronto. The Prince Albert lawyer was soon home, once again resident in The Avenue Hotel, but this time with a bride, and only briefly, while their home was being readied.

Almost immediately upon John and Edna's return, there began for him the busiest time of his career so far. During the next two years his prominence would spread to every corner of Saskatchewan.

In Regina, James G. Gardiner, still premier, called the legislature into session on September 4. His attempts to woo support from the Progressive and Independent members had failed, and Gardiner knew the jig was up. In fact, he had known that since early July, when all the non-Liberal members signed a petition to the Lieutenant-Governor calling for the resignation of his government.

At the first opportunity for a division, the election of a Speaker, the government's nominee was defeated by the Conservative choice, J.F. Bryant. With a prescience he could not then have appreciated, Gardiner persisted, forcing Anderson and the Conservatives to wrest power from him. Finally, Gardiner was again defeated, this time upon a clear motion of non-confidence. Just after midnight, on September 6, the Liberals, who had held the government of Saskatchewan since 1905, gave it up. The Anderson Conservatives, with the support of the Progressives and the Independents, were sworn into office three days later.

"LIBERAL GOVERNMENT DEFEATED" screamed the front-page headline in Regina's *Morning Leader* later that day. Underneath, another eight-column banner read: "John Pasowesty Refuses to Talk at Mother's Murder Hearing." An interesting murder case was underway at Sheho, more than one hundred miles northeast of Regina.

As Lieutenant-Governor Newlands prorogued the Legislative Assembly, his closing remarks contained an ominous reference: "I note with pleasure the steps you have taken to cope effectively with the problems resulting from the long period of dry weather in some parts of the Province." Six weeks later, on Black Thursday, October 29, the stock market collapsed into a continuing decline that became the worldwide Great Depression. In Saskatchewan, the agony to come would be compounded by the added calamity of ten years of drought.

The Dirty Thirties had arrived.

6

Rex v. Pasowesty

Farming 1,120 acres of land with horses required a fair herd of horses plus a lot of manpower. On August 1, 1929, Nick Pasowesty started his crew early, as usual. He roused his two sons, Peter and John, and the hired man at 5:30 a.m. before he himself drove the cattle out to pasture. Nick's third wife, Annie, and the hired girl were up at the same time. Mary Pasowesty, only nine, would attend school that day and was allowed to sleep later.

Nick issued the working orders to his men. Peter and John would cut hay, and the hired man would cultivate summerfallow. Three teams were needed, and seventeen-year-old John was directed to bring eight horses in from the pasture. With the day organized, Nick left on foot, driving eighteen cows ahead of him to join the balance of his herd in the pasture two miles away.

As was often the case, John was a problem that morning, moving too slowly for Nick's liking. Nick seized a stick, intending to put some speed into the lazy youth, but the boy's mother interceded. Nick and Annie quarrelled.

Nick Pasowesty was not a lazy man. The success the fifty-six-year-old Ruthenian had achieved since coming to the Sheho district twenty-eight years before was due to hard work, and he expected the same from his family. Two wives had died on his farm, and neither had been as demanding as Annie, twenty years his junior.

Nick thought about Annie as he trudged along behind his cattle. A car and a new floor in the house, she wanted, and a dress.

Could she not understand that the rains had not come and the crop was light?

Nick wondered if Annie could be part of the problem with John. Pete, his son by his first wife, was a good man, hardworking. Two quarters of the land were already really his. Never mind that he had kept Pete out of school to work. A man was better off with land than with schooling. Pete would do well. But John? That foolishness three weeks ago. Driving nine head of cattle to Invermay, selling them and buying that new Ford car. Nick has no car. Pete has no car. But the boy has to have a car.

And giving that cheque to the Doukhobor in the garage when he had no money in the bank. Where did he learn to do that? The boy had no bank account. Anyway, he should learn that the place for a man's money, if he had any, was in his pocket, where Nick's was right now. Nick had a hell of a time fixing all that up and getting his cattle back. He told John he would damn well work off the money for the Doukhobor.

The cattle saw the rest of the herd in the pasture and moved quickly through the gate. Nick Pasowesty turned back down the rutted and seldom used road allowance. He would check to see if Annie had finished the milking and then go into Sheho for the cream can ready for the next shipment.

Halfway home, a blast from a twelve-gauge shotgun took Nick Pasowesty in the back of the head. The farmer fell dead on his face. His assailant seized his heels and dragged the body one hundred feet into the centre of a small bluff.

It was the next day when Peter Pasowesty found his father's body. Late that afternoon RCMP Constable L.V. Ralls of the Foam Lake detachment investigated. He quickly found where the murderer had lain in wait behind some willow bushes next to the road. Two shotgun shells were there — one exploded, one not.

Ralls checked Nick Pasowesty's pockets. There was no money.

Later, the police found the shotgun, an old double-barrelled twelve-gauge, its three sections, barrels, stock and forearm separately hidden.

Ralls took statements from all the Pasowesty family and the hired help, but no one knew what had happened after Nick drove the cattle up the road. John had gone for the horses as instructed, but had returned one short of the eight required. Sent back, he had ridden one horse and led another home. Peter and the hired man had spent the day mowing and discing as Nick had planned. In the afternoon, John had gone off to town with a neighbour boy, Laddie Kuchinsky, with whom he spent the night.

The shotgun belonged on the farm. It was kept in the black-smith shop with a partial box of shells.

On Saturday, two days after the killing, Ralls was back on the Pasowesty farm. He wondered if perhaps the shooting was a result of trouble with a neighbour. John gave the policeman another written statement on that subject. So did Peter.

To the policeman, Peter Pasowesty "seemed as though he was trying to evade questioning and that kind of thing," so he took him into custody.

The next day Ralls thought better of his action, released Peter, and had another talk with John. Still co-operative, John gave a third written statement, this one detailing his movements on the day of the murder.

Continuing his investigation, Ralls interviewed Laddie Kuchinsky. During their afternoon together in town, the boys had spent pretty freely. They had shot some pool, had lunch at the Chinese restaurant, and enjoyed shaves in the barber shop. John Pasowesty had paid for everything, including some new head-light bulbs for Laddie's car.

John's sudden wealth corroborated a far more incriminating statement given to Ralls by Laddie. John had told Laddie, "I killed my old man and we have to take him away from there." When his friend refused to believe him, John Pasowesty asked to borrow Laddie's car that night to perform the chore himself.

"You're crazy," Laddie replied, and was about to drive off alone when John reconsidered.

"Honest to God, I didn't do it. Do you think I'm crazy?" he said.

The two carried on with their lark. The incident was forgotten until Nick Pasowesty's death was a known fact and Constable Ralls came on the scene.

Laddie's statement was enough for Ralls. He arrested John Pasowesty and took him to the detachment cells in Foam Lake

The following afternoon, John called for Ralls. "I want to tell you how everything was done," he said. The policeman knew about confessions. He carefully warned the boy that he need not say anything and that, if he did, it would be used against him at his trial. That much was standard, but Ralls was careful. He went for a witness and returned with Harold Ward, the local J.P. The warning was repeated in front of Ward, and John still wanted to talk. It was strong evidence of a voluntary statement, one that would be admissible in court.

He had shot his father, the boy explained, but in self-defence. When he had gone back for the other horse, he had encountered Nick Pasowesty with a gun. Nick shot at him, but missed. John wrestled the gun out of his father's grasp, and, as Nick began to run, shot him.

There was a serious flaw in that story, and Ralls pointed it out: there had been two shells but only one shot.

John Pasowesty promptly volunteered another version, again warned by the two men. He had taken the gun, concealed in his clothing, with him on his first trip for the horses, and hidden it out in the fields. When he went back, this time on horseback, he retrieved the gun and rode over to the route Nick Pasowesty would take back to his farm. There he lay in wait and murdered his father as he passed. "Afterward I was sorry I had shot him, but it was too late," the boy concluded.

That seemed to wrap up the case. But, a week after his preliminary inquiry, John Pasowesty, awaiting trial in the Prince Albert

Gaol, called for a policeman. RCMP Detective Corporal R. H. Smyley arrived.

"What do you want to see me about?" he asked.

"They put me in here for killing my father, and it wasn't me. It was my mother. She told me how she did it and left the gun nearby the body was killed [*sic*]."

John followed that up with a long, rambling account of his movements the day of the killing and a detailed explanation of the shooting as carried out by his mother and confessed to him.

"She told me that I should say that I have killed my old man because I might get out of it somehow because she would get some lawyers for me," he concluded.

That was enough for the Crown. Annie Pasowesty found herself charged with her husband's murder along with her son.

Whether or not Annie Pasowesty had promised lawyers for her son, his accusation against her improved the quality of his legal representation. At John's preliminary inquiry, he was defended by G.T. Killam of Foam Lake. Annie Pasowesty now consulted Killam on her own behalf. Killam could not represent both mother and son. He chose Annie, and John needed a new lawyer. A call went out from the Prince Albert Gaol for John Diefenbaker.

The first matter Diefenbaker had to deal with was Annie's preliminary inquiry, set for September 6. John would be a witness; in fact, he was all the evidence the Crown had implicating Annie Pasowesty in her husband's murder.

Corporal Smyley visited John again at the end of August to see if he was sticking by his story. He was. "She told me if I kept saying it was me, she was going to get me out because I am not old enough and that we were going to live good after she got me out."

John Diefenbaker was not free to attend his new client's preliminary inquiry in Sheho on September 6. He arranged for fellow Conservative J.A.M. Patrick, K.C., of Yorkton, to appear in his place. One suspects that Diefenbaker was in Regina that week, engaged behind the scenes in the struggle for the government of Saskatchewan. But he had given some thought to his client's vulnerability as a Crown witness, still himself under indictment for the same murder. Diefenbaker's instructions to Patrick were clear: John Pasowesty would not testify at his mother's preliminary inquiry.

And so Patrick advised Justice of the Peace W.M. Finlay when court opened in Sheho. Herman Alton Whitman, K.C., Crown prosecutor, persisted and called John Pasowesty as his first witness. The town hall, doubling as a courtroom, was crowded with the Pasowesty neighbours wearing the picturesque costumes of their homelands. In the centre, the husky seventeen-year-old stood before his mother as the lawyers wrangled over his evidence.

"Are you John Pasowesty?" demanded Whitman.

"Refuse to answer. Do not say a thing," Patrick commanded, as his client began to reply to the question.

That was as far as the proceedings got. Whitman wanted Finlay to commit John Pasowesty for contempt of court and toss him in jail until he testified. When Patrick pointed out that his client was already in jail, the prosecutor settled for an adjournment

George Thomas Killam, acting for Annie Pasowesty, was almost lost in the affair. He objected to an adjournment and demanded that the charge be dismissed against his client.

A week later, the Crown accommodated Killam and withdrew the charge of murder against his client. Annie Pasowesty was free, but her son John remained charged with the murder of their husband and father.

That left Killam without a client, but it was just as well. The change of government that took place in Regina during Annie Pasowesty's preliminary soon showed its effect in the Wynyard judicial district. On November 19, 1929, when John Pasowesty came to trial at the fall sittings of the King's Bench at Wynyard, the indictment against him was preferred by his former lawyer, now the new agent of the attorney general, G.T. Killam.

That was going a long way towards conflict of interest, even for a formality, and Killam drew the line right there. Herbert E. Sampson, K.C., a veteran prosecutor from Regina, appeared for the Crown. With Sampson was the newly-appointed agent in the Humboldt judicial district, Ross Jackson Pratt of nearby Wadena.

Anticipating an increased flow of business as a result of the new Conservative government, John Diefenbaker had formed a new law partnership in the fall of 1929. William G. Elder, another Prince Albert lawyer who came to the bar just a year later than Diefenbaker, became the junior member of the firm Diefenbaker and Elder. Rex v. John Pasowesty was the new firm's first major case, and both partners appeared at the trial.

Diefenbaker and Elder had only two arrows in their quiver as they prepared John Pasowesty's defence. First, they would try to contend that their client's confession did not qualify as a voluntary and admissible statement. Here they had a strong chance, in spite of Ralls's precautions. A judge should agree that a seventeen-year-old boy alone in jail might easily be induced to say anything. If they failed to keep out the confession, they would fall back upon John Pasowesty's story that his mother had done the murder, and that he had confessed only at her behest. The chances here were thinner, but still reasonable.

Diefenbaker knew that the odds against either line of defence succeeding were greatly increased when he learned the identity of the trial judge. Mr. Justice George E. Taylor was the terror of the Saskatchewan bar for forty years. A prosecution-minded martinet, he ran his courts with an undisguised iron fist. Not infrequently, a jury would react against his obvious bias and hostile treatment of defence counsel and bring in a verdict of acquittal merely to thwart the judge. (One of the enduring legends of the Saskatchewan bar is of E.C. Leslie, K.C., opening a case in the Court of Appeal: "My Lords, this is an appeal from a judgment of Mr. Justice Taylor. But there are other grounds.")

John Diefenbaker had experienced his share of unpleasant encounters with Mr. Justice Taylor. The defence lawyer had a thorough dislike for the jurist, and knew he was in for another rough ride.

The trouble started early, during Diefenbaker's cross-examination of Annie Pasowesty, a critical exercise because of the defence contention that she was the real murderer. The widow spoke very little English and, like most of the witnesses, testified through a Ruthenian interpreter. That made it difficult for Diefenbaker to get straight answers to his questions.

Mr. Justice Taylor was a man of little patience. When Diefenbaker repeated a question that had not been answered, the judge stepped in:

"Just what she said. Do not ask her again."

"All right, My Lord," Diefenbaker responded diplomatically, and went off in a different direction.

Three questions later, the judge again stopped the defence lawyer. Diefenbaker could not risk a confrontation, and was somewhat obsequious.

"I do not want to pursue any line that is not favoured by your Lordship," he apologized.

Diefenbaker tried to bring out the fact of Annie Pasowesty's arrest and charge with the murder. Sampson objected, and was supported by Mr. Justice Taylor.

"You were present at John's preliminary hearing at Sheho?" Diefenbaker asked.

"I was."

"Were you arrested after that?"

"That is not evidence. That has nothing to do with it, My Lord," Sampson interjected.

"I do not see what that had to do with it," agreed Mr. Justice Taylor.

"It comes up with the subsequent statement made by the accused, and acting upon the statement," Diefenbaker protested.

"It has no bearing on it at all," Sampson persisted.

Diefenbaker was cowed by the opposition, and did not press the matter. That was all the jury heard about the Crown's abortive case against Annie Pasowesty.

Diefenbaker skilfully drew admissions from the police about their treatment of John Pasowesty prior to his arrest and confession. Over a period of two days, Constable Ralls and his partner had put considerable pressure on the boy. Diefenbaker questioned Ralls.

"Did you take the accused in a car on Sunday?"

"Yes, we did."

"And you took him over to the northwest corner of the home quarter?"

"Somewhere up the road."

"Did you say: Now, we want to take those stains off your pants, and then slipped three or four patches from his trousers?"

"Yes, absolutely."

"Then did you suggest to him that there was a possibility of his finger prints being on the gun?"

"We said there might be finger prints on the gun."

"Then after you got the patches, did you say: Well, now, we want to take your boots off you?"

"No, I do not think so. I think we asked him what boots he was wearing the day of the crime."

"Did you tell him to take his boots off?"

"No, I do not think so."

"Did he take his boots off for you, or at your request?"

"He may have done."

"Did you tell him at that time the size of the footprints near the scene of the murder are about the size of your boots?"

"Quite likely."

"Did you say to him: It looks pretty black for you, John?"

"No."

"Never said that?"

"No."

"Did you suggest to the accused at all that the circumstances of the crime pointed to him?"

"No."

Then Diefenbaker moved to the arrest, emphasizing that the police had given young John Pasowesty no opportunity to seek advice from his family.

"Did you let him go in the house after you arrested him?"

"No."

"Did he ask to go in and see his people?"

"I do not think he did."

"Just think of it," the lawyer commanded.

"I do not think he did. If he did, I do not remember."

"You just picked him up, put him in the car and drove away?"

"Yes."

"Just came up, picked up the accused, and whisked him away. Isn't that correct?"

"Yes."

"After arriving in the cell, did he seem to have an appreciation of the circumstances in which he was placed?"

"Just what do you mean by that?"

"Did he seem to understand that he was arrested on a very serious charge?"

"Yes."

"He asked you to go out and get him a funny paper, didn't he?"

"Yes. He asked me to go out and get him a funny paper and some chocolate bars."

Diefenbaker's submission that the Crown had not established that John Pasowesty's confession was voluntary took the form of a running debate with Mr. Justice Taylor. The trial judge contested almost every statement made by the defence lawyer.

Diefenbaker argued that his client, an inexperienced youth with no one to seek advice from, did not appreciate either his situation or the warning Ralls gave him. Further, the lawyer contended, John Pasowesty was actuated by fear.

"Does he appreciate the warning when he comes into town and asks for a funny paper? Does he appreciate the position in which he is placed? It is a most unusual thing for a man charged with murder, realizing the seriousness of the charge against him, to say: 'Well, I would like a funny paper, and I want some candies,' or something of that sort.

"Now, I submit this is a case where the position he was in would excite fear. He had certain things to explain, and he gave an explanation at the time under the influence of that fear."

"You have got the thing wrong," Taylor interrupted, "Here was a thing which was being investigated. The attitude of the constable was to discover the truth, not to unjustly convict anybody. They had had the brother, and being satisfied, let him go." Taylor displayed his usual preference for the Crown and police side of things.

After listening quietly to Herb Sampson, the trial judge settled the issue. He was in no doubt as to the admissibility of the confession. "I must say that I feel so convinced that I could not hope that any further consideration of the matter would alter the conclusion at which I have arrived."

John Pasowesty's confession went to the jury. Diefenbaker and Elder fell back upon their second line of defence: John Pasowesty might have told the truth when he accused his mother of the murder.

The case began to get away from Diefenbaker. Herb Sampson was a tough and competent prosecutor, and he made no concessions. It was not in his interest to give the jury the statements the accused made in Prince Albert Gaol in which he placed the blame on Annie Pasowesty. As the Crown began to wind up its case, Diefenbaker tried desperately to get the Prince Albert statements into evidence. They would be effective only if they came in through a police witness. After all, the police had found them sufficiently believable to justify a charge of murder.

In his attempt, John Diefenbaker ran up against Mr. Justice Taylor, and the defence suffered a serious setback. It was the turning point in the trial.

Sampson did not call Corporal Smyley, who had taken the statements, and Smyley was not even in Wynyard. Diefenbaker had asked the Crown to produce Smyley, and thought they had agreed to do so. He requested that the Crown bring forward the witness he required. Mr. Justice Taylor stepped in, and an unpleasant exchange took place in front of the jury.

"You know how to get them [the witnesses]; to subpoena them and bring them here."

"But the deputy attorney general was down here..." Diefenbaker began.

"Do not make any more statements about that. There is a legal way in which you can get witnesses, and do not start giving evidence in this case yourself."

"With all due diffidence, I was told that all I had to do was to give them the names and they would arrange for subpoenas and everything."

"No matter what I say to you, you seem determined to make statements by way of evidence, and raise issues that should not be brought here at all. You will have your opportunity to argue on the facts, and we do not want a whole lot of cross-trails mixed up into this thing at all. You will understand that. I do not want any more of that at all. You knew that it was open to you to bring witnesses here by issuing a subpoena and bring him here [sic]. That is the legal way to do it. There is no great difficulty about issuing a subpoena by the Court and having it served on any witness you want in the province, so far as that goes. His Majesty's advisers out of their great condescension sometimes consent to bring witnesses, but if you want evidence it is your duty to get it yourself. Proceed please."

Judge Taylor loved to berate counsel, and this lecture was classic Taylor. In front of the jury, it made Diefenbaker look inept and ill-prepared. In truth, the defence was a little naive and careless in not ensuring that Smyley would be produced. But, then again, Diefenbaker had an undertaking from the Crown to produce the witness. Whether by misunderstanding, or otherwise, that undertaking was not met, at great prejudice to the accused. Mr. Justice Taylor, by refusing even to hear Diefenbaker, countenanced that prejudice.

Without Smyley, John Pasowesty's statements accusing his mother of the murder could go into evidence only through his own testimony. Not only was that the least effective way of presenting the story, it forced the accused into the witness box, something Diefenbaker wanted to avoid at all costs. Now he had no choice.

Late in the afternoon of the second day of the trial, John Pasowesty stood before the Wynyard jury and Diefenbaker carefully led him through his story. He had, the boy insisted, confessed to the murder of his father only to protect his mother. His other incriminating activities, such as the attempt to secure Laddie Kuchinsky's help in removing the body, also took place on his mother's instructions.

Once his witness identified it, John Diefenbaker read to the jury the Prince Albert statement in which the accused boy first claimed that his mother was the murderer. It now appeared to be nothing more than self-serving evidence. The opportunity was gone to hear this version from the police witnesses who found it so credible that they charged Annie Pasowesty with the crime.

It was more bad luck for the defence that Herb Sampson had the following night to prepare his cross-examination of John Pasowesty. Taking no chance of attracting the sympathy of the jury to the young accused, the prosecutor spent almost all of the third morning of the trial taking him through his story. Speaking gently, and with studied simplicity, Sampson made no attempt to trap the boy but, slowly and carefully, exposed the many unlikely features of his version of the tragic event. When the prosecutor finished, the innocent farm youth looked like a cunning psychopath.

Sampson brought out some further facts about the car John had bought with the money from his father's cattle a month before the murder. He had, John admitted, been planning on going to Alberta in that car, but the scheme blew up before he could get away.

And then came the greatest damage to Pasowesty's case. Shortly after his father had forced him to give up the car, John Pasowesty went looking for poison. He inquired at two or three stores in Sheho about gopher poison, supposedly on behalf of a neighbour. He was unable to name the neighbour.

Herb Sampson almost destroyed the defence, but only almost. There remained an element of doubt. Perhaps John Pasowesty spoke the truth. Was he really bright enough to invent such a story?

Diefenbaker and Elder had one little element of corroboration, not strong, perhaps even useless. While Annie Pasowesty was still under charge for the murder, she had encountered John. Both were in custody. In the presence of a police matron, a sobbing mother held her son in her arms and spoke to him in Ukrainian. The suspicious matron asked John what his mother had said.

"My mother said, 'John, you say you did this, you say you did it, and I will see you get free.'"

Annie Pasowesty certainly heard her son's words, and made no protest or correction. But she knew only a few words of English. Had she understood her son's accusation?

Sampson put Annie Pasowesty back on the stand to rebut her son's accusation of murder. Diefenbaker got in a couple of licks on further cross-examination. The day Nick Pasowesty's body was found, the bereaved widow promptly sent to town for ten gallons of cider and called the neighbours in to drink it. Custom of the people or celebration of a successful crime? And within a week, the same widow consulted Diefenbaker's former articling student, Mike Stechishin, then practising law in nearby Yorkton. She wanted to know how to acquire her late husband's assets.

It was the sort of case at which John Diefenbaker excelled. It contained the two elements he liked best: the Crown was vulnerable to accusations of imperfect investigation, and another person was present who could be pointed to as the real offender. But Mr. Justice Taylor had severely circumscribed the scope of the defence, so much so that the jury hardly knew that Annie Pasowesty had also been charged with the murder. Diefenbaker could not successfully attack the Crown's credibility. He would have to do his best with the victim's widow as possible culprit.

It was 2:00 p.m. on the third day of the trial when John Diefenbaker rose to address the twelve men of the Wynyard district who formed the John Pasowesty jury. He knew he had to create some serious doubts in the minds of at least a few of those men, doubts that would survive the speeches that would follow. Because the defence had been forced to put the accused into the witness box, the Crown would enjoy the advantage of the last address to the jury. Mr. Justice Taylor would supply the wrap-up, and Diefenbaker was under no illusions about the opinions the trial judge would express.

The defence counsel went straight to the core of the issue. The jury was dealing with a case of cold-blooded premeditated murder, of that there was no question. The only matter for decision was — who committed the crime? The accused John Pasowesty or, possibly, Annie Pasowesty, his mother.

"A man needs a motive to do murder," Diefenbaker contended. "No motive, no sufficient motive, can be found in the evidence to explain the killing of Nick Pasowesty by his son, John.

"Little things, yes, things in the nature of a family argument, a tiff, perhaps. But such things as this fade into nothingness when they are weighed against the great love of a son for his father, the respect and veneration in which we human beings hold our parents.

"John Pasowesty had nothing to gain by the death of his father, not only nothing to gain but much to lose. Where is the motive for murder in that?"

Diefenbaker reviewed the evidence that detailed the activities on the Pasowesty farm on the fatal morning. Peter Pasowesty and the hired man testified that John had been away only ten or fifteen minutes on each of his two trips for the horses. That was not sufficient time to carry out the murder; the distances were too great. The murder must have been done by Annie Pasowesty after the men left for the fields.

"Annie Pasowesty," Diefenbaker accused, "Annie Pasowesty committed this crime. A schemer, a plotter, she contrived an arrangement where she could kill her husband and throw suspicion upon her son. And worse. Then she induced this boy to confess to the crime, to take that responsibility upon himself and steer all suspicion away from her."

The widow, Diefenbaker pointed out, had ample motive for murder. Nick Pasowesty's considerable assets alone were sufficient motive. Then there was the evidence that suggested that the wife was unhappy in her marriage.

The lawyer stood before the jury, his eyes flashing, his voice intense. It was heavy going. The twelve Anglo jurymen, selected for their ability to speak English, might carry some prejudice against eastern European immigrants. But could they see, in the pathetic Annie Pasowesty, a woman capable of the murder of her husband, and then the selfish sacrifice of her son?

"John Pasowesty was only the dupe of a scheming woman," Diefenbaker continued. "The truth in this case lies in the statements the boy gave to the police in Prince Albert, the statements he made when at last he realized he was being used."

Perhaps it could be so, the jury must have wondered. After all, could the son have killed his father and then turned and falsely accused his mother of the crime?

Yes, said Herb Sampson, as he followed Diefenbaker before the jury, John Pasowesty was just that sort of person. His explanation from the witness box was given with such callousness, with such an absence of feeling for either his father or his mother, that it was unworthy of acceptance. As well, it was inconsistent with almost every known fact existing in the case.

That was much the attitude of Mr. Justice Taylor when he addressed the jury at the end of the afternoon, although he was careful to caution them that the decision was theirs alone.

"I can think of only one thing worse than killing one's father," the trial judge said, "and that is to charge one's mother with having done such a thing."

Taylor had quite a bit to say about John Pasowesty's demeanour in the witness box. Diefenbaker shrank and thought of Corporal Smyley, whose absence forced the accused to testify.

"But here you have had this man go into the witness box. He did not have to do so. The decision as to whether he should go into the witness box rested with the defence. The law does not require him to give evidence. He could have refrained from giving evidence and no comment could have been made by me, or anyone in the case, or suggestion made on account of his not giving evidence.

"But he did go into the witness box, and he bared himself, if I might so put it, to us, almost to his very soul, and you have to consider, at least so it would seem to me, although it is a question for you, what motives would affect him, after having seen and heard him."

The trial judge had taken a strong dislike to John Pasowesty, and he signalled that to the jury. Without being specific, he referred to the accused as "being admittedly the kind of person that he demonstrated himself to be in the witness box."

In case the jury might have undue feeling for the youth of the accused and the effect of a guilty verdict, Taylor had some words on those subjects:

"Though the very nature of man might rebel against holding and finding a lad of seventeen had killed his father, yet it is your duty to consider the facts carefully, considerately, to reach an accurate conclusion uninfluenced by any consideration of sympathy whatever.

"And if you find on the facts that he is guilty, no consideration as to the results need affect you, for the consequences that will follow from your verdict are those fixed by law, and the responsibility therefore will be taken by others and not yourselves."

It was 6:00 p.m. when the jury retired. That Diefenbaker had made some impression upon them was clear when they returned four hours later. They wanted to review the evidence of the movements of the residents of the Pasowesty farm during the morning of the shooting. In fact, they wanted to take that evidence back with them.

The testimony had not been transcribed. That would take a whole day, Taylor pointed out.

"If the stenographer could read us that evidence, that would be sufficient," said the jury foreman.

That, too, would take a lot of time, the trial judge replied. "Perhaps if I gave you what I have...?" he suggested. The jury agreed.

For three-quarters of an hour Mr. Justice Taylor delivered his interpretation of this vital evidence to the concerned jury, concluding with the caution: "My notes are not intended by me as a complete report of all that was said."

"Your notes would be quite accurate as to the length of time John was away for the horses, according to the evidence that was given?" the foreman asked. The jury was impressed by Diefenbaker's proposition.

The judge's response was strongly suggestive. "I am satisfied that I have taken down what was said correctly as to that, but while they put it that way, ten to fifteen minutes, still I would suggest to you that was not meant for any accurate statement at all. It is just a statement that men estimate about a thing afterwards, that they have kept no track of."

Taylor could not find another portion of the testimony the jury wanted, and adjourned until the next morning to enable it to be located. Again he gave the jury the evidence surrounded by his own interpretations.

The trial judge had certainly cleared up the jury's concerns. One hour after retiring the second time they were back with their verdict: "Guilty."

Diefenbaker did not remain for the fourth and last day of the case, leaving it in the hands of Bill Elder. Elder had not before experienced a murder trial. In shock and dismay at the verdict, he leaned over to Ross Pratt, the junior Crown counsel, and asked, "What do I do now?"

Pratt had an irrepressible sense of humour. "Well, one thing for sure," he replied, thinking of the automatic penalty about to be imposed, "don't ask for a suspended sentence."

Mr. Justice Taylor knew what to do, and he immediately set about doing it. He stated his opinion that the verdict of guilty was "the only reasonable conclusion that could have been arrived at upon the evidence," and then handed down sentence upon seventeen-year-old John Pasowesty.

"You will be taken from here to the jail at Prince Albert, and there be confined until the 21st day of February, 1930, and on that day be then and there hanged by the neck until you are dead, and may God have mercy on your soul."

"YOUTH SENTENCED TO HANG HERE FEB. 21," trumpeted the Prince Albert *Daily Herald* in an eight-column, front page headline. The press accounts of the story over the next few months make an interesting study in public relations.

Diefenbaker and Elder filed Notice of Appeal. On January 15 they tried to convince the Court of Appeal that Mr. Justice Taylor should not have allowed John Pasowesty's confession into evidence. They made no complaint about the judicial interpretation of the testimony when the jury returned to hear it a second time.

The appeal judges gave short shift to the defence arguments, and dismissed the appeal from the bench.

"Attempt to Save Pasowesty Starts," announced the *Daily Herald* on January 20, "J.G. Diefenbaker is Acting on Behalf of Young Slayer." The defence team was reduced to seeking executive clemency for their client. They made application for a reprieve from the federal Cabinet.

"Attempt For Reprieve of J. Pasowesty," headed another story three weeks later, "Counsel Seeks to Prove That Youth is Mentally Unbalanced." John Diefenbaker announced that he was having mental specialists examine his client. That is interesting in the light of earlier features of the case.

Diefenbaker was aware from the beginning that John Pasowesty was mentally deficient. At Annie Pasowesty's preliminary, his agent, J.A.M. Patrick, K.C., told the court, "the Crown have in their possession, and I am aware of it, that John Pasowesty has only the intelligence of a ten-year-old boy [*sic*]." The defence made no contention at trial that the accused lacked mental capacity. Why? The answer is not known. Although the profession of psychiatry was in its infancy, practitioners (then called "alienists") and facilities were available.

The Crown, anticipating some such defence, summonsed two medical men to Wynyard. Each examined John Pasowesty before the trial began and observed his conduct in the prisoner's box during the first day and a half of the case. Each testified that he was, in their opinion, legally sane. Mr. Justice Taylor, hoping to close the door Diefenbaker was now trying to open, stated in passing sentence that, although the accused was only seventeen years of age, "his development, mentally as well as physically, appears to be considerably beyond that age."

Too late for the jury, John Diefenbaker arranged for a proper assessment of his client's mental faculties.

On February 17, three days before the execution date, Ottawa granted a three week extension to permit a better examination of the Pasowesty file.

The Regina *Daily Star* reported the story: "John Pasowesty, 17 years old but with the mentality of a child of nine or ten years, according to prominent alienists who have examined him...has been temporarily reprieved...J.G. Diefenbaker, K.C., detailed to defend Pasowesty, is putting forth every effort on behalf of his client. Pasowesty has been the subject of examination by eminent experts on mental diseases and it is expected that a further mental survey will be made and the results forwarded to Ottawa."

"GALLOWS CHEATED OF YOUTH," blared another full front page headline in the *Daily Herald* on March 4, three days before the rescheduled execution date. Ottawa accepted the evidence of Pasowesty's mental condition that Diefenbaker uncovered. The death sentence was commuted to life imprisonment.

"I knew I wouldn't die," John Pasowesty sobbed when shown the telegram from Ottawa. "I don't know about spending the rest of my life in jail, but I think I'll like it better than hanging."

Years later, John Pasowesty was released from prison. He moved to British Columbia and is believed to be still residing quietly there.

In the Sheho district, the oldtimers still carry a high regard for John Diefenbaker, defence lawyer.

7

Rex v. Wysochan

Christmas is a sad time for murder. On Christmas Day, 1929, less than a week after John Diefenbaker filed his Notice of Appeal on behalf of John Pasowesty, a group of Polish immigrants were celebrating the holiday at the home of Phillip Mykolyk in Humboldt. They were startled as Stanley Kropa burst in upon them. Kropa and his wife, Antena, had left the party only a short while before and returned to their own home nearby. Mykolyk had followed the couple, urging them to return to the celebration, but Antena claimed to be unwell. It was a different Stanley Kropa who returned alone half an hour later. Dishevelled, bleeding from several cuts on his hands and head, he was almost incoherent from excitement and fear.

"Police! Police!" he stammered, "Alex has shot Antena and the baby."

Alex! Alex Wysochan, Phillip Mykolyk thought in consternation. Alex Wysochan and Antena Kropa had been having an open affair. Two weeks earlier, they had run away together, but gave up when Chief of Police Denis Palmer intervened. Why would Alex shoot Antena?

Stanley Kropa was too excited to give much explanation. As Mrs. Mykolyk bandaged his bleeding hands, he repeated only that Alex had come with a gun and would not let him out of the house. Alex, he said, had killed his wife and baby and he had to get out through the window. Nothing more.

When Chief Palmer and RCMP Sergeant Bert Evans arrived at the shack near the railroad tracks that was the Kropa home, the door was locked. They entered through a broken window.

Antena Kropa and Alex Wysochan, both unconscious and moaning, lay side by side on the floor in the tiny bedroom, a .38 calibre revolver between them. Both appeared to have been shot. Wysochan's pulse was strong but Antena's was very weak. A baby lay on the bed, unharmed. The police arranged for a sleigh to take the two to the hospital.

Phillip Mykolyk and Tony Sokolowski followed Stanley Kropa back to his home when the police arrived. Antena, seeing Sokolowski, asked in Polish, "Tony, where is my husband?" As the dying woman was being loaded onto the sleigh, she called out, "Stanley, help me, I am too hot." Just as they pulled her away, she stretched her hand out to her husband and pleaded, "Stanley, help me out because there is a bullet in my body."

Antena made it only as far as the operating room; there she died. She had been shot three times with the revolver. Dr. Harry Raymond Fleming turned his attention to Alex Wysochan, in a stupor and smelling of alcohol. Fleming concluded that the man was either in shock or under the influence of liquor.

Wysochan had a wound on his left chest, but Fleming could not determine if a bullet had penetrated. An X-ray disclosed no bullet, but then one fell from Wysochan's clothing.

The doctor was unable to get a word out of Alex Wysochan until late the next morning. Then, in response to the question, "Who did this?" the patient replied, "I didn't do it, but I suppose they'll put a rope around my neck."

Wysochan was charged with Antena's murder. More of the story emerged at his preliminary inquiry on January 3, 1930.

The Kropas, a young Polish couple in their mid-twenties, had come to Canada only six months earlier. Just two months before the shooting, Stanley found a job working on the railroad at Humboldt, where they met the twenty-eight-year-old Wysochan. A former soldier in the Russian army, with a wife and family back in Poland, Wysochan had been in Canada four years.

Antena immediately fell for Wysochan, and two weeks before Christmas she left home with him. Stanley, with the help of Chief of Police Palmer, found the runaways in a room over the local café. After some urging, Antena agreed to return to her husband. Stanley, in an act that was to prove significant, picked up his wife's suitcase and took her home.

According to Stanley, Wysochan arrived at their two-room home in the evening on Christmas Day, drunk and brandishing a revolver. At gunpoint, the Russian held the Kropas in the bedroom. He was angry with Stanley, accused him of reporting him to the police for carrying a gun, and threatened reprisal. When Wysochan stepped back into the kitchen, Stanley leaped for the bedroom door and slammed it shut. As both Kropas held the door against Wysochan, he called to Antena, "Stand back, I'm going to kill your husband like a dog."

With that, Stanley went out the window, sure he was the only one in danger. As he landed on the ground, he heard two shots, and Antena's yell, "For God's sake, what are you trying to do? You are going to kill my baby."

As Stanley raced away from his home he heard a third shot, and then, just before he reached Phillip Mykolyk's house, a fourth.

Alex Wysochan had purchased the revolver earlier in the fall, the police learned. Just a week before Christmas, a fellow player claimed to have spotted the gun in Wysochan's pocket during a card game at Humboldt's Windsor Hotel.

Wysochan spent most of Christmas Day drinking at the Windsor Hotel. When Sergeant Evans examined him at the Kropa home that night, he found him "to be in a stupor or what would be expected from a drunken man."

It seemed to be a clear cut case. Alex Wysochan was committed to stand trial for the murder of Antena Kropa and sent off to the Provincial Gaol in Prince Albert to await the next jury sittings of the Court of King's Bench at Humboldt.

Wysochan had sent most of his earnings to his wife and children in Poland and was without funds. Adrien Doiron of nearby Vonda, later Mr. Justice Doiron of the Court of King's Bench, represented him at the preliminary inquiry, but in Prince Albert the accused retained new counsel. The recently-formed firm of Diefenbaker and Elder agreed to undertake the defence without fee. Wysochan was their second murder client. They were still struggling to save the life of their first, John Pasowesty.

Wysochan's defence seemed obvious — drunkenness. The evidence at the preliminary inquiry showed that the accused had been severely intoxicated. He confessed to his friends that he remembered nothing of his visit to the Kropa home. When told that he had "shot a lady," he asked, "Whose lady did I shoot?"

Drunkenness was not a complete defence. But it would reduce murder to manslaughter if the jury found that the accused had been so intoxicated as to be incapable of forming an intent to kill, an essential element in the offence of murder. The difference between murder and manslaughter was the difference between death and life, hanging or a jail term.

But John Diefenbaker rejected the defence of drunkenness and reached for an out-and-out acquittal, a not guilty verdict that would enable Wysochan to walk out of the court house a completely free man. The fatal shots had not been fired into Antena Kropa by Alex Wysochan, he would contend to the jury, but by Stanley Kropa, the wronged husband. Kropa, in a wild act of vengeance, shot both of the lovers, then broke out through the window as a cover-up to his crime. Antena died, but, by a stroke of luck, Wysochan survived.

It was a tremendous gamble, literally a do-or-die plunge. The drunkenness defence could not be carried as a fall-back alternative because it was contradictory. Wysochan needed a clear and lucid recollection of the events of December 25. He could not tell the jury, "This is the way it happened, but, also, I was so drunk I didn't know what I was doing."

The case contained ample evidence to support the contention of drunkenness, but almost none to back up the theory that Stanley Kropa had done the shooting. With the first defence of drunkenness, Wysochan would have the choice of testifying or not. With the second, he had no option. He would have to go into the witness box and suffer all the disadvantage that followed.

The most obvious liability lay in asking the jury to measure Wysochan's credibility against Stanley Kropa's. That meant asking them to choose the paramour over the wronged husband.

John Diefenbaker was ill, and unable to devote as much time to the preparation of the Wysochan defence as he would have liked. His gastric ulcer had flared up, surely at least in part due to the tremendous pressure of the previous twelve months. The lawyer was confined to his home for a month, in bed for three weeks. Out and about only five days before the case opened, he was still weak, not nearly strong enough to undertake a gruelling murder trial.

Rex v. Alex Wysochan came on for trial at the opening of the regular spring jury sittings at Humboldt on March 18. The presiding judge was the same Mr. Justice Bigelow who had expressed strong anti-Ruthenian bias in that court house five years earlier. The Wysochan case opened just two weeks after John Pasowesty received his final reprieve.

The counsel table was staffed almost as it had been in the Pasowesty trial. Diefenbaker and Elder were on the defence side and Ross Pratt appeared for the Crown. Pratt again brought in senior counsel, this time Frank Clayton Wilson, K. C., of Yorkton.

After their experience with the missing Corporal Smyley in the Pasowesty trial, Diefenbaker and Elder took no chances. They issued subpoenas for several of the Crown witnesses who testified at the preliminary inquiry. As it turned out, the precaution was unnecessary.

"WYSOCHAN ENTERS PLEA OF NOT GUILTY," Regina's *Morning Leader* announced in an eight-column lead headline as the trial opened in Humboldt. Murder cases were big news and the lawyers were star players. Sick or not, John Diefenbaker was not going to miss the action. The next day, the press reported that "Mr. Diefenbaker is recovering from a long illness and the strain of the trial is telling severely upon him."

As soon as they opened the case to the jury, Wilson and Pratt put Stanley Kropa on the stand. Then they went straight into one feature of the evidence that has kept the Wysochan case on the curriculum of Canadian law schools ever since. Wilson asked the husband about his wife's pleas for help as she was taken from their home to the hospital.

"Objection. Hearsay evidence," came from John Diefenbaker. It was a vital point. The Crown wanted Antena's calls to Stanley in evidence. They would contend that she would hardly ask her husband for help if he had been the one to cause her injuries.

Normally "hearsay," the words of someone other than the witness, are excluded from evidence, at least as to the truth of the facts contained in such words. But the rule, like most rules of law, is shot through with exceptions. Some of the exceptions have to do with the statements of dying persons, comments contrary to the interests of the deceased. Antena Kropa's last words did not qualify as "dying declarations." Could they be admitted anyway?

No, said John Diefenbaker, they fell within the normal hearsay rule and must be excluded.

Yes, submitted Wilson, Antena's words were admissible to show her state of mind at the time of speaking. They were not tendered to prove the truth of her statements. She made no statement of fact, anyway, other than the statement "there is a bullet in my body." The Crown had ample other proof of that fact.

Yes, agreed Mr. Justice Bigelow, the jury could hear the last words of Antena Kropa as evidence of her state of mind at the time she spoke them. It followed that the jurors could draw from those words the very powerful inference the Crown wanted.

Stanley Kropa, speaking through an interpreter, carried on with his story. He told the jury how his marriage of six years had suddenly come to grief over Alex Wysochan. The cuckolded husband had been forgiving. On one occasion, he came upon Antena and Wysochan together in the Kropa bed. On another, he took his wife home from the room over the café where she was living with Wysochan. Stanley Kropa was obviously not a violent man.

Kropa repeated his description of the events of December 25. Wysochan had terrorized the Kropa family and must have shot Antena after Stanley leaped through the window. The bereaved husband had no idea how Wysochan himself came to be wounded.

Some explanation came from Staff Sergeant Bert Strong, an RCMP firearms expert who had tested the .38 revolver. It was old and decrepit, so worn that it delivered only one-half of its normal punch or penetrating power. Wysochan's heavy clothing slowed the bullet that struck him enough that it failed to penetrate his skin. The lightly-dressed Antena was not so lucky.

All the shots — the three in Antena and the one that grazed Wysochan — were fired at very close range, from between six and nine inches. The gun gave up no identifiable fingerprints. The question of who had fired the shots would not be settled that easily.

By mid-afternoon of the second day, the Crown had it all tied up. The revolver was identified as Wysochan's. He had been seen entering the Kropa home. The neighbours had heard the shots. Stanley had fled. The police found Antena and Wysochan on the floor. Wysochan must have shot Antena, and then himself. Antena died. Wilson and Pratt closed their case.

Alex Wysochan had much to explain as he took the witness stand. Using an interpreter, John Diefenbaker led his client through his version of the Christmas Day shooting.

Wysochan freely admitted his affair with Antena Kropa. It had started the first day they met. She wanted him, so he took her, was his casual explanation.

When they were found in the room over the Humboldt café two weeks before Christmas, the two lovers were planning to leave together and go farming. Some of Wysochan's belongings, including his .38 revolver, were in Antena's valise. Stanley Kropa took that valise home with Antena, and Wysochan did not see his gun again until Christmas Day at the Kropas'. No, the revolver was not in his pocket during a card game a week before the shooting. Yes, the accused admitted to Diefenbaker, he had continued the affair with Antena right up to the end.

Wysochan spent Christmas Day drinking. He was at the Windsor Hotel when Stanley Kropa, using a pretext, invited him to the Kropa house. When he arrived, Antena was crying because Wysochan had not been invited to spend Christmas with them. Antena accused Stanley of having beaten her.

Then, Wysochan continued, Stanley Kropa threw him down and began beating his head against the floor, saying, "You will run away with her no more." The beating, on top of the drink, caused Wysochan to become confused. Kropa was on top of him, he remembered, and Antena was trying to pull her husband away. Then Wysochan heard shots, he did not remember how many, and he felt something hurting him.

The accused had not fired any shots, and did not shoot Antena Kropa, he said, nor did he see Stanley Kropa go through the window. He did remember Kropa locking the door, but, feeling "pretty sick," he did not know what happened next.

At Diefenbaker's request, Wysochan bared his chest and showed the jury his bullet scar. After this flourish, the defence lawyer asked only a few more questions about his client's behaviour following the shooting, and then turned him over to the prosecution.

The timing was perfect for Wilson and Pratt. There was little more than half an hour left in the court day, just long enough to get a feel for Wysochan. Then they had overnight to prepare their real cross-examination.

Wilson began by picking a fight with the accused. The prosecutor insisted Wysochan understood English perfectly well and did not require an interpreter. Wysochan was stubborn. "I don't understand," was his only reply to all Wilson's questions, until he was asked, "You want an interpreter, do you?" To this he promptly answered, "Yes." But Wilson finally gave in and recalled the Polish interpreter.

Again Wysochan freely, almost boastfully, admitted his affair with Antena. He acknowledged that he suggested she return to her husband only after Chief Palmer took a forceful stand in the matter. Wysochan agreed that Stanley Kropa was a good man, but also admitted that he had planned to take Kropa's child, as well as his wife. No, he did not know if, after stealing the wife, he would be welcome in Kropa's home at Christmas.

The accused might have been on trial for murder, but Wilson was not above trying him for philandering. The effect on the jury had to be enormous. In the end, it came down to credibility. There were only two adult survivors of the shooting in the Kropa home, and each accused the other of being the killer. Who would the jury believe?

It was late in the third morning of the trial when the time came for John Diefenbaker to put his theory to the Humboldt jury. Again, he faced twelve men of English background who were charged with deciding upon an affair between immigrants from eastern Europe. How would men with such names as Graham, Craddock, Bradburn, Edgar, Lowe, Clark and Blair regard the passions and motives of Stanley Kropa and Alex Wysochan?

To help him gauge his effect upon the jury, Diefenbaker had an assistant. Somewhat obvious among the mostly ethnic spectators sat Edna, his bride of nine months. While the eyes of those about her were upon the lawyer, Edna focused on the jurors. As he spoke, from time to time Diefenbaker casually glanced at Edna, seeking the facial expression that told him how he was being received by the jury. Throughout the trial, that advice was an invaluable aid as the lawyer judged the nature and direction of his presentation.

Ill and dreadfully weary after the strain of the trial, John Diefenbaker drew deeply on his unusual reserves. As he stood before the jurors, the weariness fell away and his eyes flashed as brilliantly as ever. His voice recovered its power, and he commanded the attention of the twelve listening men.

"It is a matter of motive," he told them, using lines reminiscent of the Pasowesty trial.

"For a man to do murder, he must have a motive, and a motive is lacking in this case. Alex Wysochan had no reason to kill Antena Kropa. She was his love. Stanley Kropa, on the other hand, had a decided motive for murder. He was the wronged husband.

"Admittedly, Alex Wysochan dishonoured the Kropa home. Admittedly, he was immoral in his relations with Antena Kropa. But," Diefenbaker emphasized, "he is not charged with these things. He is here today charged with the killing of Antena Kropa, the woman he loved and had no reason to kill."

Diefenbaker's words became commands, personally directed to each of the twelve listening men. Somehow, as his edicts continued to flow, they were accepted by the jurors without apparent objection or resentment.

"You must accept the testimony of Alex Wysochan. It is much more probable that the shooting of Antena Kropa was done by her husband, taking vengeance for his wrongs."

Diefenbaker spoke for a full hour. With that final plea, he returned slowly to his seat. He could do no more.

F.C. Wilson followed. The prosecutor denounced the accused in such scathing terms that Wysochan lost the composure he had maintained throughout the trial, even through his cross-examination. Apparently now able to understand the prosecutor's English, he visibly winced and cast anxious glances at the jury as he was referred to as "this little rat" and "this reptile." Could such a man be trusted to tell the truth, particularly when fighting for his freedom? Wilson demanded.

"The dirty little coward," full of drink, went to the Kropa home to dispose of the husband of the woman he wanted, the prosecutor claimed, in language that would be objectionable today.

Wilson concluded with his most telling points. If Stanley Kropa had done the shooting, would he have burst out the window instead of using the door? Did the jury believe he was so cunning as to think of that as a cover-up? And was it possible that Antena would have made her dying appeal to the man who had shot her?

When they heard from both the defence and the prosecution, the jury, at their request, went off with Staff Sergeant Evans to the Kropa home, to view the scene of the shooting. During the interval, the large Humboldt courtroom, packed since the trial opened, buzzed with conversation. The spectators debated the quality of the defence and Crown speeches. John Diefenbaker's performance, they agreed, had been "masterly." It remained to be seen if the members of the jury were similarly impressed.

With the jury back at mid-afternoon, Mr. Justice Bigelow reviewed the evidence and instructed them upon the law they must apply in reaching their decision. As he did so, the trial judge did not hesitate to signal his own views, being careful, however, to tell the jury they were the sole judges of the facts.

The trial judge dealt first with motive. He disagreed with Mr. Diefenbaker, he said. If the jury believed Stanley Kropa told the truth, no motive was needed — the accused came to the Kropa home to get the husband. It was difficult to say why Wysochan then turned upon the wife. Perhaps he was infuriated by jealousy or because the husband escaped. It was difficult to analyze the mind of a man in a state like that. If a motive was necessary, possibly it lay in the love triangle.

Mr. Justice Bigelow did not think it was likely that Stanley Kropa would have gone through the window except to save his life. Further, he asked the jury, did they not think that, if the husband had held the gun, he would have made a better job of Wysochan? The trial judge thought it more reasonable that the accused had shot Antena as Stanley escaped, then turned the gun upon himself.

The judge referred to Antena's dying pleas and agreed with the prosecution. "Mr. Wilson has very properly argued that that would be a most unusual and unreasonable, and, I think, improbable thing for her to do, if it was her husband who had shot her." He gave the jury their choice of possible verdicts. They might acquit Wysochan entirely, if they accepted enough of his story to be in doubt about his guilt, or they might convict him of murder.

Then, for the first time in the case, and almost incidentally, the judge put forward the defence of drunkenness. The jury might convict Wysochan of manslaughter, he said, if they concluded that he did the shooting but had been so drunk that he was incapable of forming an intention to kill.

At 4:30 p.m. the jury retired. At 6:00 they returned to review some of the evidence about the movements of Wysochan and Stanley Kropa on the night of the shooting. At 10:00 that night, with not an empty seat in the courtroom, the jury reported that they had not reached a verdict. They adjourned for the night.

John Diefenbaker had indeed made an impression upon the twelve men who were deciding the fate of his client. His plea had survived the vicious comments of the prosecution and a very unfavourable charge from the trial judge. Would it survive the night?

In the cells in the court house basement, Alex Wysochan startled the guards as he sang "Nearer My God to Thee" in his native Polish.

Ross Pratt was examining a witness in another case the next morning when, shortly after 10:00, the Wysochan jury returned. Their verdict: "Guilty of murder."

Mr. Justice Bigelow decided to complete the case before him and sent Wysochan down to the cells to await his sentence. Just before noon he was brought back.

As the bells of a nearby church tolled high noon, the stern jurist delivered the dreaded death sentence: "You shall be taken from here and be conveyed to the Provincial Gaol at Prince Albert and there confined until the 20th day of June, 1930, and on that day, between the hours of 1:00 o'clock and 6:00 o'clock in the morning, you shall be taken to the gallows and there hanged by the neck until dead. And may God have mercy upon your soul."

Alex Wysochan's military training was apparent as he stood at parade attention to receive his sentence. Then he threw a venomous glance at Wilson, the prosecutor whose vicious words had done him in.

Mr. Justice Bigelow told Wysochan that he "fully concurred with the verdict." Any clemency would have to come from Ottawa, "but I do not hold out any hope for you at all," the judge said. He would not recommend leniency, he added.

John Diefenbaker and Bill Elder sat slumped in dejection. Twice in four months they had heard the death sentence imposed upon a client. As they thought back over the case, a drunkenness defence and a manslaughter verdict looked like an excellent option to have passed up.

"Mr. Diefenbaker, are you ready?" Mr. Justice Bigelow was in a sentencing frame of mind. John Diefenbaker had another client on the list. They had entered a guilty plea the afternoon before, after the Wysochan jury went out, and the judge was now ready to hear submissions as to sentence.

Diefenbaker, weary, ill and depressed, drew himself to his feet. The show must go on. He did the best he could in the circumstances.

"Thirty days imprisonment at Prince Albert Gaol. With hard labour." Mr. Justice Bigelow was in fine form. He adjourned for lunch.

The next day Alex Wysochan, manacled and guarded, was taken to Prince Albert by train. A large crowd gathered at the Humboldt depot to stare at the spectacle. The convicted murderer had recovered his spirits. "Goodbye, Mr. Sergeant," he smiled to Staff Sergeant Evans, shaking his hand. "The stunted little Polack," as the press described him, carried no hard feelings.

From his Prince Albert law office, John Diefenbaker announced that he would appeal Wysochan's conviction. The appeal took place on May 26. At that time, Diefenbaker concentrated on the admissibility of Antena's last words and the lack of fairness in the trial judge's instructions to the jury. Herb Sampson responded for the Crown and the Court reserved its decision.

Chief Justice Haultain handed down the Court's judgement on June 10: "Conviction affirmed." Antena's words were admissible as "evidence more or less strong of a certain feeling or attitude of mind, and it was for the jury to decide what inferences might be drawn from them." As to Mr. Justice Bigelow's charge to the jury: "While on certain points the charge was not favourable to the accused, the jury were adequately instructed as to the defences open to him, and were invariably told that they were after all the sole judges of fact, and that they should not convict if they had any reasonable doubt of the prisoner's guilt."

Just ten days remained to the fixed execution date. Alex Wysochan's only hope now was that the federal Cabinet, on its automatic review of his case, would see fit to grant him a reprieve. On June 19, the last day, the answer came. There would be no clemency. Alex Wysochan would be executed in the morning as directed by Mr. Justice Bigelow.

Arthur Ellis, self-styled "Official Executioner to the Dominion of Canada," arrived in Prince Albert two days early to check the local facilities. The Gaol, built in 1923, had provision for executions but no one had yet been hanged on its premises. All previous death row inmates had won reprieves.

The *Daily Herald* reported that Wysochan was downcast when told he would not be reprieved. "However," the paper went on, "it is understood that, like many of his nationality, he is apparently unmoved and will in all likelihood go to his death just as stolidly as he now awaits it."

Alex Wysochan, anything but "unmoved," spent his last hours with Reverend Father H.J. Baillargeon, to whom he continued to protest his innocence, although he confessed his drunkenness. "I do not remember all that happened, but I know that I am innocent and did not shoot anybody."

In a rite that he perfected in a lifetime career of six hundred executions, Ellis came to the cell just before 6:00 a.m., pinioned Wysochan's arms behind his back and walked him to the gallows. There he bound his legs, adjusted the noose, placed the black cap over his head and stepped back to spring the trap.

"Save my soul, Father," cried Alex Wysochan as he dropped to his death.

Homestead bound. William, Mary, John and Elmer Diefenbaker shortly before leaving Ontario for the West, *circa* 1902

Freshman John Diefenbaker, University of Saskatchewan, 1912.

Lieutenant John G. Diefenbaker just prior to embarking for overseas service, Regina, Sask., August 1916

The law is a serious affair . John Diefenbaker upon graduation from Law School, 1919.

The new lawyer in town: John Diefenbaker, Wakaw, Sask., Fall 1919.

The 1919 Wakaw football team. Diefenbaker is in the back row, third from left.

The Man From Prince Albert shortly after his arrival there in 1924. A formal studio portrait of a smiling barrister, a rare pose for the serious young lawyer.

"I killed him. I shouldn't have done it, but I'm not sorry." Isobel Emele, twice successfully defended for murder by John Diefenbaker.

Conservatives on the march. Delegates surround party leader J. T. M. Anderson and newly nominated candidate John Diefenbaker, Prince Albert, 1929.

William and John Diefenbaker, father and son, flank two Prince Albert cronies and a fine catch of lake trout, Prince Albert National Park, 1930.

Newly appointed King's Counsel and counsel to Bryant Commission poses with proud wife and mother, Saskatoon, 1930.

The Lord of Prince Albert: T.C. Davis

Early years in the M. P. office.

John G. Diefenbaker, K. C., M. P., strides down the walk of the Prince Albert Court House, 1947. (*Saskatchewan Archives Board*).

8

A Provincial Reputation

The provincial government of J.T.M. Anderson, sworn into office in Regina on September 9, 1929, was not, strictly speaking, a Conservative government. Dependent upon two other distinct political groups, the Progressives and the Independents, it was known as the "Co-operative," or the "Anderson government." Yet for all practical purposes, including those of patronage, it was a Conservative administration.

Saskatchewan Conservatives, in power at last, set about to even the score for their years of suffering under the arrogant domination of the Liberals. Particularly in the later Gardiner years, Liberal politics had permeated every facet of Saskatchewan life. Not only was the holder of the lowest public office certain to be a Liberal party man, but hardly could a new pastor be chosen for the church until the applicants had been blood-tested for their political views.

Political tradition dictated that, as the defeated government candidate in Prince Albert, John Diefenbaker was entitled to rule upon all provincial government appointments in the riding. He accepted the role with relish, taking over from the hated Davis. The former attorney general, still an MLA, was back in his law practice. Davis retained control over the local patronage of the Ottawa Liberal government until 1930, when it, too, was defeated.

The Conservatives were quick off the mark. Within ten days of the swearing-in of the Anderson government, Diefenbaker was approving applications for appointment as Commissioners for Oaths, the lowest-ranking of all offices. The holder was entitled only to a very modest fee for swearing affidavits, but the appointment was a handy accessory in real estate and insurance offices. Diefenbaker saw that Samuel J. Branion received his reward. The Prince Albert mayor replaced J.H. Lindsay, K.C., as agent for the attorney general and became responsible for all criminal prosecutions in the district. Lindsay was the president of the local Liberal association.

The new attorney general, Murdoch A. MacPherson of Regina, had the pleasant task of drawing up Saskatchewan's first list of Conservative lawyers for the coveted appointment of King's Counsel in the New Year's honours list. The K.C.s wore a more expensive gown and were accorded a certain precedence in court. Diefenbaker, just ten years at the bar, was included among the thirty appointed, as was Branion.

From Wadena, Ross Pratt wrote Diefenbaker a letter of congratulation with a humourous reference to their recent experience together in the Pasowesty trial: "Am very glad indeed to congratulate you on being officially set apart as one of those who are 'learned in the law,' Judge Taylor to the contrary notwithstanding."

In 1930, the Conservative Party scored a second great victory: on July 28, R.B. Bennett defeated the government of Mackenzie King. With their party in power in both Ottawa and Regina, Saskatchewan Conservatives were in political utopia.

John Diefenbaker chose not to further blunt his spear against Mackenzie King, and wisely side-stepped the Prince Albert nomination in the 1930 campaign. George Braden of Rosthern came forward on behalf of the Conservatives and did surprisingly well, cutting King's majority from 4,000 to under 1,200. But King, leader of the Opposition rather than prime minister, continued to represent Prince Albert in the House of Commons.

Although he accepted a reduced role, Prince Albert's leading Conservative did not sit out the 1930 federal campaign. Joining his successor, Braden, on the platform, John Diefenbaker indulged himself with replays of the previous year's provincial election, deriding "Jimmy" Gardiner and T.C. Davis. Braden's major campaign rally in Prince Albert was addressed by such prominent imports as Saskatchewan Conservative President Dr. D.S. Johnstone of Regina, and Arthur Marcotte of Ponteix, soon to be a senator. But Diefenbaker was accorded the role of main speaker. With quips, humour and statistics he brought the crowd of two thousand to its feet in an enthusiastic demonstration.

Diefenbaker seized upon Mackenzie King's claim that the Conservatives had preached "the parting of the ways" during the 1911 Reciprocity election. "I preach the meeting of the ways," Diefenbaker replied. "Let us join both doctrines, Liberal and Conservative, and part with Mr. King, never to meet again." The former candidate concluded with an emotional appeal, asking his audience to vote "not for Liberals, not for Conservatives, but for Canada." The crowd loved it.

The federal election was not the only event dominating the political stage in 1930. Immediately after gaining office, Saskatchewan Conservatives made it plain that they would not be content with just the spoils of office — they also wanted to shoot some prisoners. J.F. Bryant, no longer Speaker but in the Cabinet as minister of public works, continued to gather affidavits alleging that the Gardiner government had meddled politically with the provincial police. With the Liberals out of office, the evidence became easier to uncover. In February 1930, Bryant presented his material to the legislature, and touched off an uproar. The Conservative members demanded investigation by a committee of the House. The Liberals, fully aware they would have a majority of the committee against them, resisted. Finally, T.C. Davis proposed that the accusations be referred to a Royal Commission to be composed of not one, but three judges, and the compromise was accepted.

In June, the commission was appointed, consisting of Judges James McKay and Percy E. MacKenzie of Saskatchewan's Court of Appeal and J.F.L. Embury of the King's Bench. The next step was the appointment of legal counsel to the commission, for "the Crown and the defence," as the Regina *Leader* termed it, but actually for the Conservatives and the Liberals. Since all lawyers would be paid by the government, the appointments were huge political plums; legal incomes were already pinched by the Depression. But both sides wanted the best talent they could get; a great deal was at stake.

Diefenbaker's association with Bryant in the Arm River by-election now bore him fruit. He worked with Bryant planning for the commission beginning in June and, early in August when the appointments were announced, he was confirmed as junior counsel on the Conservative side. Senior counsel was Colonel C.E. Gregory, K.C. The Liberals nominated Percy McCuaig Anderson, K.C., and Bamm David Hogarth. All but Diefenbaker were from Regina, where the commission would sit.

His selection for such a prominent and responsible undertaking was indeed an accolade for Diefenbaker. The Bryant Charges Commission, as it came to be called, was the biggest show of the year in Saskatchewan. Obviously, the Anderson government had confidence in Diefenbaker's ability and regarded him as a loyal party man with a future.

The Bryant Charges Commission worked through the fall of 1930. For several weeks, Colonel Gregory and John Diefenbaker paraded past the three commissioners a sorry story of partisan politics carried too far. The entire province watched, eager for the blood of Gardiner or Davis, but eventually grew weary as none was drawn.

Few leading Liberals escaped implication. Diefenbaker was relentless as he searched out the details of the political usage made of the provincial police. On September 30 he examined Kenneth McRae, for ten years a constable in the force.

"Did you during that period have any occasion to do any political work?"

"Sure."

"You were doing what kind of political work?"

"I was canvassing, of course."

"For whom?"

"For Billy Patterson."

"Patterson, was he subsequently a Minister of the Crown? [In 1935, Patterson became Premier.]"

"Yes, sir."

"At whose request were you doing the political work?"

"Mr. Patterson's."

"What work did you do at his request?"

"Well, he wanted me to go through my district and canvass for him. He wasn't well known east of Kipling, he wasn't well known, he was a stranger in that constituency."

"To whom were the expenses, if any, incurred in doing this work charged?"

"Charged to the usual account, of course."

"What was the usual account?"

"The administration of justice."

McRae testified that C.A. Mahoney, commissioner of the force, ordered him into the 1919 by-election in Assiniboia on behalf of William Richard Motherwell. Motherwell had been a provincial Liberal minister and was seeking election to Ottawa. Although defeated in the by-election, Motherwell later became federal minister of agriculture.

On Mahoney's orders, McRae went into the riding where he took further instruction from a local Liberal MLA.

"Tell us what happened," Diefenbaker pressed.

"I was told to stay there, until after the election if I wished to, that everything would be O.K. He had made arrangements with either Mahoney or the attorney general's department. He asked if I had my uniform, and I said, Yes, it was in my grip."

"What did he tell you to do, and what did you do?"

"He gave me a sum of money and I was supposed to take a livery car from Estevan and go as far as Stoughton and from Stoughton I was to start my electioneering as Motherwell had a meeting there that same night, and from there I was going to go west towards Fillmore."

"Where were you to take the money to?"

"I was supposed to divide the money with whomever I liked. Say, I was to give $5 to Tom and Dick or John if he would go out and get in a vote or two, and work for the Liberal party."

"You say you went to Stoughton?"

"Sure, and the livery man wouldn't drive me any further on account of the weather, wouldn't stay with me any longer."

"This livery man, how much did he charge you?"

"Twenty five cents a mile."

"Did you pay him?"

"Sure."

"What money did you use to pay him with?"

"Why, the government money, of course."

Diefenbaker was after T.C. Davis, and he came close, but on an uncomfortable topic. Commissioner Mahoney had instructed the force to investigate the Ku Klux Klan and report to him in confidence. Those reports were passed to Attorney General Davis who hoped to find evidence of Conservative connections to the Klan. The commissioners criticized the former attorney general for his actions.

Although all Saskatchewan believed he was the inspiration behind the Liberal excesses, former premier Gardiner escaped direct implication. His decision to disband the provincial force in favour of the RCMP gave him a measure of protection from the revelations.

As the hearings wore on, they took on the aura of a Damon Runyon saga. Colourful names such as "Bill the Barber," "Stud Watson," "Tub Hall," and "Smokey Johnson" wove through the evidence.

The depth and reach of the Liberal political machine was illustrated by Smokey Johnson's testimony. Smokey, a former inmate of Regina Jail, claimed: "It was well known in the jail that different treatment was meted out to the Liberal and Conservative prisoners. The Conservatives were put on the rock pile and the Liberals had all the best jobs." The commissioners were unable to substantiate Smokey's allegation.

Gregory and Diefenbaker began to lose witnesses. "Irish" Jim Gallen, a former sergeant in the police force and once an active Liberal, appeared before the commission in early November, 1930. After one day in the witness box, he thought better of it, and disappeared. Later, Gallen wrote Diefenbaker, asking him to "overlook the action of a poor unprotected male from the Shamrock Isle." Gallen had been frightened, his "sleep was disturbed by visions of Ellis [the hangman] examining my neck and considering what drop I should have." He implied that some kindly advice from Colonel Gregory caused him to leave.

Gallen was not the only witness the Commission missed. A.L. Geddes, K.C., the former deputy attorney general, disappeared before the inquiry opened, supposedly in a drowning accident that no one believed.

Somehow given the privilege under the commission's terms of reference, the Liberal defence understandably declined to call any of their former ministers. The inquiry began to run out of steam.

After fifty-five full days of hearings, Gregory and Diefenbaker were only halfway through Bryant's charges. The Conservatives called it quits to enable the commissioners to report to the 1931 session of the legislature.

The commission's findings, filed in late February, verified much of Bryant's charges, but contained no major revelation. With the public opinion of Gardiner's government confirmed, it could be said that the Liberals escaped with their reputation intact.

The lawyers had trouble collecting their fees. The commission recommended that the two leading counsel, Gregory and Anderson, be paid $150 per sitting day, and the junior counsel, Diefenbaker and Hogarth, $100 per day. Diefenbaker was awarded $1,000 for subsistence in Regina. The totals came to $9,000 for Gregory and Anderson, $6,500 for Diefenbaker, and $6,000 for Hogarth. Diefenbaker grumbled about his bill relative to Gregory's: "Got less; worked longer."

That was an embarrassing amount of money in Saskatchewan in the 1930s, and the government refused to pay it. In 1932 the accounts still were not settled. When someone sued, all the lawyers were paid in full.

As late as 1938, the Liberals were filing the accounts in the legislature, trying to embarrass Diefenbaker with what, by then, had become exorbitant fees. But Diefenbaker had earned his money, and J.F. Bryant, himself a lawyer, knew it. Pleased with the outcome, he thanked Diefenbaker "for the very splendid manner in which you conducted the case. I appreciate very much the fact that you have given such careful and close study to the details of the evidence, and feel that great credit is due you for bringing out the evidence as you did, particularly in view of the fact that you received a good deal of discouragement at times."

Diefenbaker was a busy man in late 1930. At the same time as the Bryant Commission was holding its hearing, Diefenbaker was involved in his third murder case in a year. It was an unusual and heart-rending case, and this time he won. The story began at Wakaw.

In 1927 John Bajer abandoned his farm and his family, and moved to Windsor, Ontario. Nadia, his wife, and their two small children were left behind, without support, in a one-room shack on the outskirts of Wakaw. Nadia did what she could to maintain her children and herself. She performed housecleaning around the town and took in washing. One of her laundry customers was Stanley Lepine.

Soon Stanley came to expect the use of Nadia's body as part of her services. For this, he sometimes paid Nadia fifty cents or a dollar extra, important money to the destitute woman. Early in 1930, Nadia found herself pregnant. When she shared this problem with Stanley, his response was unsympathetic. He brought Nadia some pills with instructions on how to take them. Stanley, Nadia later explained, "wanted to get rid of the child."

Nadia was afraid to take the pills and returned them to Stanley on one of his visits. He threw them in the stove, picked up his last load of laundry, and left. At the end of July, Nadia, by then very pregnant, sent her daughter to Stanley to say that her mother wanted to see him. He did not come.

On September 9, Corporal E.J. DesRosiers of the Wakaw RCMP detachment received a report. Nadia Bajer was no longer pregnant, but there was no sign of a baby about her house. Desrosiers went to investigate.

Nadia at first denied having given birth to a child, but then admitted she had, about midnight on August 31. She had been alone except for her sleeping children. Unable to lie down because of the pain, Nadia said she had been walking when the child was born. It fell to the floor.

"The child cried when it was first born, but it stopped and later it died," Nadia explained.

"The child must have bumped its head," DesRosiers suggested.

"I put a piece of cloth in the baby's mouth to stop it from crying as I did not want anyone to know that I had had a baby," Nadia further offered.

With that, Nadia showed DesRosiers where, in the middle of the night, she had buried the child, tucked into a shoe box.

Dr. Frank Coppock was present when the box was exhumed. It contained a seven-pound female child which he thought was full-term. There was a bruise on the head. Also in the box was a six-foot length of cord, and, in the child's mouth, a three-by-eight-inch piece of cotton cloth. There were indications that the cord had been around the child's neck. There was a groove around the front of the neck and on the right side that seemed to fit the cord.

It was Dr. Coppock's opinion that the child had died of suffocation. The cotton cloth in the mouth was, he felt, sufficient to have caused death. Nadia Bajer was arrested and charged that she "did murder a newly born female child of which she had been delivered, by suffocating the said child." A fast preliminary inquiry was conducted on September 11, only two days after Corporal DesRosiers first dropped in on Nadia. She was remanded, in custody, for trial at the October jury sittings in Prince Albert. Nadia got word to Diefenbaker and Elder and the firm was off and running on another murder case.

When the case came to trial on October 9, the defence team had done their homework. The actual or probable cause of the death of Nadia's child, and Dr. Frank Coppock's opinion, came under close scrutiny.

Mr. Justice MacDonald presided. The Crown's case was presented by Samuel J. Branion, in his second year as agent of the attorney general. Prince Albert had not seen a murder trial for some years, and the curious crowd overflowed the courtroom.

Branion's case contained no surprises and went in swiftly, except for the medical testimony. John Diefenbaker, primed by his own medical witnesses, was waiting for Dr. Coppock.

Yes, Dr. Coppock admitted, certain symptoms usually found with instances of strangulation, such as black and blue spots on the body and protruding eyes, were missing in this case. But this did not, in his opinion, prove that strangulation had not been the cause of death.

"Please state the medical reasons supporting your conclusions," Diefenbaker commanded.

"In my opinion, without a doubt, the child died from strangulation caused by the rag in its mouth," Dr. Coppock insisted.

"Why?"

"What other reason was there for the child to die?"

"Would you have concluded that asphyxiation was the cause of death had you not found the rag in the child's mouth?" Diefenbaker zeroed in.

"No," the doctor admitted. The child had been dead ten days when he performed his examination. The doctor thought that by then some of the effects Diefenbaker was quoting to him out of medical texts would have subsided.

Dr. Coppock backed up even further. The child had died of a lack of air. But, he suggested, that could not have been caused by a sudden cutting off of the air supply, for such an action would produce symptoms which, as Diefenbaker had pointed out, were not evident in this case.

Dr. Richard L. King, the Wakaw coroner, was present when Dr. Coppock examined the child. He, too, thought the infant had died of strangulation due to the rag in its mouth.

Bill Elder took Dr. King through the same list of missing symptoms John Diefenbaker had put to Dr. Coppock. "The absence of symptoms is not incompatible with asphyxiation," the coroner maintained.

When Branion closed the Crown case at four o'clock in the afternoon, Diefenbaker and Elder went straight into their defence. In an unusual move, the first defence witness was the justice of the peace who had conducted Nadia's preliminary inquiry. A.E. Danby, the hotel proprietor in Wakaw, had been Prince Albert's chief of police. He had seen several cases of death by suffocation or strangulation, and Nadia's child showed none of the symptoms he would expect to find. Danby was no medical expert, but he was still a very effective witness to put before a Prince Albert jury.

Dr. Robert G. Scott was a medical missionary who had been head of Wakaw's Anna Turnbull Hospital since 1908. A beloved figure, he had attended at hundreds of childbirths. Although he had worked against Diefenbaker in the 1925 and 1926 elections, he was nevertheless very helpful in the witness box during Nadia Bajer's trial.

"The blood becomes noticeably darkened as a result of asphyxiation," Dr. Scott testified. "Lividity could be expected to be found in the child's back and shoulders if it had been strangled."

It was Dr. Scott's opinion that Nadia's child had bled to death as a result of a disorder common to childbirth. His reputation made him all but invulnerable, and Branion wisely was very circumspect in his cross-examination.

Two more medical men followed; both cast doubt on asphyxiation as the cause of death. The groove in the child's neck was from natural causes, not from the cord found in the box, they told the jury.

With that, the defence closed its case. There was no question of putting Nadia on the stand. Her story had already been conveyed through Corporal DesRosiers, and the poor woman was in no shape to testify. The sight of the dejected Nadia in the prisoner's box, wracked with sobs, produced all the sympathy the defence needed.

As if all concerned in the trial felt an urgency to end Nadia's ordeal, the case pressed on. At 5:30 in the afternoon, Diefenbaker, first in the order, rose to address the jury. By now a crowd of several hundred had gathered at the Prince Albert court house, spilling out of the courtroom into the corridors and onto the walks and street out front.

The situation was tailored perfectly for the eloquent defence counsel. Elder had done an excellent job on the medical homework, and a huge hole was shot through the prosecution's theory of strangulation as the cause of death. The jury was waiting to be led through that hole, and Diefenbaker was just the man for the occasion. His audience, in the jury box and throughout the court house, were not disappointed.

He began with a vivid description of the hovel in which Nadia and her two children subsisted, abandoned by their husband and father and forced to fend for themselves. On the night the child had been born, Nadia was alone, deserted by the father of the child. In terror, she tried desperately to protect her family from the ostracism that surely would come if her condition became known.

It was good material, and effective. Diefenbaker's rapt listeners were somber and sympathetic. For Nadia, a few feet behind her counsel, it was too much. She succumbed to continuous sobbing, taking everyone's emotions to the edge.

"He gave her *pills*," the lawyer spat the word into the well of the courtroom. "Pills, when she needed succour, food, clothing. Pills, when she needed honour and protection.

"She had the courage to refuse, the courage to admit her sin, the courage to confess her wrong. Would such a woman then take the cowardly course of murdering her own child and covering up the crime?

"This is not a case of trying to cover up murder, but of a woman trying to hide her shame. Yes, Nadia Bajer buried a body. Early in the morning she laid her child away, but not a child whose life was taken by her hands.

"Scientific medical evidence has shown that the prosecution has not proven that the child died because of a rag in its mouth, a rag placed there to stop the child from crying. Nadia Bajer's child died from natural causes."

As John Diefenbaker slowly returned to his seat at the counsel table, there was no room for increase in the dramatic effect. Nadia's sobs were the only sound in the completely silent courtroom.

"Mr. Branion," called Mr. Justice MacDonald finally. It was a tough role that the prosecutor faced. It was all over, and Branion knew it, but the form had to be observed, and he went through the motions.

Mr. Justice MacDonald did likewise. Pressing the case on with the same urgency, he completed his charge at 8:30 in the evening and allowed the jury to retire. In addition to a verdict on the main question of murder, MacDonald asked them to answer two questions: had a child recently been born to Nadia Bajer? and did she by some secret disposition of it conceal its birth?

No one was surprised when the jury took only fifteen minutes to reach its verdict: "Not guilty." The two questions were answered in the affirmative, rendering Nadia guilty only of the offence of concealing childbirth.

Speaking to sentence on the lesser offence, John Diefenbaker pointed out that his client, the sole support of her two children, had been in jail for a month. She was truly repentant, he said, and had suffered enough. Branion agreed, and so did Mr. Justice MacDonald, who handed down a suspended sentence.

"Repentant" was hardly the word for Nadia Bajer. The tear-stained and emotionally drained woman was helped from the courtroom, free to return to Wakaw and the life of a social outcast. The crowd surged around Diefenbaker, full of congratulations.

It was the first win in three attempts for Diefenbaker and Elder, and they deserved it. Although it might have been a hard case to lose, they had handled it carefully and well, leaving nothing undone. It was doubly satisfying to have won at home in Prince Albert. The glory lasted for weeks down on Central Avenue.

As the end of the year 1930 approached, and John Diefenbaker took stock of his personal situation, he had good reason for pride and comfort. On all fronts — professional, political and personal — he could count secure achievements.

In the six and a half years since his move to Prince Albert, Diefenbaker had established himself as the city's leading counsel. The more lucrative commercial work still evaded him, controlled by the better-connected firms, but he was busy and well paid. During the last year his reputation had spread province-wide with the three murder trials and the Bryant Charges Commission. The future was extremely promising.

With Conservative governments entrenched in both Ottawa and Regina, Diefenbaker's political connections could hardly be improved upon. He had not achieved elected office, but he enjoyed stature and prestige in his party, and could reasonably expect reward and further prominence.

And on the personal side, the lawyer was proud and pleased with his wife and his married status. Edna was his delight. With her ability to walk straight into people's hearts, she opened doors and friendships the austere Diefenbaker could never find himself.

Financially, the lawyer was not as strong as he would have liked, but that would come. The thing was to keep advancing, keep improving one's position to take advantage of tomorrow's opportunities.

Diefenbaker's firm grossed just under $14,000 during 1930, but his take-home net was only $4,500. The two lawyers, Diefenbaker and Elder, employed a clerical staff of nine full-time and part-time employees on a total payroll of $3,000. Elder's salary, rent and other office costs, plus travel, court house and agency fees, lifted the entire expense of the office over $9,000. The billings for the Bryant Charges Commission swelled his 1931 gross up to $17,000, a level not reached again for ten years. He owned a quarter-section of land near Wakaw, a small rental house in Prince Albert, and no other properties other than the modest home he and Edna lived in. He had no other investments or business interests whatsoever. Similarly, he had no debt.

Because he did not have market investments, not even a broker's account, Diefenbaker was not directly affected by the stock market crash of October 1929. The decline that followed the crash was slow in reaching western Canada, and even slower to find Prince Albert. In fact, the city was feeling so confident during 1930 that it voted approval for the paving of Central Avenue, accomplished that summer.

By the end of the year, however, Prince Albert, like the rest of Saskatchewan, was experiencing a phenomenon until then almost unknown in the developing West — serious unemployment. More than seven hundred unemployed men, two-thirds of them transients, were registered in the city. Still, Prince Albert was remote from much of the real hardship, which was centred in southern Saskatchewan.

The farm economy showed signs of trouble again but, although wheat was in more trouble than ten years earlier, no one believed the problem would be of long duration. Production in 1929 was only half of the 1928 bumper crop, but in 1930 it was again over 200 million bushels, almost up to the ten-year average.

The price of that wheat was more discouraging. It held up during 1929, but in 1930 began a steady slide. On Boxing Day it dropped to fifty cents a bushel, a record low, and tentacles of fear gripped brave New Year's smiles. Net farm income in Saskatchewan in 1930 was only one-fifth of the level two years earlier. It was the last time for several years that it would even be in the black, but no one could foresee that.

In many areas of southern Saskatchewan, the drought, first noticed in 1929, continued into 1930. Fifty rural municipalities suffered two successive crop failures, and Premier Anderson's government began to address the desperate and growing need for a program of public relief. A government relief camp was established in 1930 at Waskesiu, in the Prince Albert National Park.

As the winter of 1931 deepened, what began as a curiosity of nature became a disheartening calamity. During the summers of 1929 and 1930 the rains had failed to come to much of the southern plains. Now, for the first time, the snow, too, failed.

Across the three prairie provinces, the land, normally silent and protected beneath a winter blanket of white, lay uncovered and vulnerable to the western winds. Drought-dry and exposed, the soil began to shift, and then to lift in great towering black blizzards as the heartland blew eastward and away. Following some signal storms of the previous summer, duststorms descended in fury upon the western plains of North America and became the hallmark of their Depression years.

9

The Conservative Years

Although the Depression bruised everyone in Canada, fate dealt its blows in very unequal doses. This was true even on the prairies, where economic blight was compounded by a nature turned cruel. The farmers on the light soils of the south watched their farms turn to desert before their eyes, a disaster escaped by the homesteaders in the parkland region.

So it was with Canada's political parties. It was the misfortune of the Conservatives to be in office when the depression arrived, and they took the brunt of the public's vengeance for a world gone wrong. In Saskatchewan, where the greatest hardship was endured, the party was also in power provincially, and for fifty years was not fully forgiven. The party John Diefenbaker had chosen as promising the fastest political advancement suddenly and unpredictably became a victim of fate, and a liability to an ambitious man.

Premier Anderson's government, as befitting a new administration, had quickly embarked upon a series of fresh initiatives and reforms, but before long it was forced to deal with a Depression agenda of disappearing revenues and unheard of demands for public assistance. Anderson set up a commission to inquire into the Liberal tradition of using the provincial public service as a party employment centre. A civil service commission was established, offering open competition for civil service positions and promotions based on merit, a real innovation in 1930.

Campaign promises were kept. A long-running dispute with the federal government over Saskatchewan's natural resources was settled; control over resources was brought home to the province. Highway construction was modernized by the introduction of power equipment. A royal commission inquired into public concern over foreign settlers and indiscriminate immigration. The new government's first legislative sessions amended the School Act to prohibit the display of religious symbols, the wearing of religious garb and the use of French in public schools.

It was a government of energy and promise, but, as the province and its revenue dried up, policy options disappeared. Premier Anderson and his Cabinet became fully engaged in coping with a crisis that took Saskatchewan to the edge of famine.

The drought that began with the black blizzards of winter continued through the growing season of 1931. The crops failed totally throughout all of Saskatchewan south of Saskatoon, the first failure of such general magnitude. There had been losses in 1929 and 1930, but in much smaller areas, and it had been reasonable to view the problem as temporary and local. Now, a vast area of the province suffered three consecutive crop failures, another region two failures, and almost all of the grain belt lost the 1931 crop. The extent and impact of the disaster was acknowledged by Premier Anderson, who assured a frightened Saskatchewan that "no one will starve."

In many rural areas, food, clothing, fuel and livestock fodder almost disappeared. In August 1931, Anderson created the Saskatchewan Relief Commission, "for the purpose of relieving distress and providing employment." Voluntary agencies marshalled contributions of food and clothing for the impoverished in Saskatchewan. Fruit, vegetables and fish from Ontario and the Maritimes were shipped to the West.

Many Westerners made their first acquaintance with the dried codfish, an intimidating and entirely inedible mystery to the uninitiated. Special recipes for preparing the cod were distributed, but not nearly as widely as the fish, which quickly won a place among the legends of the West. Stories abound of perplexed homesteaders who shingled their roofs with the board-like commodity, or used them for signposts.

But there was very little humour along the western road allowances as the tragedy deepened. Years of work, planning and hope shrivelled together with the faltering crops and disappearing soil. Families who once took pride in their economic achievements now became concerned with survival.

Reinhold Drews of Aberdeen was one whose prosperity quickly turned to disaster that threatened to overwhelm him. Having established his initial homestead, in 1928 he bought another half-section of land a mile or two away. The purchase was on credit, the standard agreement for sale, but presented no problem to Drews. He was a good farmer, a careful man who managed his affairs properly. He had to — Drews was the sole support for his wife and large family. He was well regarded in Aberdeen, not many miles east of Saskatoon.

But, as so often happens, when luck turned bad it turned very bad indeed. Two years after Drews undertook his additional debt, a fire started in a strawpile on his property and spread into the crop of his neighbour, Agnes Longueil. Longueil sued and came away with a judgment for $300. With the crops failing, the judgment was enough to sink Drews.

When he travelled back and forth between his lands, Drews passed Longeuil's home. In June and July of 1931, as the wheat in the fields wilted and died and his prospects grew bleaker, the overstressed man brooded until his normal good sense worked loose. Carrying a can of gopher poison, Drews broke into Longueil's home during the family's absence and dosed several containers of food. It was an amateurish break and entry and, when the family returned, the broken window through which Drews had entered alerted them. The poison was spotted and avoided. Because of the bad feeling, Drews was suspected right away.

When the police arrived, Drews made no attempt to deny his behaviour. He told the investigators exactly what had happened, as nearly he could remember. He could not recall all of his actions, but was certain enough to admit his guilt.

The Crown charged attempted murder. Drews, anxious not to place any further financial stress upon his family, appeared without a lawyer in front of Mr. Justice Bigelow. He pleaded guilty and threw himself on the mercy of the court.

"Have you anything to say why the sentence of the Court should not be pronounced upon you, according to law?" Mr. Justice Bigelow put the formal question to the frightened farmer.

"Not very much. Present hard times lot to do with it, too." It was not much of a plea in mitigation.

"I beg your pardon?" asked Mr. Justice Bigelow.

"Present hard times have a lot to do with this case. This thing would have been settled, and gone and forgotten, you see. Kept worrying me, of course." It was a very barebones explanation.

"I beg your pardon?" asked the judge again, not being very helpful.

"They kept worrying me, and of course it was unpaid, and, as it happened, I don't remember me going there."

"Is that all?"

"No more."

Fortunately for Drews, the prosecutor, George Arthur Cruise, K.C., was concerned about the case and the accused. He made sure that Mr. Justice Bigelow was aware of how out of character this behaviour was for Reinhold Drews, who was "not an ordinary criminal."

"The people who know this man seem to agree that he was not himself, not his proper self when this thing happened. I don't know how it works out, but they say he was not the same man that he was before this thing happened. They think he had brooded over this thing till, they think, it affected his mind to some extent, and they say he is a man who could not do that thing if he were quite right."

To confirm what he had just said, Cruise handed Mr. Justice Bigelow two letters from people who knew the unfortunate Drews. It made little impression on Bigelow.

"I have heard of nothing except that you have had a good reputation in the community so far, and that you have not been in difficulties before, all of which speaks well of your past history." Mr. Justice Bigelow began with encouraging words, but they did not continue.

"I cannot take the responsibility of passing a short sentence upon you, even with your previous good character. I do not think I would be doing my duty to the community to let you free again in a short time. A man with tendencies like that, of such a vindictive nature, might easily go out in the community again and perpetrate a similar offence, and some one, the next time, is liable to die. I cannot take that responsibility.

"The sentence of the Court is that you be imprisoned in the penitentiary at Prince Albert for the term of fifteen years."

When he got to Prince Albert, Drews reconsidered his decision about legal counsel and called John Diefenbaker. There was little Diefenbaker could do other than appeal the sentence, which seemed unduly severe, and he promptly did so. Two months later, the Prince Albert lawyer and Regina prosecutor Herb Sampson again duelled in the Court of Appeal.

It was not much of a duel. The judges of appeal listened for an hour and a half as Diefenbaker contended that the sentence was excessive considering the circumstances, and that the rehabilitation of Reinhold Drews would be better accomplished by leniency. When he had exhausted his arguments on his client's behalf, the court thanked Diefenbaker and dismissed his appeal without calling upon Sampson.

Another Diefenbaker client, Dymtro Stefaniuk, was more fortunate. At 2:00 a.m. on a cold mid-November night, 1931, Corporal DesRosiers of the Wakaw RCMP detachment peered into an open grave in the Sokal rural cemetery. There, six feet down, by the light of a flickering lantern, he saw a man kneeling on the edge of an open casket.

Piled about the man was a large number of boxes and parcels. DesRosiers watched as the shadowy figure took articles from the boxes and parcels and stuffed them alongside the body in the casket, stopping occasionally to hug and kiss the body. DesRosiers noted that the corpse was in an advanced state of decomposition.

"What are you doing there?" The policeman decided it was time to interrupt.

"This is my wife. She died on the 18th of January, 1931, and was buried here on the 20th. I feel pains in my heart and I feel better after I have seen her." It was a completely matter-of-fact reply.

As his eyes became accustomed to the dim light from the lantern, DesRosiers saw that the man was surrounded by women's clothing, apples, oranges, peanuts and candy, pillow cases and a variety of other items.

"Why don't you take them home instead of leaving them in the coffin?" he asked.

"I couldn't afford to dress my wife when she was living and I promised to dress her when she was dead." Again the response was matter-of-fact.

With that, the man kissed the corpse from head to foot, emptied the last of his parcels into the coffin, replaced the lid on the casket and climbed out of the grave. Then he helped the policeman fill in the hole.

Dymtro Stefaniuk appeared to be quite normal and acted as if his behaviour were entirely natural. Although he knew he would have to file some sort of charge, DesRosiers allowed the bereaved husband to return to his nearby farm home.

Two days later, DesRosiers charged Stefaniuk with indecently interfering with the dead body of his wife, Sofia, contrary to Section 234 of the Criminal Code. The policeman and the accused appeared before Justice of the Peace A.E. Danby, and a quick preliminary inquiry was held.

After DesRosiers had testified as to what he had seen in the Sokal cemetery, Danby read to Stefaniuk the statutory ritual about his right to remain silent, and asked the question: "Having heard the evidence, do you wish to say anything in answer to the charge?"

"I can't say anything," the accused replied. "What Mr. Des-Rosiers says is true."

Danby committed Stefaniuk for trial by jury and John Diefenbaker was called in. One look told the lawyer that this was a case for a guilty plea.

Diefenbaker quickly arranged to have his client re-elect his method of trial, giving up the jury in favour of a "speedy trial" in front of District Court Judge A.E. Doak. On December 17, Diefenbaker and Stefaniuk appeared before Judge Doak, pleaded guilty and asked for lenience. The lawyer used an excellent argument he had developed for the Court of Appeal a month earlier on behalf of Reinhold Drews, but of course did not mention how that court had reacted to his plea.

Judge Doak had no trouble understanding Dymtro Stefaniuk's aberrant behaviour, and granted him his freedom on a suspended sentence. Another victim of the times returned to his home and community.

Prince Albert, although removed from the worst effects of the drought, had its share of destitute families and plenty of examples of the hurt and humiliation inflicted by unemployment. In September 1931, the month in which John Diefenbaker was retained by Reinhold Drews, two hundred unemployed men gathered at the city's Memorial Hall to draw attention to their plight. Prince Albert had been forced to cancel its modest relief works program when funds ran out. Men cried on the steps of city hall when they could get no work to feed their families. Some worked all day without food so that the subsistence level relief wage could be saved for their children.

The 1931 census identified 9,905 residents in Prince Albert, and this number grew throughout the Depression due to migration from the blown-out southern rural regions. The city's finances, still strained from the La Colle Falls hydro disaster, could not cope with the influx of poor and unemployed. The Depression stopped work on the new railroad station under construction in Prince Albert. It would be twenty-nine years before the station was finally completed.

As affluence evaporated and rewards went only to the very strongest, the mediocre career of Diefenbaker's brother Elmer made his fraternal responsibilities all the harder to bear. Younger brother Elmer, who had achieved only limited success as a local insurance agent in Prince Albert, slipped into financial difficulty.

Elmer was a pleasant, well-meaning, not very ambitious, bore. Like a pilot fish accompanying a shark for the morsels of food spilled by the predator, Elmer provided the insurance required by the Diefenbaker law practice.

John, who had sold insurance himself while at Wakaw, turned the opportunity over to Elmer when he moved to Prince Albert. The law office had a modest need for administration bonds and the like, and could easily steer its clients who required fire and liability coverage in Elmer's direction. Elmer operated out of the Diefenbaker offices on Central Avenue.

The brothers, as bachelors, had lived together at the Avenue Hotel, and then at the Donaldson boarding house. When John married, he attempted to move Elmer into his new home, but Edna put her foot down and refused. Elmer went back to the boarding house. Later, he moved into the National Hotel, somewhat seedy quarters.

Accepted practice in the insurance industry required the local agent, who sold the policy, to collect the premium, deduct his commission of 20 or 25 per cent, and remit the balance to his general agent. As business tightened, Elmer dipped into the share of the premiums belonging to the general agent, Massie & Renwick. The penalties could be severe, but certainly would include termination of the agency account. Elmer would be out of business.

John came to the rescue, but it was not easy. Elmer owed Massie & Renwick over $550, more than John had on hand in the fall of 1931. He paid the company $200, guaranteed the balance, and promised to clean up the account by spring. The following spring, John Diefenbaker found Massie & Renwick pressing him for payment. Funds were even tighter than the previous fall, but, finally, he was able to clear the debt.

Meanwhile, the Depression continued to deepen. As new adversities arrived, they piled upon a people already so benumbed by tragedy as to be hardly able to appreciate their ever-worsening conditions.

Something was salvaged of the 1932 crops, but it was only a slight improvement on the total failure of 1931. Prices continued to fall. In December 1932, the price of wheat sank to its lowest level in three hundred years. In Prince Albert, that translated into an elevator price of twenty-two cents per bushel. But that was the price for the almost mythical Number One grade of wheat. After a day spent driving a hundred-bushel wagonload to town, a farmer lucky enough to have that quality of grain could expect a cash ticket for $22. If, as was more likely, his crop was Number Two feed oats, the wagonload might bring only $2.50. At Wakaw, Dr. Robert G. Scott reported: "We are in a bad fix here. Money is almost never seen now. Farmers cannot sell butter at 10 cents a pound, nor eggs at 5 cents a dozen, or less."

It was little wonder that provincial "net farm income" — defined as total gross income less operating and depreciation charges — plunged into the minus column in 1931. It stayed in the red for four years. Saskatchewan dropped from Canada's fourth-wealthiest province to its poorest.

The firm of Diefenbaker and Elder did not withstand the strain of reducing revenues. In the summer of 1932, Bill Elder left. He later became Prince Albert's magistrate. The friction between the partners was ostensibly over money, and was unpleasant, as such divorces frequently are. Elder complained privately that he and Diefenbaker possessed incompatible ethical standards. Diefenbaker remained silent. Whatever the reason, John Diefenbaker was again a sole practitioner.

The Co-operative government headed by Premier Anderson also experienced disharmony. Strangely, however, it was the Conservative Party that showed signs of coming unglued, rather than the three-party coalition that held the government together.

Some of Anderson's more progressive programs ran counter to the beliefs of the reactionary or "true blue" wing of the Conservative Party. Provisions in the government's debt-adjustment legislation for deferral of payment were seen as interfering with the sanctity of contract. Many of the debts being deferred were owed to prominent Conservatives.

Nor was this all. A period of crisis-level unemployment was not the best time to attempt a patronage-free civil service. With their new Civil Service Commission, the Conservatives cut themselves off from hundreds of jobs that otherwise might have gone to their friends and supporters. Not popular in party ranks, the restriction was, according to a Regina Conservative MLA, "one of the greatest mistakes the government made."

James Gardiner and the Liberal opposition gave no quarter as they watched the Anderson government struggling to cope with the problems of the Depression. A suggestion from Anderson, that partisan politics be set aside and an all-party coalition formed to deal with the emergency, was received with derision.

In the spring of 1933, Premier Anderson induced the Liberal member from Kinistino to cross the floor and join his Cabinet. It was then still a requirement that a new Cabinet member secure re-election after his appointment, and a May by-election was called for Kinistino. By tradition, such by-elections were not contested and the candidate was allowed to win by acclamation. Not so in 1933. The Liberals nominated in Kinistino and, assisted by insurgent Conservatives, trounced the government candidate.

The message was clear. The Anderson government had become a lame duck administration, and awaited only the formality of defeat at the polls before it went out of office. The Liberal opposition, under Gardiner and T.C. Davis, became a government-in-waiting. The Liberals, certain that the government was mortally impaled upon the Depression, refused to permit it to free itself until it was fully dead. When coalition support deserted Anderson on crucial votes, enough Liberals MLAs discreetly absented themselves to ensure the survival of the government. Gardiner and Davis did not want the election to come too soon.

Undeterred by the bleakness of the Conservative prospects, John Diefenbaker sought advancement within the party. At the Conservative convention held in Saskatoon on October 11 and 12, 1933, he put his name forward for the position of vice-president. Three other delegates did the same.

The Prince Albert lawyer did not overwhelm the convention. He was elected, but not until the third ballot. Perhaps it was a matter of too many lawyers. The convention elected a new president, Diefenbaker's agent from the Pasowesty case, J.A.M. Patrick, K.C., of Yorkton, who succeeded the retiring Dr. D.S. Johnstone.

Johnstone was a leader of the "true blue" element, those who preached adherence to traditional Conservative philosophy. The past president participated in an unpleasant episode at the gathering. Vocally critical of the policies of the Co-operative government, the "true blues" provoked Premier Anderson into handing his resignation to the convention. The resignation was promptly rejected by the delegates, who gave Anderson a standing ovation, while Johnstone and other "true blues" pointedly remained seated. It was a serious sign of disunity in a government party heading into an election year.

In the spring of 1933, John Diefenbaker was joined by a law student just out of the University of Saskatchewan law school. John M. Cuelenaere, whose father was the hotel-keeper at nearby Leask, arrived pursuant to an arrangement made a couple of years earlier, which Diefenbaker claimed to have forgotten.

It was a fortuitous arrangement. Cuelenaere became an outstanding lawyer. His research and work on the legal side of the cases which came to the office bolstered the area in which his leader was the weakest. The association between Diefenbaker and Cuelenaere lasted far longer than any other professional relationship John Diefenbaker entered into. Sadly, however, it ended in bitterness more than thirty years later when both men had achieved prominence and responsible public office.

About the time Cuelenaere came, Diefenbaker took advantage of the Depression to apply to his landlord, the Banque Canadienne Nationale, for a reduction in his rent. Diefenbaker wrote the bank's manager:

"I spoke to you sometime ago in regard to the question of the rent being paid by me and the impossibility of being able to continue under the present terms. When I asked you to enlarge my office, business conditions as you know were very good but since that date conditions have changed to such an extent that business is only about half of what it used to be and I have had to reduce my staff accordingly.

"I do not wish in any way to be unfair but conditions being what they are I suggest to you that in view of the fact that I have been your tenant for well on to ten years I am entitled to some consideration. I suggest to you that having regard to conditions you reduce the rent on the premises occupied by me to $50.00 a month which rate of rent is to be in effect for one year, after which period new arrangements can be made. On the other hand, if you are not in agreement to this my next suggestion is that you partition off the space between my outer office and the premises formerly occupied by the Dwyer Elevator Company and that the rental for the reduced portion be $40.00 per month.

"I have endeavoured to carry on during the past six months according to the strict letter of the agreement but I realize now very clearly that I cannot continue on this basis and that to do so would be ruinous to me. I trust, therefore, that you will give consideration to this application, letting me know your decision at as an early date as possible [sic]."

The bank manager was unmoved. The rent remained at $60 per month, although a $5 decrease was implemented the following year.

Perhaps, however, the manager had reason to suspect the veracity of the lawyer's statements. In fact, rather than "only half of what it used to be," Diefenbaker's gross in 1933 was down only ten per cent from its 1930 level, and his net income was off only $400, from $4,573 to $4,142. In truth, John Diefenbaker was doing very well in Depression-ridden Saskatchewan. While he had not done as well as many of his contemporaries during the more affluent 1920s, he out-performed them all in the tougher times. An income of more than $4,000 in 1933 Prince Albert was close to munificence.

During the Depression, Saskatchewan's birth rate sank with its economy. Few couples could afford children. John and Edna Diefenbaker faced no such financial limitation, but the ambitious lawyer did not want his style cramped by a family. Edna would have liked a child, but was overruled.

As John Diefenbaker approached his fortieth year, maturity erased the last effeminate aspects of his visage. His features became more pronounced and less attractive, a process that continued throughout his life. The full head of hair remained, but the forehead was higher, and the face more exposed. Determination shows in every photograph.

Today, the lawyer would be described as a "workaholic," a "Type A personality." He was driven to succeed — his work was his life. Although Edna persevered in her attempts to engage her husband in social affairs, her achievements so far were minimal. Diefenbaker carried his work home and closeted himself with his files and books. To a great extent, Edna was forced to make her own social life.

During this period Diefenbaker abandoned even his occasional summer holidays in the United States. Only politics took him away from Saskatchewan, and that but rarely. Until 1936, when he made a trip to Europe, he made no time for travel in his busy life.

But there was always time for his parents, particularly his doting mother. Whenever a call came from Saskatoon, Diefenbaker would drop everything and go. On at least one occasion, he took his father on a Waskesieu fishing trip. A photograph of the group suggests that William, stiffly dressed in a three-piece suit, was less than an avid fisherman.

In 1933, a redistribution of federal constituencies to accord with the 1931 census was debated in Parliament. Prince Albert was affected. Saskatchewan would retain its twenty-one seats, then the third-largest provincial caucus in Canada, but a population shift meant moving one riding from the south to the north. The new constituency of Rosthern was created, immediately south of Prince Albert.

The Conservative majority sought to improve their party's position in the surrounding ridings by transferring unwanted Liberal voting blocs into Rosthern, a strategy termed "hiving the Grits." The proposed removal of a substantial number of Liberal votes from Prince Albert, and the addition of some Conservative votes, was more than enough to wipe out Mackenzie King's 1,200 vote majority. King was worried.

There is no evidence that John Diefenbaker was involved in these proposals, but he must have been interested if he harboured a desire to be the Prince Albert member. In any event, his name popped up during the House of Commons debate.

The suggestion was made that constituency boundaries should be drawn upon ethnic lines. King demurred, saying, "We ought to regard the citizens of Canada as Canadians, and Canadians only, irrespective of what their origin might be." Then, by way of example:

"When I was opposed in the by-election in Prince Albert in 1926, whoever was responsible for the choice of the Conservative candidate in that constituency chose Mr. J.G. Diefenbaker to oppose me. It would seem he was of foreign origin. This gentleman, or at all events, his father, whom I knew years ago, strangely enough came from the same county of Waterloo as I do myself."

In years to come, Mackenzie King, who had some of his facts wrong, would become much better acquainted with his Prince Albert opponent "of foreign origin."

Whether or not he was keeping an eye on the federal seat, John Diefenbaker had not lost interest in elective office. Late in 1933 he became a candidate for mayor of Prince Albert.

Hugh Sibbald, who succeeded Samuel J. Branion as mayor in 1929, announced his retirement. Harold J. Fraser, a lawyer with six years service as an alderman, seemed certain to replace Sibbald, at least until eight days before the election, when John Diefenbaker announced for the office. The late entrant proposed a simple platform. He would demand more public works from the federal government, and he would seek a 1 per cent interest reduction on the city's outstanding debentures. Diefenbaker pointed out that 45 per cent of tax revenue was consumed by interest payments. His program was attractive to the financially-strapped voters.

To the city's establishment, however, Diefenbaker's proposed confrontation with the bondholders smacked of repudiation, something Prince Albert had been trying to live down since the failure of 1918 had ruined its credit. Central Avenue businessmen lined up behind Fraser. So did T.C. Davis and the local Liberals who were not about to allow the Conservative Diefenbaker any easy advancement. Fraser's near-acclamation turned overnight into a one-week furious campaign. The *Daily Herald*, since 1929 owned by W. L. Davis, T. C.'s brother, sided with the establishment against Diefenbaker.

The vote, on November 27, was the heaviest ever polled to that time in a Prince Albert municipal election. Fraser won with a 48 vote edge, 1,068 to 1,020. Diefenbaker did not give up easily or graciously. The next day he issued a statement:

"The determination with which the financial magnates of the city fought my candidature yesterday is convincing evidence that they were fearful and alarmed at the prospect of the investigation into city finances which would have been made had I been elected mayor.

"But even as a private citizen it is not my intention to give up the fight. I shall make every effort during the next few months to ascertain the entire and exact financial set-up of the city and the connection with and participation therein of certain people and interests in this city."

Fraser slyly thanked Diefenbaker "for the many kind references which he made in regard to myself throughout the campaign."

Diefenbaker was convinced that Prince Albert's "financial magnates" were deliberately keeping the city's finances in poor condition to depress the prices of its outstanding bonds, which they were then secretly buying at heavily discounted prices. He demanded from the city full information on transactions involving debenture stock since 1919. After some debate on city council about the propriety of disclosing the information, it was made available to Diefenbaker. He found it very disappointing. Prince Albert residents had bought only $10,000 worth of debentures in the previous four years, and none of those who did had any obvious connection with the city. Local citizens actually sold twice as much debenture stock as they purchased in the period.

Nothing further was heard from John Diefenbaker on the subject, and he never again showed any interest in civic affairs.

It was appropriate to use political connections to advance business and professional interests, and John Diefenbaker did so. In the fall of 1933, he wrote the Honourable T.J. Murphy, Minister of the Interior, at Ottawa: "I notice by the local press that Mr. Mulcaster [another Prince Albert lawyer] has been granted a fiat to proceed with an action against the Department of Indian Affairs in regard to the administration of certain Indian reserves within the federal constituency of Prince Albert. As no doubt the Department will be represented by counsel in the litigation now commenced, I am writing you for the purpose of asking that you give my name consideration when counsel is appointed."

As 1934 opened, the five-year mandate of Premier Anderson and the Co-operative government was running out. It would expire in June. The Conservative Party began to move into a full state of election readiness. In Prince Albert, Samuel J. Branion was nominated, this time without opposition from John Diefenbaker.

As an officially-nominated candidate on the government team, Branion had to give up his appointment as agent of the attorney general. He was succeeded by John Diefenbaker.

Accepting appointment as Crown prosecutor was very much out of character for Diefenbaker. The appointment applied only to the Prince Albert judicial district, and would not prevent him from accepting defence retainers in other districts, but in practice it meant that he was abandoning his hard-won role and image as champion of the accused: Prince Albert's pre-eminent defence counsel.

Very little criminal defence work was lucrative, and the Depression had dried up almost all the fees that had been available. People in trouble with the criminal law are usually very poor credit risks, and defence lawyers have to be ruthless about fees. Diefenbaker had learned that aspect of his practice very well, but obviously decided that the modest fee tariff of the attorney general's department was more attractive than the generally unpaid glamour of the defence.

Premier Anderson issued writs for the election to be held on June 19, 1934. Supporters of his government believed optimistically that Saskatchewan voters would recognize that responsible action had been taken to meet the problems of the Depression. But dissension still existed. Former party president Dr. D.S. Johnstone and the "true blue" Conservatives openly attacked the Anderson administration.

There was a wild card in the election in the form of the Farmer-Labour Party, which had been formed in Regina the previous year, the forerunner of the Co-operative Commonwealth Federation (CCF). The Farmer-Labour group nominated fifty-three out of a possible fifty-five candidates, one more than the Conservatives, and it was thought that they might split the anti-government vote sufficiently to re-elect Anderson's government. The Gardiner Liberals were seriously worried by this prospect.

"The Depression is the main plank in the platform of the Liberal Opposition," John Diefenbaker stated, not at all inaccurately, as he spoke in the campaign. "The Liberal Party in this province has been stirring up trouble and searching for something to criticize for months, but had to resort finally to a world condition and blame that on the present government."

Citing increases in world trade, production of lumber, minerals and electricity, Diefenbaker claimed that Canada was "emerging from the Depression. Wouldn't you think," he asked, "that the Liberal Party would be pleased at these signs of prosperity?"

Saskatchewan voters were hurting too much to be mollified with statistics and reason. On June 19, they hurled the Anderson government from office. Not one supporter of the government was re-elected. The Liberals, who campaigned on the slogan "Liberal Ways Bring Better Days," took fifty seats, and the Farmer-Labour group had five.

One month later, on July 19, James Gardiner and his Liberals were sworn into office to succeed the Anderson government. T.C. Davis, who had taken Samuel J. Branion's deposit, returned to the portfolio of attorney general.

John Diefenbaker did not wait for that last event. On June 25, he filed his resignation as agent of the attorney general, to be effective immediately. His career as a Crown prosecutor was over before it had begun.

For John Diefenbaker and the Saskatchewan Conservatives, the light had been snuffed out after just five years in the political sun.

10

Rex v. Steve Bohun

Detective Constable Arthur Cookson had been with the RCMP only two years, but murder investigations were nothing new to him. Still, three cases in one week was a bit of a record. It put a strain on the three-man criminal investigation division at North Battleford, where Cookson was stationed.

When the call came from Redberry, forty miles to the east, Cookson was one hundred miles west, on the Alberta border, working on the first murder. By the time he got to Redberry, it was June 14, 1933, and the case was two days cold.

Peter Pommereul had been found lying behind the counter in his combination general store and post office, shot in the side of the head with a .22 calibre gun. The postal inspectors had already determined that $324 in postal funds was missing.

No one had been seen coming or going, and no strangers had been noticed about the tiny village, not even the hoboes so common since the onset of the Depression.

A glint of sunlight on the wooden floor of the store exposed a spent .22 long-rifle cartridge case hidden in a crack. No other clues.

Pommereul's store was on the edge of the village. As Cookson stood on the front steps, he noticed that the field across the street was in summerfallow, recently cultivated. Inspection disclosed two sets of footprints, one approaching the store and one leaving. Both showed a distinctive heel mark. Whoever made the footprints had been running when he left.

With the help of several townsfolk, Cookson followed the footprints. They lost the trail whenever their quarry crossed grassland or pasture, but picked it up again in the fields. They followed the trail for three miles before darkness forced them to adjourn.

As Cookson was about to leave Redberry for the night, a telephone call came for him, and he drove six miles north to talk to sixteen-year-old Fred Harach. Fred had helped Cookson follow the tracks. When they adjourned, Fred had carried on to his home, spotting the tracks now and then in the gathering dusk. They seemed to lead right to his father's farm.

"This got me thinking," Fred told Cookson. "In the morning, two days ago, Steve Bohun came over here to borrow my .22 rifle. He said his father wanted him to shoot a pig.

"Steve promised he would have the gun back by noon, but he didn't. I was mad. I couldn't understand why he had not brought the rifle back as he said he would."

An angry Fred went over to the Bohun farm to see about his rifle. He spoke to Steve's father, who knew nothing about butchering a pig, or about Fred's rifle.

"Steve left this morning and I don't know where he went," the elder Bohun told Fred.

Even angrier now, Fred returned home. Part way there, he saw Steve Bohun coming towards him, across the fields, alternately running and walking. Fred waited. When Steve came up, out of breath and sweating profusely, he admitted he had lied to get the gun. Wanting a day to himself, he had gone shooting gophers and lost track of the time. Suddenly realizing that it was well past noon, he hurried back to return Fred's .22.

That cleared up, the two boys sat in the pasture taking potshots at some ducks in a slough. Steve provided the ammunition.

With this information, the police went straight to the Bohun farm. Steve was not home. The boy and his father had had a row two days before; Steve had left in a huff, and his parents had not seen him since.

Nineteen-year-old Steve was in love, his father related, and wanted to marry, right away. He had insisted that his father set him up with a half-section of land. The youth would not listen to his father's explanation that conditions did not permit such generosity.

Annie Barchuk had not been seen for two days either. Her parents told Cookson that Steve Bohun had taken her for a walk, and they had not returned. The Barchuks were worried. Annie was only seventeen and, although she had been going with Steve for some time, they had not before been away overnight.

Some hours later, at 2:30 a.m., Cookson found Steve Bohun and Annie Barchuk asleep on the floor of an otherwise uninhabited house. Spotting a blackjack strapped to the boy's wrist, Cookson quickly handcuffed him.

"What are you arresting me for? I didn't shoot the old man." No one had mentioned a shooting.

From under Steve Bohun's pillow, Cookson recovered $322 in bills.

Annie was pregnant, she told Cookson, and she and Steve had to get married. They were leaving that morning for Saskatoon. No, she did not know where Steve's money had come from. When told of Pommereul's murder, Annie became very distraught.

The next morning, Cookson took Steve and Fred Harach out to the pasture where they had been potshooting ducks. Four .22 casings were recovered.

"I am guilty," said Steve, looking at the shells.

"What do you mean, you're guilty?" Cookson asked.

"Well, I shot Pete Pommereul," Bohun admitted.

That night Steve Bohun fully confessed to the killing of Peter Pommereul. He gave a detailed written statement to RCMP Constable Bovan.

Steve needed money so he and Annie could marry. Aware that Pommereul kept cash in his store, the boy borrowed Fred Harach's .22 and went to Redberry. In the store, he asked Pommereul for some tobacco, kept on a low shelf behind the counter.

As the storekeeper bent and turned, Steve put the rifle to Pommereul's head and pulled the trigger. The boy scooped up the cash and ran.

The day after his confession, Steve took Cookson and his fellow investigators out and showed them the route he had taken across the fields to Pommereul's store and back. The tracks Cookson had followed were Bohun's tracks. The police had taken plaster casts of the tracks, and now took the opportunity to get a sample of tracks made by Bohun. They directed him to walk across a freshly-cultivated garden plot. All of the casts matched perfectly with the shoes the youth was wearing.

Art Cookson's case was complete. Everything, including the ballistics, matched up.

That afternoon, Steve Bohun was visited by his parents for the first time since his arrest. An emotional and noisy dialogue in Ukrainian ensued. Mrs. Bohun fainted. The boy wept. Pulling himself together, Steve Bohun proclaimed himself innocent. He claimed the police had beaten him to make him confess. The statement he had given Constable Bovan was entirely untrue. The father was sympathetic. He patted Steve on the shoulder, told him not to worry and promised to have a lawyer come around.

After the parents left, Cookson and the other investigators held counsel. They decided to take Steve back to Pommereul's store on the chance that the scene of the crime would cause him to reconsider and confirm his confession. It turned out to be a terrible mistake.

At the store, Steve was sullen and resentful, shrugging off the police suggestions about how the killing had taken place. Suddenly, Cookson says, the handcuffed youth dropped to his knees and threw himself forward into a large sack of potatoes. His nose began to bleed profusely, all over his shirt. The police quickly stopped the bleeding, but the damage had been done. They had to get a clean shirt on Bohun immediately.

Constable Bovan had remained outside. When Cookson brought the bloody Bohun out, Bovan was at first speechless and then caustic.

"What the hell have you been doing? Christ, what did you hit him for?"

"I tried to explain what happened in the store," Cookson now says, "but, to this day, I'm not sure Bovan believes me."

A clean shirt was found for Steve Bohun, but before the bloody one could be disposed of, Alfred Svoboda, a lawyer from nearby Blaine Lake, showed up. As soon as Svoboda heard the story from Steve he demanded, and got, the bloody shirt.

Cookson was worried, plenty worried, and with good reason. Any serious suggestion of police brutality would jeopardize the admissibility of Bohun's confession, and might well contaminate other evidence as well. The bloody shirt could cause a lot of trouble in the hands of a skilled defence lawyer.

A few weeks later, Arthur Cookson's worry turned to genuine alarm. Steve Bohun's father took Alfred Svoboda off the case and retained John Diefenbaker.

"I had heard of Diefenbaker's reputation," Cookson says today. "I knew I was in for a very rough time when the case came up for trial in the fall."

The court house stands in "old" Battleford, the original community which arose next to Fort Battleford on a high plateau commanding the sweep of the North Saskatchewan River.

When Chief Justice J.T. Brown opened the sittings on September 26, the John Diefenbaker who arose to enter a plea of "Not Guilty" on behalf of Steve Bohun was a very different defence counsel from the one Brown had assisted at Humboldt fourteen years earlier. Now supremely confident, the lawyer was impressive, and quickly became the dominant figure on the courtroom floor. His handsome features and dark, curly hair were accentuated by the wing collar and flowing black silk robes of the King's Counsel. Detective Constable Arthur Cookson, watching the opening of the case, felt his stomach twist.

Cookson was soon sent out of the courtroom. When the jury was selected and Crown prosecutor R.B. Mills had called his first witness, Diefenbaker made the standard request for the exclusion of witnesses until they had testified.

The first day was occupied with background evidence and plans of Redberry and the Pommereul store. Late in the afternoon, the jury also was sent out of the courtroom as Chief Justice Brown began to inquire into the admissibility of Steve Bohun's confession and his several verbal admissions of guilt. This, as both Cookson and Diefenbaker very well knew, was the heart of the case. If the defence counsel could raise doubts in the mind of the trial judge about whether Steve Bohun had freely volunteered those statements, they would be excluded from the jury.

The Chief Justice reviewed nearly all the Crown case before making his decision to admit the confession and verbal statements of guilt. The jury played bridge for forty hours before they were called back to the courtroom.

On Wednesday morning, the second day of the trial, Arthur Cookson was the first witness into the stand. As the chief investigator, he was the main Crown witness on the subject of Bohun's statements. Cookson still remembers that day very, very well.

Mills was a quiet and thorough lawyer. He spent almost an hour taking Cookson through his experiences with Steve Bohun during the investigation. Then he turned the policeman over to the defence.

"I was not an inexperienced witness, but it was my first time in King's Bench," says Cookson. "Dressed in scarlet tunic, breeches, high boots and spurs, I was anything but the serene and confident Mountie I appeared to be.

"Any moment, I expected that bloody shirt of Steve Bohun's to be flung in my face, and an explanation demanded.

"It was his eyes, most of all," Cookson says, as he recalls his contest with John Diefenbaker.

The defence lawyer rose slowly from his place at the counsel table, apparently deep in thought. As if stalling for time, he asked

Cookson a number of routine and repetitive questions, all the while moving slowly towards the witness box.

"What did you say your name was?

"You are a member of the Royal Canadian Mounted Police? For how long? You are a detective?"

Arriving at the witness box, Diefenbaker rested his right arm on its railing, and, now only a couple of feet from Cookson, fixed him with a piercing glare.

"Do you understand the nature of an oath?" he demanded loudly. It was one of his standard opening gambits, almost certain to unnerve any witness.

And then it began. For an hour and a half, John Diefenbaker paced slowly up and down before Arthur Cookson, penned in the witness box, probing, attacking, pleading, criticizing and confusing, trying to create the impression that Steve Bohun had been manhandled and threatened from the moment of his arrest.

"His eyes were steely, his lips somehow became firm, and his jaw jutted out at me. He was very fierce and intimidating. And all the while I was waiting for that damn shirt to jump out at me," Cookson remembers.

Diefenbaker took the investigator back to the arrest, his first encounter with Steve Bohun. Yes, Cookson, admitted, the boy had probably been sleepy after they awakened him.

"And you immediately demanded to know where the money you found had come from? And about the .22 rifle? And about where he had been? Didn't you?"

He had questioned Bohun, Cookson agreed.

"Questioned? You were pushing, pressing strongly for answers, for a statement, were you not?"

"We pressed him, but mildly," the policeman tried for a compromise.

Using a technique he had learned in this very courtroom from a Winnipeg lawyer who beat him in a contested divorce case, John Diefenbaker stood facing the rapt spectators. With his back to Cookson, he continued to throw questions at him, increasing his psychological mastery of the situation.

"And having arrested him, in the middle of the night, you took him straight to the scene of the crime, to Pommereul's store, did you not?"

He had done that, Cookson agreed.

"And there you showed him the blood stains still upon the floor, the blood of the dead Peter Pommereul, didn't you?" Diefenbaker was setting up his prey.

That, too, had probably happened, Cookson admitted.

"And then, Constable Cookson, then you tried to force this young boy to put his hands upon those blood stains. What do you say to that?" Diefenbaker whirled and pointed a long finger and arm at the investigator.

"I did no such thing." The policeman was vehement in denial and he rose from his seat in indignation.

But the accusation itself left a vestige of doubt. Of course, the police would deny any such action. But there was an intriguing element to the suggestion. Might it have happened? It was a very clever ploy by the defence lawyer.

And still the bloody shirt had not come forward. Cookson was sure Diefenbaker was holding it in reserve, like a secret weapon.

In spite of it all, the defence pried no damaging admissions from the policeman. Weak and exhausted, Cookson left the stand. His stomach was so sore that he was sure he was developing an ulcer. For weeks, his nervousness returned every time he approached a courtroom.

Cookson survived, but the written confession the police had secured from Steve Bohun did not. With his skilful cross-examination of all the police who had been involved, and by masterly use of the power of suggestion, John Diefenbaker had succeeded in creating a doubt in the mind of Chief Justice Brown.

The next morning, after hearing more than a day's testimony and a forceful argument from the defence, the trial judge excluded the Bohun confession. He also excluded the statement "I shot Pete Pommereul" made by the accused when the .22 shell casings were found. All that remained was the comment "I didn't shoot the old man" that Steve blurted out to Cookson at the time of arrest.

In a decision perhaps a little too favourable to the defence, also excluded were the plaster casts taken from Bohun's tracks in the garden plot. Explaining that the accused had been commanded to provide his footprints, the Chief Justice reasoned that even this physical evidence had been improperly secured.

As Cookson listened to the Chief Justice deliver his decision, his concern for the fate of his case was mixed with admiration for John Diefenbaker. The defence counsel had turned an impossible case into a potential winner. But, as the jury finally returned to hear the evidence which had been judged admissible, he still had a long way to go.

The ballistics testimony identified the rifle Fred Harach had loaned to Steve Bohun as the murder weapon, and tied it in with the shell casings found in the pasture and on the floor of Pommereul's store. Then a new dimension entered the case. Mills called Dr. Arthur Rose who had treated Steve Bohun at the Hafford hospital in 1926. The boy, then twelve, had been kicked in the head by a horse. He had remained unconscious for hours.

Diefenbaker was aware that his client suffered some mental deficiency. He had a witness of his own on the subject, and had done some medical homework. He had some questions for Dr. Rose.

"Could the boy's injuries have caused a serious and permanent impairment of his mental processes?"

"Indeed, they probably did," Rose agreed.

Mills finally closed the Crown case at 2:00 p.m. on Saturday, September 30. John Diefenbaker called his witness.

Dr. Samuel R. Laycock was a highly regarded professor of educational psychology at the University of Saskatchewan. Laycock had performed psychological tests on Steve Bohun. In his opinion, the accused had a mental age of about nine years and ranked as "high-grade feeble minded." According to Dr. Laycock, "no child of the mental age of Steve Bohun would be fully able to appreciate the nature and quality of the act which he was alleged to have committed."

Chief Justice Brown stepped in. He wanted some explanation of the reaction of the average Saskatchewan child of nine or ten to right and wrong.

"Would such a child know inherently, because he is a human being, that murder without provocation is wrong?" the trial judge asked.

"Questionable," Laycock replied.

John Diefenbaker, at the conclusion of the case, entered the defence of insanity, contending that Steve Bohun, within the legal definition, "was incapable of appreciating the nature and quality of his actions, or of knowing that they were wrong."

With that, the case went to the jury. It had been a long trial and, even without the confession, there was a good deal of evidence. Diefenbaker, lacking two of his favourite defence features — an absence of motive and another possible suspect — chose a careful review of the case in support of his plea, "Not proven." On the evidence the Crown had placed before the jury, there was, he submitted, a reasonable doubt that the shooting of Peter Pommereul had been done by Steve Bohun.

But insanity was Diefenbaker's strongest argument. If the jury found that his client had, in fact, shot the storekeeper, he asked them to consider the testimony of Dr. Rose and Dr. Laycock.

"Mentally crippled as a boy, distraught over the pregnancy of his young love, in his mind abandoned by his father, Steve Bohun could not appreciate the action he took, in the legal sense. Neither did he really know it was wrong."

Diefenbaker addressed the jury for an hour and a half, an unusually long summation for him. He had a sympathy-evoking cause, and he played it well. The watching Cookson began to doubt the outcome.

Richard Burkett Mills was a painstaking prosecutor. Dispassionate and fair, he also reviewed the evidence in detail. It pointed to no other conclusion than the guilt of the accused, he argued, and that guilt was established well beyond a reasonable doubt. As to insanity, Mills pointed out that the onus of establishing Bohun's lack of mental capacity was on the defence. And, he argued, there was no satisfactory evidence before the jury upon which they could base such a finding.

Chief Justice Brown agreed with Mills on the insanity question and went further. Dr. Laycock was not a medical man, the Chief Justice stated, and, therefore, his evidence was not satisfactory as to Bohun's possible insanity. There was no proper evidence before the jury that would justify them in reaching a verdict of not guilty by reason of insanity.

And so, the Chief Justice spiked the best defence John Diefenbaker had, though it was one he had not presented strongly.

Chief Justice Brown had pressed the case to completion. It was after 6:00 p.m. when he began his charge to the jury. Out of deference to their weariness, he spoke only forty-five minutes, but, even so, the twelve men had been sitting for five straight hours when they retired at 7:00 p.m.

In spite of the removal of his insanity defence, John Diefenbaker was still confident. The evidence would remain in the minds of the jurors, and would, at least, elicit their sympathy. The jury, Diefenbaker knew from experience, would be out for hours, perhaps days, as it sifted through all the evidence. He went off to his hotel for some rest.

Shortly before 10:00 p.m. that Saturday night, Detective Constable Arthur Cookson knocked on the door of John Diefenbaker's hotel room.

"Excuse me, Sir. I have been directed to tell you that the jury has reached a verdict. Will you come back to the court house with me?"

The defence lawyer was astonished and dismayed. "I can't believe it. Only three hours?"

Diefenbaker looked at Cookson, his adversary three days before. "A verdict at this time can mean only one thing," he muttered as he closed the door to follow.

It was as the lawyer feared. The jury found Steve Bohun guilty of the murder of Peter Pommereul. They added "a strong recommendation to mercy on account of his age and inferior mentality."

"Do you have anything you wish to say, Mr. Diefenbaker?" asked Chief Justice Brown.

"No, My Lord," the weary lawyer replied.

Steve Bohun remained calm, as he had during the entire five-day trial. The almost studied composure of the young accused provoked comment among the trial-watchers.

It was past ten o'clock on Saturday night after a long and tough week. Chief Justice Brown adjourned the court. Sentencing would wait until later in the court sittings.

One week later, at 12:15 p.m. on Saturday, October 7, another jury returned a verdict of murder. William Bahrey was convicted of the killing of his brother. Chief Justice Brown proceeded directly to sentencing. Bahrey would hang at Prince Albert on February 23, 1934.

While he was about it, the Chief Justice called up Steve Bohun and passed sentence on him, too: "You are to be kept within the confines of Prince Albert Gaol until Friday, February 23rd, 1934, and on that date you are to be taken and hanged by the neck until you are dead, and may God have mercy on your soul."

"Your case will be drawn to the attention of the Minister of Justice in Ottawa, in accordance with the jury's recommendation for mercy," the Chief Justice told Bohun. The youth, standing alone, without counsel or family, received this news, as he had the sentence, with stoic calm.

Steve Bohun's bloody shirt never did surface. Arthur Cookson learned after the trial that Alfred Svoboda, angry at losing a fee-paying case, had refused to give up the shirt, resisting all John Diefenbaker's efforts to secure it.

Arthur Cookson went on to enjoy a distinguished police career, capped by seventeen years as chief of police in Regina. Retired in 1971, he now lives in Calgary.

"LOCAL JUDGE REPRIEVES BOY SLAYER," The Saskatoon *Star Phoenix* announced on Thursday, February 22, 1934, in an eight-column headline. A photograph accompanying the story was captioned: "J.G. Diefenbaker, K.C., lawyer, of Prince Albert, who saved Steve Bohun, 19 year-old slayer, from going to the scaffold early Friday, when he secured a two-week stay of execution from Mr. Justice Donald Maclean this morning. The boy was scheduled to die Friday morning for the murder of Peter Pommereul, Redberry postmaster, whom he robbed."

In a curious repetition of his actions in the Pasowesty trial, John Diefenbaker waited until his client was convicted of murder before he arranged a thorough assessment of his mental condition. Two medical doctors examined Steve Bohun, and a test was made of his intelligence. Armed with the new evidence, Diefenbaker applied for a stay of execution.

In his argument before Mr. Justice Maclean, Diefenbaker explained his apparent delay. It was his understanding, the lawyer said, that in such cases it was the practice for the Crown to appoint a commission of doctors to examine the accused. This had not been done for Steve Bohun, he complained. Diefenbaker gave no reason why the defence had not secured such an examination.

The results of the belated examinations of Steve Bohun would have been very effective before a jury. Dr. Alexander Brodie, physician for the Prince Albert Gaol, reported: "Steve Bohun is of low mentality, his mental age is that of a boy of approximately 12 years and, in my opinion, he does not appreciate the difference between right and wrong."

Dr. J. Angus McDonald, another Prince Albert medical man, was even firmer about Bohun: "I have concluded that he has a feeble mentality, that he has very little appreciation of his present position, and, as a result of questioning him, I can say that he does not appreciate the difference between right and wrong, nor does he know that the killing of another human being is wrong."

Adolph Pachal, an educator with post-graduate training in intelligence testing, identified Steve Bohun's intelligence quotient to be 57, "very definitely a feeble-minded subject." Pachal applied the then-accepted racial bias: "In view of the fact that he is of Ukrainian antecedence, and liberal allowances are made for such facts as language, his intelligence would be that of a boy of nine years."

But Pachal had much more to say: "I examined him by questioning him, and came to the conclusion that he had no conception whatever that he is under sentence of death, or that he has any grasp of the meaning of his coming execution, and that he cannot in his own mind associate any connection between the crime for which he was convicted and the punishment he is to receive."

Steve Bohun's schoolteacher reported that the boy had been in Grade Five when he was kicked in the head by the horse. After the accident, he lost so much knowledge that he had to start again in Grade One. Steve slowly advanced back to Grade Five, but was not able to progress further.

All of this was powerful evidence, late as it was. John Diefenbaker asked Mr. Justice Maclean to delay the execution so the material could be sent to Ottawa for review. Steve Bohun had already been refused clemency on a first review resulting from the jury's recommendation for mercy.

Mr. Justice Maclean granted Diefenbaker's request. The execution date was postponed until March 9.

Steve Bohun's plight caught the public's attention. Two hundred Prince Albert citizens signed petitions to Ottawa asking that the boy's death sentence be set aside.

On March 3, Dr. Harvey Clare, superintendent of the Homewood Sanitorium at Guelph, Ontario, and a prominent psychiatrist, visited Steve Bohun in the Prince Albert jail. Dr. Clare refused to confirm that he was on special assignment from the minister of justice in Ottawa.

On March 7, John Diefenbaker was formally advised that the federal Cabinet would not interfere with the rescheduled execution. He telephoned the news to Steve Bohun's father. Mr. Bohun did not think he would be able to make it to Prince Albert in time to see his son before the execution.

Arthur Ellis, who had hanged William Bahrey on February 23, the date initially scheduled for both Bahrey and Bohun, returned to Prince Albert.

Annie Barchuk — who by now had given birth to a son — did not make a planned last visit to Steve. Nor did Steve leave any last message for Annie. Showing no emotion whatever, to the surprise of the few present, Steve Bohun was hanged at 6:00 a.m. on Friday, March 9, 1934. He was pronounced dead nine minutes later. His neck had been fractured. His family did not claim his body.

11

Rex v. Napoleon Fouquette

The impact of drought and price collapse was worse in Sas-
katchewan than in any other province. Successive crop failures af-
fected an area of cropland, concentrated for the most part in
Saskatchewan, equal to one-quarter of the total improved farm
acreage in Canada. The drought area during the decade comprised
the farms of approximately one-half of all Saskatchewan farmers.
In 1931, one half; in 1933, 1934, and 1936, one third; and in 1937,
two-thirds of the farm population in Saskatchewan were destitute.
— G.E. Britnell and V.C. Fowke, *Canadian Agriculture in War and*
Peace

The year 1934 turned out to be the halfway point in
Saskatchewan's agonizing odyssey through the Depression. It
was also the year in which the realization came that "next year"
was not going to bring a miraculous recovery, and that serious
long-term programs were needed to deal with the disaster.

In May 1934, a month before the Saskatchewan election, a
monumental duststorm, probably the worst of all time, swept the
western plains of North America from the Rockies to the Great
Lakes and New York. Huge dust clouds were sighted at ten
thousand feet over the Atlantic Ocean. During the rest of that
summer, winds blew the soil so relentlessly as to destroy gardens
and crops. The lack of plant exhibits forced the cancellation of
many rural fairs across the Canadian Prairies.

In both the United States and Canada, the national governments began to stir into action. The New Deal initiatives of
Franklin Roosevelt, now in his second year of office, attracted
attention in Ottawa. Early in 1935, Prime Minister R.B. Bennett

embarked upon a series of reforms modelled upon the American experiment, and somewhat out of character with his previous philosophy. Although Bennett was not motivated entirely by self-preservation, certainly the fate of the Anderson government in Saskatchewan helped draw his attention to the depth of the problem.

In Regina, James Gardiner's Liberals resumed office as if ending an insignificant interregnum presided over by Anderson. Cementing the considerable enmity of the Conservatives, they proceeded to dismantle the public service commission and to replace scores of civil servants with Liberal Party supporters. Partly because Gardiner had an antipathy towards power machinery, and partly to restore a good patronage source, the Liberals returned the highway program to locally-hired horse-drawn equipment. It was "business as usual" for the Liberal Party in Saskatchewan as it prepared for the federal election of 1935.

Part of Attorney General T.C. Davis's first legislative program was an amendment to the Jury Act to reduce the composition of Saskatchewan juries from twelve to six. Justified as an economy measure, the six-man jury was to have an impact upon the career of John Diefenbaker, who worked with juries more than most.

The Prince Albert lawyer had his office scaled down to mid-Depression efficiency. Total personnel consisted of the two lawyers — Diefenbaker and John Cuelenaere — and two secretaries. The payroll in 1935 was under $2,000, including $835 for Cuelenaere, $750 for the senior secretary, and $346 for the junior. Total expenditure for the year was $7,512, or an average of $625 per month. Gross receipts were just over $12,000, enabling Diefenbaker to maintain his net income at about $4,500, a very satisfactory achievement.

It was often touch and go, however, and the lawyer had to keep a very careful eye on the operation of his practice. Collections were sporadic and frequently the monthly receipts were insufficient to cover the month's overhead. Generosity and soft-heartedness had to be avoided, with only rare exceptions. Diefenbaker had learned to disregard any sympathy he might feel for the financial side of his client's plight and to insist upon his fee, and, usually, insist upon it being secured or paid in advance.

In one case, the lawyer secured his fee for a serious criminal defence by taking title to the accused's farm near Blaine Lake. The defence was successful, but the client's gratitude, as so often happens, evaporated. Some years later he accosted Diefenbaker in his office, demanding return of the title. The situation was close enough to physical violence that the lawyer called in a law student for support, but he held firm on the deal.

Diefenbaker worked exceedingly hard and, in a habit that remained with him all his life, was never without his files and books, whether at home or while travelling. It put a strain upon his marriage as he isolated himself from the fun-loving Edna, immersed in his work or his reading.

Another strain was Diefenbaker's domineering mother, living in Saskatoon but a constant interruption in his life and, particularly, his marriage. Mary Diefenbaker developed an unwholesome dependence upon her eldest son and indulged herself constantly by calling him to her side. John, completely devoted to his mother, responded unfailingly, cancelling engagements on a moment's notice to drive or catch a train to Saskatoon. Often this occurred at such special times as Christmas, leaving Edna alone and doubly disappointed.

An austere and imperious woman, John Diefenbaker's mother was never addressed otherwise than as "Mrs. Diefenbaker," and she accorded equal formality to her son's contemporaries. Emmett Hall was always, from their first meeting, "Mr. Hall." To her son's wife, she was an imposing, selfish, heartless mother-in-law.

There was much of Mary Diefenbaker's personality in the makeup of her son, John. From the beginning of their marriage, Edna set herself the task of smoothing out the less-pleasing side of her husband and making him more interested in, and liked by, others. Slowly, she transformed him from an aloof and selfish man into one who could mix and make friends. But people never warmed to John Diefenbaker the way they did to Edna, who attracted and radiated affection wherever she went.

As 1935 wore on, the term of R.B. Bennett's government began to tick away, as Anderson's had the previous year. A number of federal judicial appointments were available in Saskatchewan, and would be filled before the election. The more prominent Conservative lawyers began the sometimes not-so-discreet, behind-the-scenes campaigning that passes for judicial selection in Canada. The contest was even more than usually fierce because of the impact of the Depression and the number of lawyers who had served in Premier Anderson's government and had been at loose ends since its defeat.

John Diefenbaker was only mildly involved in the contest. A new position on the Court of Appeal was to be filled, and there were several vacancies on the District Court. The Court of Appeal appointment was slated to go to former attorney general Murdoch A. MacPherson, K.C., and Diefenbaker was not interested in the far less prestigious District Court positions. A hoped-for opening on the King's Bench attracted him, but it did not materialize.

The appointments were made on August 10, 1935, four days before Parliament was dissolved. Surprisingly, the Court of Appeal appointment went, not to MacPherson, but to Percy H. Gordon, K.C., a former Regina lawyer of far fewer political credentials who had moved to Toronto. Among those who became District Court judges were former Cabinet minister J.F. Bryant, K.C., and Conservative Party president J.A.M. Patrick, K.C., of Yorkton. Patrick's judicial appointment forced him to resign the presidency of the provincial party, and John Diefenbaker, vice-president since the fall of 1933, became acting president.

Since his appointment as counsel to the Bryant Charges Commission in 1930, John Diefenbaker had received no particular patronage from the Conservative governments in either Regina or Ottawa. His tenure as agent of the attorney general in the spring of 1934 had been of such short duration as to be not worth counting. The last days of the Bennett government brought him a similarly short-lived favour.

In September 1935, Diefenbaker was appointed Prince Albert solicitor to the Canadian Farm Loan Board. W.J. Scott, the board's in-house counsel, wrote the new representative offering to "show you the odd short-cut or give you the odd tip on the expeditious manner of handling loans with the least expense and to the greatest profit." In conclusion, Mr. Scott extended "his personal congratulations to you on this appointment and hope you may make a lot of money out of it."

Scott's kind words, although surely well meant, were in reality cruel jest. The October 14 election was just a month away and both Scott and Diefenbaker must have believed that the Conservatives, and Diefenbaker's new appointment, would not survive.

Following the election of "Bible Bill" Aberhart and his Social Credit Party in the Alberta election of August 1935, the Social Credit hordes poured across the border to contest the Saskatchewan ridings in the October federal election. With very little time, candidates were found for each of the twenty-one constituencies. In Prince Albert, they nominated R. Bedard, a farmer from MacLeod, Alberta. The Conservatives nominated in Prince Albert on July 22, choosing Tom F. Graves, a rural merchant and farmer. Twelve names, including John Diefenbaker's, were put forward, but all except Graves and one other withdrew.

Diefenbaker was pressed to accept the nomination. The *Daily Herald* reported "a popular wave of feeling" for the lawyer, who declined. It was clear from his explanation that he did not regard 1935 as a good year for Conservatism: "I think this is a time for us to have a farmer as a candidate. A farmer might unite us and then we could get some place."

Another speaker described Diefenbaker as "the victim of insidious propaganda started by the Liberals who recognize him as their most formidable opponent in this constituency."

Diefenbaker's appraisal was correct. On election day, October 14, Social Credit and Bedard outpolled the Conservative Graves by 3,185 to 2,880. Redistribution forgotten, Mackenzie King swept the seat with more than 9,000 votes.

Across Saskatchewan, the Conservatives lost all but one of the eight seats they had won in 1930. Social Credit had two seats, as did another new party, the Co-operative Commonwealth Federation (CCF) which elected two members, Major James Coldwell and T.C. "Tommy" Douglas, both of whom had been defeated in the 1934 provincial election. The remaining sixteen Saskatchewan seats were taken by the Liberals, including Lake Centre, where Russell Hartney, the lawyer with whom Diefenbaker had first articled, ran a distant last for the Social Credit.

Canada accepted the Liberal slogan, "King or Chaos," and gave Mackenzie King 173 seats. The Bennett Conservatives were reduced to 40. Social Credit had a total of 17, and the CCF 7. The Reconstruction Party of H.H. Stevens, who had split from the Conservatives and contributed to their loss, collected one seat.

The member for Prince Albert was once again the prime minister, and another Conservative government became a victim of the Depression. Diefenbaker, as acting president of the Saskatchewan Conservative Association had, it seemed, presided over the demise of his party.

As John Diefenbaker looked over the debris of two elections in sixteen months, he could see nothing but continuing Conservative ruin. In the provincial election of 1934, the party, although wiped out, had won more than 26 per cent of the vote. In the federal election just past, the Conservatives retained one seat and their overall support dropped to 18 per cent. They were overtaken by the CCF, with 20 per cent, and almost beaten by the newly-arrived Social Credit, with 17 per cent.

The Prince Albert lawyer made a very sensible decision in the circumstances; he would take a holiday to Europe. A "pilgrimage" to the dedication of the Vimy War Memorial in France was being organized for the following summer. He would join the tour.

Re-established as prime minister, Mackenzie King conscripted Saskatchewan Liberal Premier James Gardiner to his Cabinet, as he had done with Charles Dunning almost ten years earlier. On October 31, 1935, the fifty-member Liberal caucus met to select a successor to Gardiner. The choice was between two men, Attorney General T.C. Davis and Natural Resources Minister William J. Patterson. Both men were regarded as able administrators, Davis as the more combative and aggressive. The milder Patterson was the more popular in caucus and he became the new Liberal leader and Saskatchewan premier.

In Regina's Assiniboia Club, then the unofficial seat of Saskatchewan governments, whether Liberal or Conservative, Court of Appeal Justice W.F. Alphonse Turgeon, himself a former Prince Albert MLA and long-term attorney general, harrumphed prophetically about the Liberals' decision: "They wouldn't go for Davis because they were afraid he would go off half-cocked, so they went for Patterson and they'll find he won't go off at all."

The political career of John Diefenbaker's Prince Albert adversary had finally passed its peak. Denied his party's leadership, Davis remained a few more years as attorney general, and then passed out of the still-ascending Diefenbaker's path.

To Detective Corporal E.J. DesRosiers, it appeared to be just another unsophisticated and unpleasant murder, the result of too much Saturday night revelry in Leask. Certainly, there was nothing at first apparent to the RCMP investigator to suggest that he had met the toughest case of his career.

It was 5:00 a.m. on Sunday, July 28, 1935. DesRosiers, promoted out of the Wakaw detachment and into the criminal investigation division at Prince Albert, stood in the alley behind Matthew's Hardware Store in Leask, a town fifty miles southwest of Prince Albert. Lying before him was the body of Ernest Fouquette, a local farmer, badly beaten about the head. Dr. J.D. Duncan had already fixed the time of death at half an hour after midnight.

Fouquette, DesRosiers learned, was a sixty-two-year-old French Metis, a successful farmer operating five quarter-sections of choice land. Fouquette had been married for twenty years, but a year earlier his wife, Annie, twenty-five years younger, had left him, taking with her their nine children. Annie and the children were living in destitute circumstances in a shack in Leask while Fouquette continued to live on the farm.

Annie Fouquette had earlier retained John Diefenbaker to pry some support out of her husband, and the Prince Albert lawyer had sued successfully. He secured a judgment for $800 and an order for continuing support of $60 monthly. Fouquette refused to pay. Diefenbaker took steps to enforce the judgment.

The sheriff seized the farmer's equipment, livestock and other chattels, and arranged to auction the property to satisfy the judgment. On the day of the auction, Fouquette's neighbours came to his support. Dragging up a stone boat loaded with a steer, dead, bloated and covered in tar, they announced that all successful bidders would also win a ride strapped to their steer. The sale faltered and died. When he received a bid of only fifty cents for Fouquette's car, the sheriff gave up and cancelled the sale.

The situation remained in stalemate. Although Fouquette made some payments on the judgment, he refused to pay the monthly support. Since the aborted sale, the farmer had been harassed by thieves and vandals. Grain was stolen from his bins, and his horses turned loose from their pasture. The neighbours thought Annie Fouquette was a sore loser.

Dr. Frances McGill, provincial pathologist, performed the post mortem and told DesRosiers that she had never seen a head so badly battered. Fouquette's skull had been literally crushed from several powerful blows. The nose was broken, and one tooth knocked out.

Someone with a bloody hand had gone through Fouquette's pockets. His wallet was gone, but DesRosiers had difficulty believing that robbery could be the motive for such a savage killing. His case began to look a little less like a Saturday night event got out of hand. DesRosiers arranged to have the coroner adjourn the inquest for a few weeks while he continued his investigation.

It had been a normal summer Saturday night in Leask. The town had been full of cars and wagons and people, visiting and shopping. The beer parlour in the hotel, which was owned by John Cuelenaere's father, did a brisk business and the stores, as usual, stayed open until midnight.

Ernest Fouquette had been on Main Street that Saturday night. He had been drinking, but none of the many who had seen him thought he was drunk. Nobody could remember seeing anyone with Fouquette, nor had he been noticed after midnight.

Annie Fouquette had also been downtown that night. So had her seventeen-year-old son Napoleon and several of her seven daughters. Annie's brothers, Nick and Bill Litwinic, and her sister, Anne Grovu, with her husband, Nick Grovu, had all been there.

But Annie Fouquette, her children and all her relatives had been out of town, by one means or another, by 11:30, at least an hour before Ernest had been killed. Every one of them was positive on that point.

DesRosiers and his fellow investigators piled up interview after interview, statement after statement. The shifting and conflicting stories told them they were up against a cover-up. Two witnesses reluctantly admitted they had been pressured to give false time estimates, and told of being in fear of Annie Fouquette and her relatives. But it was far from clear who had actually killed Ernest Fouquette.

Annie Fouquette and her family moved back into the farm home just as soon as Ernest's funeral was complete. Napoleon had a cut and bruised knuckle that looked to DesRosiers like the result of punching a man's tooth out. The boy said a wrench slipped while he was working on a tractor.

The police decided upon a strategic manoeuvre. They enlisted George Milledge Salter, K.C., who had succeeded Diefenbaker as Prince Albert's agent of the attorney general, and determined to call everyone remotely connected with that Saturday night in Leask as a witness at the inquest. There George Salter could interview them under oath, and perhaps some truth might emerge.

On November 4, 1935, Coroner Dr. Richard Lionel King called the inquest to order in Leask's Legion Hall. More than 250 spectators, all the hall could seat, watched and listened as the first of 42 witnesses took the stand. The town was agog. Cuelenaere's hotel was sold out.

The crowd was not disappointed. Salter had a circus on his hands. His central witnesses all suffered an amazing loss of memory. On the second morning of the inquest, Coroner King lost his patience.

"I know a whole lot are going to be arrested for perjury and I'll give the warrant for you. I won't sit here and listen to this stuff. You tell the truth."

Annie Fouquette was on the stand at the time.

"I'm trying," she said.

"No, you're not," complained Coroner King, "you took the oath to tell the truth and you're contradicting yourself all the time."

In spite of the many contradictions, Annie Fouquette stuck to her contention that she had left Leask for her brother's farm at least three-quarters of an hour before her husband's murder.

Salter asked Annie about the judgment against Ernest Fouquette that John Diefenbaker had secured for her. She personally was not anxious to get paid anything on that judgment, she said.

"I don't mind if something is paid, but it's Mr. Diefenbaker who wants it paid," she explained, to the amusement of the spectators. The whole town knew better.

By day three of the inquest, which ran all week, several residents of Leask placed bets on which witness would most often use the response, "I don't remember." Salter complained that a "don't remember" disease was attacking the witnesses.

DesRosiers had two star witnesses who testified that they had heard, but not seen, Ernest Fouquette and his son Napoleon speaking in the lane behind Matthew's Hardware a few minutes before the murder must have happened.

Then the lid blew off the hearing. At the end of his testimony, Nick Grovu, brother-in-law to Annie Fouquette, asked permission to "say another word." Coroner King granted permission, but, for several minutes, Nick was struck dumb and was unable to say anything. Finally, he blurted out that his wife was trying to "provide an alibi for Napoleon Fouquette," and had been asked to do so by one of the boy's sisters.

Anne Grovu loudly denied her husband's statement, and the inquest was in a frenzy. One of the jurymen complained to King, "What's the use of wasting our time on all this perjury?"

By the time King and Salter managed to close down the proceedings, more than five hundred people were jammed into the Legion Hall. The jury brought in a verdict of "murder by a person or persons unknown," stated that Mrs. Nick Grovu had committed perjury, and expressed suspicion that others had as well. King agreed, and asked the police to arrest Annie Fouquette, Anne Grovu, and William Litwinic, a brother to the two women, and charge them all with perjury.

It was great drama, but it had not accomplished very much for DesRosiers's case. It was still not very clear who had killed Ernest Fouquette, although there was now some circumstantial evidence against Napoleon. The trouble was that DesRosiers and his investigators believed the real villain was Napoleon's mother, Annie Fouquette, and they were completely without evidence against her.

DesRosiers huddled with his superior, Detective Sergeant J.S. Wood. They decided to charge Napoleon Fouquette with murder, in spite of the fact that their evidence was not nearly strong enough to convict. Something might turn up. And maybe the mother, Annie, might come forward rather than see her son at risk for a murder conviction.

Wood went out, arrested Napoleon, and took him down to the Leask lock-up. The seventeen-year-old seemed unconcerned. He slept well, had a good breakfast, and greeted his worried family with a big smile. The police, he assured them, "had nothing" on him, and could "hang nothing" on him.

Maybe so, but the situation was serious enough that even Annie Fouquette thought it called for a lawyer. She went to see John Diefenbaker.

Less then three weeks later, the circus was back in town. On November 26, the preliminary inquiry opened in the Leask Legion Hall. The cast was the same, except for the addition of Diefenbaker and a change of presiding officer. On the bench was J.E. Lussier, Diefenbaker's associate from the Bourdon case, now a magistrate.

The crowd returned in greater numbers. Leask merchants blessed the name Fouquette; business was great. At the Cuelenaere hotel, John Cuelenaere's younger brother, Marcel, who would also become a prominent member of the Saskatchewan bar, helped with the heavy load of guests. He remembers the overfull hotel, and the excitement throughout the town.

It was a perfect situation for the flashy defence lawyer from Prince Albert. Diefenbaker sailed through Salter's case as if he were on a Sunday cruise, probing here, attacking there, but mostly just grandstanding in front of the appreciative crowd.

A preliminary inquiry is intended as a disclosure of the Crown's case to determine whether there is sufficient evidence to justify putting the accused on trial. In practise, the procedure is a dry run for the real event, and the defence can experiment almost at will. Mistakes are not costly at this level, and can be avoided later. The prosecution case will need to be very weak, indeed, before the average magistrate will decline to send the accused up for trial.

Diefenbaker knew the police had only a thin case against Napoleon Fouquette. He went looking for items of evidence that might disprove his client's guilt.

Fouquette's jacket had cleared an examination for bloodstains performed by the pathologist, Dr. McGill. It occurred to Diefenbaker that the murder should have been a messy event, that such serious wounds as Ernest Fouquette had suffered would have spouted blood over his attacker. He had not, however, done his medical homework.

"There are no main arteries in the head, Mr. Diefenbaker," Dr. McGill pointed out, "Therefore the blood would not spurt very far."

The defence counsel persisted, but the pathologist was a feisty lady; she snapped back.

"You ask me sensible questions, Mr. Diefenbaker, and I will give you sensible answers."

The lawyer moved on to safer ground.

When Salter brought forth his star witness, Tony Verreault, Diefenbaker went after him as if they were already in front of the jury. Verreault described the conversation he had heard in the lane behind Matthew's Hardware shortly before the murder.

"Who is the father of them kids? Who is to support them, your mother or me?"

Those words, said Verreault, had been spoken by Ernest Fouquette. A reply was made in the voice of Napoleon Fouquette.

For three and a half hours, the amused audience followed as the defence lawyer subjected Verreault to a wide-ranging cross-examination. The witness admitted he had been attentive to two of Napoleon's sisters, but denied he had proposed marriage and been refused. No, he had not spoken to a priest about a marriage ceremony. Yes, Diefenbaker finally dragged out of the witness, he had proposed marriage, "but had not been very serious." No, Verreault insisted, he had never threatened violence to Mrs. Fouquette or to Napoleon.

On the main point, Verreault was emphatic and unshakable. He was positive that the two men in the alley had been Ernest and Napoleon Fouquette.

Verreault had not told DesRosiers about the conversation he had overheard when first questioned by the police. "Why not?" Diefenbaker wanted to know.

"Because I was scared of them all."

"What do you mean by that? Who is 'them all'" the lawyer pressed.

"Mrs. Fouquette and her relations," the witness replied.

As the relentless Diefenbaker closed in on Verreault, the witness began to retreat into "I don't remember"'s. The lawyer had heard of the problem at the inquest. "Are you catching the 'don't remember' disease?" he asked Verreault. As laughter swept the courtroom, George Salter spoke up.

"Mr. Diefenbaker, you don't know anything about that disease. You should have been at the inquest."

Salter was less congenial when Diefenbaker went after Des-Rosiers.

"Remember, Corporal DesRosiers, a man's life depends upon your evidence," the lawyer stated sonorously. It was not the first time he had used the warning, and the prosecutor objected, provoking an angry exchange between counsel.

Nick Grovu, who had startled the inquest with his accusation that his wife was making an alibi for Napoleon, had a difficult time at the hands of Diefenbaker. Since the inquest, Grovu had moved to Saskatoon, "to be away from my wife's relatives." Nervous and hesitant as the cross-examination began, Grovu was soon contradicting himself. Before long, Diefenbaker had the witness so tangled in his own story that his credibility was gone.

The defence lawyer was running a large risk. He was doing an effective job on the Crown witnesses, but it did not count. There was no jury watching, and by the time the case got to a jury these witnesses would be practised and more difficult to trap.

Diefenbaker was gambling that, if he could expose the weakness of the Crown case, it would never make it as far as a jury. If Lussier committed for trial, as was likely, the prosecution could still throw in the towel and stay the charge.

Diefenbaker knew that the police were more interested in Annie Fouquette than in Napoleon. He also knew Annie Fouquette better than the prosecution did. He had acted for her for nearly two years. The lawyer did not believe that Annie Fouquette was going to soften as DesRosiers hoped.

Diefenbaker was partly right and partly wrong. Lussier did commit Napoleon Fouquette to trial for the murder of his father, and Annie Fouquette came apart. Calm and almost arrogant throughout the inquest and the five-day preliminary, the mother broke down completely as her son was taken back to jail, and she had to be helped from the hall.

"This is the worst case in my experience," Lussier said in explaining his decision. "The police have encountered a solid wall of opposition in their efforts to solve this mystery, and I commend them for the fair and clean way in which they have conducted their investigation."

Annie Fouquette soon recovered her composure. Her determined denial of any implication in her husband's death never wavered. DesRosiers's case did not improve, and he was unable to dig out any more evidence. The police decided to stall for time.

Napoleon Fouquette came up for trial at the King's Bench sittings in Prince Albert on February 25, 1936. Mr. Justice George E. Taylor presided, a stroke of luck for the prosecution.

George Salter asked Mr. Justice Taylor to set the Fouquette case over to the next sittings of the court, due in April. The Crown, Salter explained, needed "an opportunity to obtain further evidence," an embarrassing admission.

Diefenbaker pointed out that his client, only seventeen-years-old, had been in custody four and a half months and "is being held on suspicion only." If the case was to be adjourned, the defence counsel wanted Napoleon "to have his freedom pending his trial."

Taylor granted the requests of both the Crown and the defence. Salter got his adjournment, and bail was set for the accused.

The amount was fixed at $20,000. Although Taylor permitted any number of sureties necessary to total that amount, Diefenbaker's clients would have had to round up almost the entire population of Leask to find that much net worth in 1936. Napoleon Fouquette stayed in jail.

The trial judge was back in Prince Albert on April 28. This time the Crown folded. George Salter entered a stay of proceedings, and Annie and Napoleon Fouquette, both smiling and happy, walked out of the court room together. Diefenbaker's gamble at the Leask preliminary had paid off.

But by then the lawyer was involved in another case, one that had stolen the headlines at the end of the Fouquette preliminary, back in November.

Those headlines had read: "TRAPPER REPORTED MUR-DERED NEAR GOLDFIELDS, Police Mushing From Chipewyan to Seek Partner."

12

Rex v. Harms

Micky Lindgreen was just one of the many who did what they had to in order to survive the Dirty Thirties. As a single mother with a three-year-old son, she found the going even tougher than most. Still, keeping house for a trapper on the north shore of Lake Athabaska was not a bad deal. It was a primitive life, but the lake was bountiful, and there was no hunger. And Ira Allen was a pretty good man.

The North was sprinkled with refugees from the Depression who had filtered into the bush, taking up life as trappers and hunters. Many succeeded; some were never heard of again. John Harms and John Anthony were two strange examples of the type.

John Harms wandered in first, in 1932, all the way from Colorado. A large man in his mid-fifties, it was rumoured that he had been a deputy sheriff in the States. He did have a Smith & Wesson .38 Special, a favourite gun with many police forces. Harms frequently carried the revolver in a shoulder holster. Micky Lindgreen had seen it several times.

The American built a cabin on Spring Point, two miles down the lake from Micky Lindgreen, and established a trapline. His brother joined him for the first two years, but moved on. John Harms had been alone a year when John Anthony joined him in the summer of 1935.

The new mine at nearby Goldfields, just coming into production, attracted a number of job-seekers and opportunists. The twenty-five-year-old Anthony had left his wife and small child on their blown-out farm near McLeod, Alberta, to try his luck in the North. His family would join him if he found work. Hearing of the trapper looking for a partner, Anthony approached Harms and they struck a deal.

It was an unlikely arrangement; more than thirty years lay between the slightly-built Anthony and the muscular veteran with the rough disposition. All went well at first, but in the fall, when they went out to Fort Chipewyan for grub, a letter was waiting for Anthony. His wife was refusing to join him in his new life. Anthony became as miserable as Harms. It was not long before the two developed a running quarrel over a mink skin that Harms claimed Anthony had held from him — more than enough for murder in the tension of cabin fever.

Micky Lindgreen heard all about that mink on Saturday, November 23, 1935, when Harms and his dog team pulled in for a visit. Ira Allen was out on his trapline, a route that took from a week to ten days to cover, depending on weather and luck. Harms, in ugly humour, spent the morning grousing to Lindgreen while consuming several bottles of homemade beer that he brought with him. He had brewed the beer, Harms said, in celebration of a moose taken by Anthony, who was expected along sometime that day.

Anthony did show up at noon, and Lindgreen fed both men. At one o'clock, Anthony and Harms climbed on the toboggan behind Harms's dogs, and headed for Spring Point, a forty-five-minute run.

Two hours after leaving, Harms was back, alone. Anthony had hurt himself, had taken a fainting fit, the trapper told Lindgreen. He insisted the woman return to his cabin with him. Reluctantly, Lindgreen dressed herself and her child and they settled in for the ride behind Harms's dogs. What followed was an episode of True Grit, northern style.

Lindgreen quickly learned that she and her son were in the presence of an abnormal and capricious man. On the trip across, Harms, standing at the back of the toboggan, reached down and took the head of Lindgreen's child in his huge hand, seemingly intent upon crushing it. The terrified mother tore the hand away.

At Harms's cabin, Lindgreen instinctively avoided his attempts to get her to enter first. The winter dusk was settling, and the cabin was cold and dark. When Harms lit a match, Lindgreen, from the safety of the doorway, took one look, then snatched up her son and bolted for the bush. As she ran, she heard the whine of a bullet and saw the slug smack against the glare ice just ahead of her and ten feet to the left. She reached the cover of some willows and stopped for breath.

Murder! My God, he's killed him, Lindgreen thought as she struggled to control her panic. In the flare of the match she had seen the body of John Anthony lying on the cabin floor, the side of his head covered in blood.

The terrified woman and her small son watched from the willow bluff as John Harms, lashing his dogs, drove towards them, then passed by, following the main trail, not bothering to search for their tracks. He was heading for Ira Allen's cabin.

The dark of the sub-Arctic night closed around Lindgreen as she considered her plight. Her choice was to join Anthony or to follow Harms back to her own cabin. She took the latter course, but cautiously. Avoiding the overland trail, she skirted along the lakeshore, stumbling over the jumble of compressed and upturned ice.

When Lindgreen reached her cabin, she nervously reconnoitered. Harms had pulled his team up at the rear cabin door and was lying in the toboggan, apparently asleep. There was an opportunity to slip in the other door, and Lindgreen seized it, immediately locking the door behind her with two knives jammed in the frame. Then she grabbed a hammer and spiked up the rear door. Harms did not awake.

Lindgreen breathed a short sigh of relief. She was only somewhat safe, and very much under siege. Within half an hour, Harms was awake and banging on her door. She made no answer.

In the middle of the night, Harms was back, and again at daylight. He tried to batter the cabin door in with a pole but failed. Although he banged upon the windows, strangely, he did not break them.

The terrified woman took stock of weapons in the cabin. The only firearm was a single-shot .22 rifle without sights that her small son used as a plaything. She found six cartridges, but she would not likely get a chance for a second shot, and only a well-placed or lucky bullet from the little gun would stop the bear-like Harms. There were several knives in the cabin, but they were of less use than the .22. Lindgreen knew she would have to be very, very alert.

All day Sunday the nervous mother peered carefully from her cabin window, shushing her child anxiously as she watched a besotted Harms out front. The trapper had built a fire beside Ira Allen's woodpile and settled in. Perched upon caribou skins spread upon the snow, he thawed and drank frozen beer and roasted chunks of moose meat. Harms stayed until dark, but the exhausted Lindgreen never relaxed her vigil or her grasp upon the little .22. When the polar early night fell, the trapper climbed into his toboggan and drove off behind his dogs.

In the morning he was back. Banging upon Lindgreen's door, he tried to engage her in conversation. He was going to travel to the cabin of another trapper, fifteen miles away, he said. Lindgreen thought Harms was showing signs of sobering up. She admitted her presence in the cabin, but she stayed put.

Late Tuesday morning, Harms again appeared on Lindgreen's doorstep. He had lost his eyeglasses, he told her through the door, and was having trouble travelling. He would go to his shack on Scorched Dog Island, on the south shore of Lake Athabaska. When Ira Allen returned from his trapline, she should send him for the police, he said. With that he left.

Two hours later, Lindgreen again heard dogs outside the cabin, but this time it was Ira Allen, and a relieved Lindgreen opened the doors to him. The next morning, Wednesday, they drove to the settlement at Goldfields to report the killing of John Anthony.

When the news reached the press rooms five hundred air miles to the south, the reporters leaped into action. Limbering up their best purple prose, they filled their columns: "To get their man a mushing police patrol bucked miles of upended lake shore ice, and dared a sub-Arctic blizzard that swept over the trailless ice of Lake Athabaska, while over the trapper's lonely island hideout circled a Canadian Airways pilot like an eagle that sought its prey."

To be sure, Sergeant Vernon F. Vernon of the nearest RCMP detachment at Fort Chipewyan, Alberta, seventy miles west of Scorched Dog Island, took John Harms very seriously. He received the homicide report on November 29, and set off by dog-team, reaching the cabin where Harms was holed up on December 2. A passing Canadian Airways flight the day before had spotted Harms waving a white flag. Vernon commandeered the ski-equipped bush plane and pilot to assist him with the arrest, but Harms came out to greet them, and surrendered quietly.

Harms and the policeman took dinner in the cabin, after which the trapper volunteered his explanation of the shooting.

Since the end of September, when Anthony had heard that his wife would not join him in the North, the younger man had become "more bullheaded." Once, when the two were separated in the bush, Anthony had shot in Harms's direction. On the day of the fatal shooting, after the two had returned from the Allen cabin, Harms suggested they split up. He would not again go into the bush with Anthony.

The trappers were drinking the homemade beer. Harms went back of the kitchen stove to get two more bottles. When he turned back, Anthony was standing in front of him with his hands up "as if he was going to choke me."

"I will kill you with my bare hands," Harms claimed Anthony had threatened.

At that, Harms said he drew his revolver and told Anthony to stand back. The younger man kept coming and Harms fired one shot. Anthony fell on his face. Harms felt for a pulse and found none.

From that point on, Harms claimed, he did not remember very much of what he had done that day. He took some more beer, and he thought he had gone over to Allen's cabin. Later, in the middle of the night, Harms awakened in his own bed, with his dogs still in harness. He drove back to Allen's. There he built a fire in front of the cabin and stayed because a storm had come up and he was afraid to start back again. Finally, he crossed over to Scorched Dog Island where he waited five nights until the police came.

Sergeant Vernon carefully wrote down all John Harms had to say, and the trapper signed the statement. Then the policeman took his man into Goldfields by plane, charged him with murder and left him in custody. Finally, Vernon went off to inspect the abandoned and frozen cabin at Spring Point.

John Anthony was lying on the kitchen floor alongside the table. He had been shot in the mouth and had died instantly.

The case presented a problem to Attorney General T.C. Davis. His department did not have enough officials in the newly-opened North to handle the required inquest and preliminary inquiry. Some fast appointments were arranged. The new log hotel at Goldfields served as a court house. On December 12, the bar became a courtroom, filled with prospectors and miners all in town for the event. John Harms chose not to attend, and was excused. He waited out the formalities while lying on his bedroll on the floor of the hotel dining room, smoking cigarettes, apparently unconcerned and unmindful of the crowd around him.

Saskatchewan's remote North was divided between the judicial districts of Prince Albert and Battleford. Spring Point fell in the Battleford section, and John Harms was remanded to its February King's Bench sittings. He would await his trial in Prince Albert Gaol. From there he contacted a lawyer, John Diefenbaker.

Diefenbaker did not hesitate to undertake the defence of John Harms, even though the trapper was unable to raise much by way of fees. Harms had asked Sergeant Vernon to arrange the sale of his trapping and fishing equipment, dog-team and cabin, all of which he had priced below $500. The trapping season was just underway when the shooting took place, and Harms had taken little fur. He was able to give Diefenbaker a retainer of $35 only, pending the sale of his gear.

The lawyer pondered his case. What would his defence be? In Wysochan and Pasowesty, a third person had either been present at the killing or nearby with opportunity. Here there was no possibility of an attempted shift of blame.

In Bourdon, the explanation had been self-defence, or accident, and the sympathy had gone to the elderly accused because he was so clearly the physical underdog. Just the opposite was the case with Harms. Diefenbaker's client was much older than the dead Anthony, but still in the prime of life, and tougher, more experienced and forty pounds heavier. Any jury would be slow to believe that John Harms had reasonable need to resort to a .38 Special to protect himself against an unarmed John Anthony.

There was another possibility. Murder may be reduced to manslaughter if the killing was the result of an action taken during sudden provocation, provocation sufficient to reasonably cause a loss of self-control. Again, though, would a jury consider that Anthony's supposed threat was enough to flood an ordinary person with such anger that he would pull and fire a pistol? Not likely, Diefenbaker thought.

But John Harms had been drinking, and had certainly been intoxicated to some degree, enough to affect his thought processes. Perhaps it could be contended that the mind of John Harms, made fuzzy by his home-brewed beer, perceived more danger in John Anthony than a sober man would see. And, similarly, such a mind might be more easily provoked to sudden passion, the kind of passion that killed.

Finally, Diefenbaker considered the defence of drunkenness, the defence he had passed up in the Wysochan case. Although not permitted as an excuse for crime, drunkenness, like provocation, might reduce murder to manslaughter. Could he persuade the jury that Harms had been so affected by his beer as to be incapable of having an intention to kill when he fired his pistol at John Anthony?

Diefenbaker knew there was almost no chance of a complete acquittal. But John Harms might escape the gallows if the jury could be convinced that one of the above defences should reduce the conviction to manslaughter.

Diefenbaker had the problem of how to put his client's story in evidence before the jury. The Crown would have to put in the fairly complete statement Harms had given to Sergeant Vernon, but any amplification would have to come from Harms himself. Should he testify?

To the defence lawyer the decision was obvious. Harms was far too vulnerable to the prosecutor's cross-examination to risk going into the stand. His size, strength and experience would be emphasized. He would have to explain why he had not chosen a number of alternative and less deadly weapons that had been at hand when he shot Anthony. And his background would be carefully examined. If Harms had served as a peace officer in the United States, no jury would believe that he had panicked and overreacted when threatened by an unarmed and smaller man. No, the defence would rely on Harms's statement and keep the accused out of the stand. That decision had the additional benefit of giving him the last word to the jury, an advantage Diefenbaker always strove for.

Mr. Justice Henry V. Bigelow, the judge at the Wysochan trial, was to preside. That did not augur well for Diefenbaker and Harms. Bigelow, Diefenbaker knew from bitter experience, was a stern, even harsh jurist who believed in imparting his opinions to his juries. Walter L. Clink, the local agent of the attorney general, would prosecute.

The trial opened on Tuesday, February 4, 1936, and, remarkably, closed that same day. It was John Diefenbaker's first murder case before a six-man jury — the economy measure introduced by T.C. Davis the previous September.

The six men selected to try John Harms must have wondered at the casual, almost lackadaisical methods of his defence counsel. Diefenbaker behaved as if a great deal of the evidence brought forward by Clink had nothing to do with his client. Except for Micky Lindgreen and Sergeant Vernon, Diefenbaker showed almost no interest in any of the Crown witnesses.

Diefenbaker led Micky Lindgreen, the first witness, through a detailed description of Harms's behaviour on the day of the killing. Lindgreen admitted, with a little hesitation, that the trapper had not appeared normal, either before he left her cabin with Anthony, or later, when he returned for her.

"And as soon as the accused drank the beer at your place on that day he began to act, as you say, not normal?"

"Yes."

"When he first came over was he not acting normal?"

"Yes, he was acting normal."

"But after he drank those four or five bottles of beer he commenced acting abnormal?"

"No, he just got a little more grousing. He didn't appear to be intoxicated." Lindgreen would be only so helpful.

"When you went across to his place after he told you something had happened, he acted in a very wild manner didn't he? He tried to crush your child's head?"

"For an instant he did."

"And is it not correct that he had a look in his eye as if he was going to crush that head?"

"Yes." On that point Lindgreen had no doubt.

"You mean to tell me at that time you thought he was fully normal?" Diefenbaker had his witness.

"Not at that moment."

"You thought he was out of his mind?" The lawyer pressed.

"Not out of his mind. He was not acting quite normal." Lindgreen was sliding away again. The witness was more helpful when Diefenbaker queried her about the type of man John Harms was.

"He was very quarrelsome when he was under the influence of liquor?"

"Yes."

"And quick to take offence? Was he quick to take offence?"

"Rather."

"He would flare up and get in fighting shape over a very small incident?"

"Yes."

"Seemed to have a very bad temper?"

"Yes."

"Easily annoyed when under the influence of liquor?"

"Yes."

When Sergeant Vernon followed Lindgreen to the stand, Diefenbaker, of course, did not object to the policeman putting John Harms's statement before the jury. He wanted his client's story to come forward that way. But the lawyer had a few questions in expansion of the conversation at Scorched Dog Island, when Harms was arrested.

"You say he seemed very glad when you arrived?"

"Yes, he seemed relieved."

"And he told you he had been drinking very heavily?"

"He told me he had got pretty drunk afterwards and he doesn't remember a thing. His mind is a blank."

"Afterwards" was no good. Diefenbaker needed Harms drunk when he shot Anthony. He took Vernon back to some earlier testimony.

"As to what took place at the time of the shooting, he made the statement, 'I don't know what I did'?"

"No, he didn't say. I remember asking if he aimed and how many shots he fired, and he said only the one shot. And with regard to aiming, he said, 'I don't know what I did'"

Sergeant Vernon was a skilful witness. Diefenbaker soon let him go.

After that, the defence appeared to be through, and Diefenbaker stated, "No questions," after each of the last seven Crown witnesses. The remaining police testimony, the medical evidence, even the report from the provincial analyst concerning the superior alcohol content of Harms's beer, went by without comment or question from the defence. It might have been a mistake. Cross-examination can often be used to emphasize the defence theories in a case.

At 4:15 that afternoon, Clink closed the Crown case. "The defence rests," Diefenbaker advised the court. There would be no defence evidence. Clink rose to address the jury.

Half an hour later, John Diefenbaker followed Walter L. Clink before the jury. He spent forty-five minutes explaining his theories of self-defence, provocation and drunkenness to the six men. Pointing to Harms's statement to Sergeant Vernon as the only evidence of what happened in the cabin on Spring Point, he argued that it supported his theories. Diefenbaker asked for a verdict of manslaughter.

But Mr. Justice Bigelow had some comment to make to the jury about that statement of John Harms's: "You don't have to take that as true because he told it to the police officer. You may or may not believe any of it....You have a perfect right to ask yourselves whether you believe any of the evidence that man told in his own favour....He is a very partial witness when telling what occurred to the police officer."

After those and a few similar remarks the platform upon which the defence theories rested began to look very shaky. The trial judge went on to instruct the jury on the law governing those theories. Drunkenness will not assist an accused pleading self-defence or provocation, he said. A man who flies into a rage because of drink will receive no consideration. The state of mind to be measured is a reasonable or ordinary one. Drunkenness, however, was an element to be considered in deciding whether Harms had been capable of forming an intention to kill Anthony, and might reduce murder to manslaughter.

Bigelow began his charge to the jury after Diefenbaker sat down at 5:30 p.m. When 6:00 p.m. came, he stopped, due to the lateness of the hour, although he had barely touched the evidence. "I am not going to deal with the evidence any further because I don't think it will be of any service to you," he told the jury, and sent them off to consider their verdict. Court was adjourned until the next morning. The jury would have to hold its verdict until then. "I think the officers of the court will not want to be around the court house all this evening," the judge explained, not mentioning that he was happily including himself in the kindness.

The jury was left to struggle with the case as best it could, not knowing what aspects of the evidence might be considered in relation to what defence theories. They had been told what the law was, but not given much help in applying it to the case in front of them. Mr. Justice Bigelow seemed to be infected by the same casualness with which John Diefenbaker treated the case.

By 10:00 the next morning the jury had done its duty and was ready with its verdict: "Guilty of murder." Mr. Justice Bigelow immediately handed down sentence.

"You have had a fair trial. You had able counsel defending you, and everything that could be said or done fairly on your behalf was said or done by him, and in other respects your trial has been fair, and the verdict is one that has been justified by the evidence. There is only one sentence I can impose upon you: the death sentence....You will be taken from here and conveyed to the Provincial Gaol at Prince Albert and there confined until the 8th day of May, 1936, and on that day between the hours of six o'clock in the morning and twelve o'clock noon you shall be taken to the gallows and there hanged by the neck until you are dead. May God have mercy upon your soul."

With those words spoken, Bigelow turned to the next case, an uncontested divorce.

In the prisoner's dock, John Harms was no longer the powerful man of the North. Noticeably grayer and older-looking, he swayed, and his hands gripped the dock rail "like a vise," according to a local observer. He was escorted to solitary confinement at Prince Albert while awaiting execution.

"HARMS SENTENCED TO DIE ON GALLOWS, MAY 8," blared the headlines. Below, more purple prose described the trial.

"In one day, the court heard of the age-old struggle with the wilderness for food and fur in the Athabaska country, and of feasting following the capture of a moose that for a time blotted out the weeks-old quarrel between the partners over a fur catch. The court heard, too, of an orgy in Athabaska homebrew that left its victim crazed, and of the suspicion engendered in the lonely cabin, that suddenly blazed into hatred and spent itself in a single puff of revolver smoke as the drink-mad Harms faced his partner in a last man-to-man struggle for mastery."

An appeal was very much in order, but an impediment was Harms's complete lack of funds. Not only had Sergeant Vernon been unable to sell the trapper's cabin and equipment, he had been presented with a demand from John Anthony's father claiming all sale proceeds.

Diefenbaker filed a notice of appeal and applied to have the Court of Appeal appoint him as counsel to John Harms. This was done, and enabled the defence to secure transcripts of the trial evidence at no cost. It also entitled counsel to a fee set by the court. After the hearing of the appeal, Chief Justice Haultain fixed Diefenbaker's counsel fee at $75.

"APPEAL AGAINST NORTHLAND MURDER CONVICTION," the headline read in the Regina *Daily Star*. Below a photograph, the caption identified "J.G. Diefenbaker, K.C., of Prince Albert, who will be in Regina this week as defence counsel in the Harms appeal against a death sentence. He is one of Saskatchewan's outstanding lawyers and a prominent Conservative. Twice he has opposed the present premier of Canada in the Prince Albert constituency and though not elected made a good showing. He is well-known and well-liked all over the province."

The appeal was argued April 6 and 7. John Cuelenaere, proving his value to the Diefenbaker law office, had made a microscopic examination of Mr. Justice Bigelow's charge to the jury. Armed with Cuelenaere's research, Diefenbaker presented to the appeal judges a masterly exposition of the possible and probable deficiencies in the jury charge. He secured their agreement on five of his grounds of appeal, the most basic being the trial judge's failure to put the defence case properly to the jury. The court found little fault with Mr. Justice Bigelow's statements of the law, but wondered if he had taken time to explain adequately their possible application to the evidence before the jurors.

During Diefenbaker's submission that Harms might well have become intoxicated by consuming several bottles of his homemade beer, an exchange took place among the appellate judges that shook the lawyer's confidence in his case.

"In Milwaukee," observed Chief Justice Haultain, a stout trencherman himself, "people drink sixty or seventy bottles of beer a day."

Mr. Justice MacKenzie appeared somewhat dazed by this information. Shaking his head sadly, he said, "It does make a man look like a piker, doesn't it."

On April 20, eighteen days before the day fixed for Harms's execution, the Court of Appeal handed down its decision: Mr. Justice Bigelow's summing-up was defective and unsatisfactory, and there must be a new trial.

"HARMS, CONDEMNED SLAYER, WINS NEW TRIAL," the newspapers announced, "Overcome at News of Fresh Chance for Life 18 Days Before Date of Execution, Prisoner Leaves Death Cell."

John Diefenbaker took the good news to his client in the Prince Albert Gaol. Harms was overcome. Tears coursed down his cheeks as he struggled to speak.

"I had always hoped," he finally sobbed.

The new trial began on June 2 before Mr. Justice H.Y. MacDonald. This time everyone — the Bench, the Crown and the defence — took care to ensure that the jury understood the legal issues of the case. In his opening, Walter L. Clink, again prosecuting, stated that intoxication was "one of the very important elements," and asked the jury to pay particular attention to this phase of the evidence.

John Diefenbaker might have treated Harms's first trial a little too casually, but he did not repeat the mistake. Having enlisted John Cuelenaere's help in preparing the submissions to the Court of Appeal, he kept Cuelenaere with him through the new trial.

A second trial normally can be expected to require less time than the first, but such was not the case with Harms's. Even though the Crown omitted two of its earlier witnesses, the evidence was not complete until the late morning of the second day.

Diefenbaker's strategy remained unchanged, but he took much greater care to ensure that his theories were understood by the jury. This time he had the provincial analyst emphasize that the beer Harms had brewed, at more than 6 per cent alcohol by volume, was 50 per cent stronger than the commercial varieties available. And the pathologist was asked to explain the effects of alcohol consumption upon human reactions and co-ordination.

More time was spent with the jury, too — an hour more, in fact — as Diefenbaker painstakingly explained how so much of the evidence supported his theory of a seriously intoxicated Harms.

Mr. Justice MacDonald also was more thorough, spending twice as much time with the jury as Mr. Justice Bigelow had. Taking a little licence with the law, the trial judge even extended the jury's options by suggesting that they might find Harms had been so drunk at the time of the shooting as to induce a condition of temporary insanity.

Harms's second jury had little trouble grasping what was expected of them. They left the court room at 4:00 p.m. on the second trial day, and were back in an hour and a half with a verdict of manslaughter and a recommendation for mercy. It was a popular verdict. As soon as court closed, dozens of spectators crowded around the jurymen, congratulating them on their finding.

From the same dock where he had heard a death sentence imposed upon him just four months earlier, a haggard but obviously grateful John Harms gazed adoringly upon his defence counsel, John Diefenbaker.

MacDonald added his congratulations to the jury, saying he agreed with the verdict, and sentenced John Harms to fifteen years imprisonment. It was over for the Athabaska trapper.

"HARMS SENT TO PENITENTIARY FOR 15 YEARS," was the Saskatoon *Star Phoenix* headline. "Escapes Gallows When Convicted of Manslaughter." The final lurid chronicle continued:

"Strangest of all the northland stories is that of John Harms, the Athabaska trapper. It will live long in those lonely spaces where time means only Summer and Winter, plenty and scarcity and life and death.

"When the full import of the verdict was borne in on the mind of the man who has endured the ordeal of two murder trials, and lengthy incarceration in a death cell, he looked at his counsel, J.G. Diefenbaker, K.C., Prince Albert, with just such a gaze as a drowning man, clutching at a straw, would turn upon his rescuer."

The Northland, which John Harms never saw again, was ablaze. Drought had extended far into the forest region, and raging fires were consuming huge stands of timber. On June 2, while John Diefenbaker addressed the second Harms six-man jury, Attorney General T.C. Davis flew over the north country, inspecting the new disaster.

"Completely beyond control," Davis was quoted in the same *Star Phoenix* that reported the Harms verdict. "Only general rains can save large areas of timberland." Davis described emergency measures being taken in hopes of saving Prince Albert National Park.

In Prince Albert, the paper reported, more than one hundred youths marched upon city hall. They protested the giving of work and wages to the many single transients stranded in the city. And in Saskatoon, the establishment of a distributing station for grasshopper poison was announced. Farmers drove into the city for the mixture of arsenic, bran and sawdust that they hoped would save their meager crops from the swarms of invading insects.

Although it was only early June, people noticed and commented upon the unusually high temperatures. It was the first touch of a heat wave that would render prairie residents prostrate for nearly two months.

The summer of 1936 had begun.

13

The Tough Years

Against the backdrop of a land ravaged by natural disasters, the world of politics played out its own hand. As acting president, John Diefenbaker was the only officer on the bridge of the foundered Saskatchewan Conservative Association. The double blows of the provincial defeat in June 1934, followed by the federal loss in October 1935, shattered the party. By the spring of 1936, funds, members and interest had evaporated, and the organization was all but moribund.

The Prince Albert lawyer was almost the only prominent Conservative official in the province whose financial affairs were strong enough to enable him to devote any time or attention to party affairs. Party leader J.T.M. Anderson, his Cabinet and others connected to the former government were forced by the hostile electors to seek new employment at the worst possible time, the depth of the Depression. Other members of the party's executive were also struggling economically.

Diefenbaker, in spite of the Depression, continued to do very well financially. In April 1936, he purchased a new Buick sedan for $1,600 and completed his arrangements to travel to Europe in July. Both transactions were far beyond the contemplation of almost all his professional peers, or anyone else in Saskatchewan at that time.

From the president's office, Diefenbaker began manoeuvring to succeed Anderson as leader of the Saskatchewan Conservatives. The former premier had not formally announced his resignation, but intended to do so as soon as the party was ready. Since

Anderson had ceased to act, there was pressure within the party to hold an early leadership convention, certainly not later than the summer of 1936. The calling of that convention was the responsibility of the acting president.

As early as May, the press reported that Diefenbaker was "making a strong bid for provincial leadership of the party." The announcement provoked little reaction. No one else wanted the job, but there was no enthusiasm for Diefenbaker's candidacy. He put the convention off until fall and continued with his plans to spend the summer in Europe.

At the end of June, shortly before leaving for overseas, Diefenbaker asserted himself as acting president and gave the organization something to do while he was away. The party secretary sent all the provincial constituency representatives a letter composed by Diefenbaker:

I am instructed by Mr. J.G. Diefenbaker, K.C., acting President of the Association, to advise you that a Provincial Convention will be held some time this fall, probably September or October, for the following purposes:
1. To select a Provincial leader.
2. To elect officers of the Association.
3. To discuss the future policy of the Conservative Party in Saskatchewan.

Mr. Diefenbaker wishes to have a completely new organization in the Constituencies so that the Conservative party may present a united front at the forthcoming election. Please call the constituency conventions as soon as possible. Do everything possible to secure a complete representation of the constituency at your Convention. Do not forget to secure the cooperation of all classes and races and include representatives of the young people and women.

Then followed a lengthy list of activities for all ridings and a proposed schedule of financial contributions to sustain the party's central office. Given the plight of the party and the province, the suggestions were, for the most part, completely impractical. They served, however, to give the image of a dedicated and energetic president. Diefenbaker then went off to Europe. Edna was not included in the trip, at the time quite an acceptable, almost to-be-expected arrangement. Wives shared only certain aspects of their husband's lives.

Diefenbaker joined a group of Prince Albert veterans crossing the Atlantic on the S.S. *Montcalm*. After taking part in the dedication of a memorial to fallen Canadian soldiers at Vimy Ridge on July 26, he went on to Berlin to look in on the Olympic games. Like many of the visitors to Germany that summer, Diefenbaker fell victim to the Nazi propaganda and came away with a distorted opinion of the country's accomplishments under Hitler.

By late August, John Diefenbaker was back in Saskatchewan. Resuming his quest for the leadership of the Conservative Party, he called the convention for October 28 at Regina.

Diefenbaker's availability for the almost vacant leadership was by then well known across the Conservative Party, but little encouragement came back to him. The hierarchy was looking for someone a little more prominent, a little more experienced. Robert Weir of Melfort, former minister of agriculture in the Bennett government, and Murdoch A. MacPherson, the Regina lawyer who served as Anderson's attorney general, were the most desired candidates. Even Anderson himself, in spite of the total defeat of 1934, still had considerable support.

Diefenbaker had no choice but to wait things out. Finally, a week before the convention, with no other candidates in sight, he began openly to line up delegates, although somewhat diffidently. Even with Edna's brother, Jack Brower of Langham, he seemed to feel a need to colour the situation, and explain his own candidacy:

> Dear Jack;
>
> I am very anxious that as many delegates as possible go to Regina for the Convention. There is going to be a close fight and I would like to see you and others from Langham there.
>
> Dr. Anderson, Mr. MacPherson and Mr. Weir are not going to stand, so I trust that you will be able to get together a half dozen or so who will be pledged to me. See what you can do around Langham, Borden and Radisson.

To other possible delegates the candidate was more direct, if a little hasty:

The question of leadership is going to be decided, and it is my present intention to allow my name to be submitted in nomination, and if you can attend and see your way fit to support me, it will be much appreciated, and, if so minded, if you can get other delegates from your Constituency to attend, so much the better.

Diefenbaker was unable to muster much support. Even his old friend Bert Keown, of Melfort, his colleague on the Olson appeal, was lukewarm to his candidacy:

Dear Bert;

I am a little worried about the attendance at the Convention, and would like to see you do something towards securing an attendance from the Melfort and Kinistino constituencies.

Mr. Weir has been in Town several times but has not called at the office, and I do not feel like calling upon him and asking his assistance towards securing representation.

You know the position of affairs is this — that unless a substantial attendance is secured at the convention more harm will be done than good.

I would like to know whether you are still prepared to put my nomination before the Convention.

The latest reports are that Mr. MacPherson will not stand due to the fact that he has received a Wheat Pool solicitorship, and Dr. Anderson is definite in his refusal to stand.

Please let me hear from you by return, and if you have any suggestions to make as to what I ought to do, kindly let me have same.

Would you be willing to write to a number of your friends on my behalf? If you would I would appreciate your doing so at once, as I know that your assistance will be a very great help to me.

I would like to see you in Regina on Tuesday next, at which date there is a meeting of former Federal and Provincial candidates called for the purpose of generally canvassing the situation and to assist the Resolutions Committee in preparing planks for the platform.

With kindest regards, I am
Yours Sincerely,
John G. Diefenbaker

Keown withheld his support. Diefenbaker was on his own.

Nearly six hundred Conservatives attended the one-day meeting, held in Regina's city hall. As a political leadership convention, it was a bust. For John Diefenbaker it was an exercise in embarrassment and determination. But, overall, it was a creditable achievement for the down-and-out Conservative Party.

Former premier Anderson had secured employment as manager of a Saskatoon life insurance agency and submitted his resignation as party leader, over considerable protest from some delegates. With that formality attended to, Diefenbaker, who chaired the convention in his capacity as acting president, asked for nominations for vice-president. He needed to turn the meeting over so that he could become a candidate.

A vocal delegate immediately demanded to know why a vice-president was necessary, since the president was already in the chair. Diefenbaker did not want to explain, and stood in embarrassed silence until Frederick B. Bagshaw, K.C., filled in. The convention then accepted nominations for leader.

A parade of proposals and refusals followed. Name after name was put before the meeting and was quickly removed by the nominee. Former leader Anderson was first; he declined. Then F.R. MacMillan of Saskatoon and Murdoch A. MacPherson of Regina; they both declined. Then Ernest E. Perley, the lone remaining Conservative MP, who also declined.

Next was John Diefenbaker, nominated by a Prince Albert delegate.

Then came more names; Netson R. Craig of Moose Jaw, Robert Weir of Melfort, Robert L. Hanbidge of Kerrobert, Bert Keown, Diefenbaker's hoped-for nominator, Ariel Sallows of North Battleford, and W. Wallace Lynd of Estevan. All declined.

Eleven names were put before the convention. Ten declined the honour, and only John Diefenbaker was left.

"I'm not here to put my qualifications before you," the sole remaining candidate told the crowd, "but, if you think I can lead this party to victory, I'll lead the party. If you think I'm not the man, then I'll get behind the man you choose, and give him my wholehearted support....

"I will stand," he concluded.

The convention accepted the new leader with enthusiastic applause. The selection was made.

"Well, now we've got someone on first base," said Frederick B. Bagshaw from the chair.

Diefenbaker told the delegates that he wanted "a party platform based on Conservative traditions of the past, yet brought up-to-date to conform with present day conditions....It might be termed radical," he said, "radical in the sense that the reform program of the Honourable R.B. Bennett was radical."

"Young Lawyer Who Battled Premier NEW PARTY HEAD," ran the headline in the Liberal-leaning Regina *Leader Post*.

"Youthful of appearance and personable of voice and manner, is J.G. Diefenbaker, K.C., new leader of the Conservative Party in Saskatchewan. At 40 years [*sic*], Mr. Diefenbaker is one of the youngest men to take office as party leader of the Conservatives in Saskatchewan. He carries his forty years lightly, is darkly slim and erect, and thunders forth his convictions and ideas in resonant tones of purposeful youth."

The Conservative *Daily Star* carried an interview with the new leader's wife. Edna responded appropriately:

"His heart is in his work. He will try even harder now that he has been chosen leader. I know he will be happy at it, too. His happiness will be mine, too," Edna responded as the reporter tried to pry into her feelings. "It's no use interviewing me. I don't know anything about politics. I leave it all to him."

The Saskatoon *Star Phoenix*, another Liberal paper, commented in an editorial entitled "The New Leader":

> There has been little doubt these last few months as to who would get the bid to lead the Conservative forces in Saskatchewan, providing always that Dr. J.T.M. Anderson could not be persuaded to return to the political arena. Nevertheless, congratulations are due to Mr. John Diefenbaker, K.C., of Prince Albert, for the honour which has been conferred upon him by his fellow political workers....
>
> The party, probably, is more fortunate than Mr. Diefenbaker. The party gets a man well equipped for leadership, but the leader gets a party which seems little inclined to follow any single lead....

> There seems to be another division in the party as well. This one
> is over matters of change in policy. There is a general feeling that
> the party must shift its ground considerably to the left of tradition-
> al Conservatism. The question which will bother the convention
> and the leader is: How far to the left?

The editor put his finger upon a problem that bothered John
Diefenbaker and the Conservative Party for many years to come.

As John Diefenbaker returned to Prince Albert, he took an additional measure of satisfaction from his election. He had finally
succeeded where T.C. Davis had failed, in securing the leadership of his chosen party.

Even the dogged Diefenbaker must have questioned his own
sanity at undertaking the burden of the Conservative Party when
he did. The political prospects were dreadful and continued to
deteriorate as the Depression, incredibly, deepened still further.
The Conservative Party Diefenbaker now headed was still tarred
with blame for the disaster.

In Europe during most of July and August, John Diefenbaker
had escaped most of a record heat wave that parched and
paralyzed the Prairies for more than two months. Beginning in
June, by the end of that month the furnace-like winds had blasted
the crops in their fields. For the first time since the Dirty Thirties began, Prince Albert and northern Saskatchewan experienced real drought.

By July, Regina residents were bedding themselves down in
the parks at night in futile attempts to escape the oppressive heat.
The record temperatures extended across the Great Lakes and
into southern Ontario. For a full week in July, the Fahrenheit
thermometers registered more than one hundred degrees from
Calgary to Toronto. Hundreds died from heat prostration.

In the West, the unrelenting heat wave continued well into
August. The crop yields dropped to their second-lowest level
since the Depression began. It was no longer possible to feed the
cattle population in Saskatchewan and Alberta.

What little growth survived the heat and the drought was consumed by grasshoppers, whose population exploded geometri-

cally year after year throughout the Depression until their numbers grew beyond reckoning. In his account of western land reclamation, *Men Against the Desert*, James H. Gray describes the death of a single flight of grasshoppers driven over Lake Winnipeg. Trapped by a cold wind, the insects fell into the water and were blown onto the shoreline where, for twenty miles, their bodies piled up to a depth of several feet. Touring in such huge swarms, the insects descended without warning, devoured everything edible and much that was not, then as suddenly departed.

As northern Saskatchewan began to experience the worst effects of the Depression, the financial strain brought the city of Prince Albert close to another fiscal collapse. Still burdened with the debt of the La Colle Falls debacle, the city was unable to cope with the rising requirements of relief, and seriously considered default.

The census of 1936 showed Prince Albert with a population of over eleven thousand, an increase of more than 11 per cent since 1931. Most of the new arrivals were unemployed migrants from the Prairies' dried-up south country, and the city did not appreciate its status as "the fastest growing city on the Prairies."

A Prince Albert alderman proposed the deportation of all non-naturalized immigrants who applied for relief. City council approved the idea, and resolved to take it to the organization of urban municipalities, where it might acquire enough impetus to become national policy.

As the inferno of 1936 faded, the following year opened with ominous signals that nature had not yet fully tested the endurance of the prairie population. The desert-like drought of 1936 continued throughout the fall, and then into winter. No snow fell, and the land lay exposed and exhausted, waiting for a spring that could not be green. Temperatures, which tested the upper ranges of thermometers during the previous summer, now fell into record lows — and stayed there. Saskatchewan shivered as it waited for the certain calamity coming.

And when spring arrived and turned into summer, there was no rain. The crops failed all over Saskatchewan — even in the usually secure northeast region — and the failure was earlier, and more total, than ever before. In June, the duststorms began, and they blew all summer. As far east as Winnipeg, the sun was obscured by the haze of dust blown in from southern Saskatchewan. The grasshoppers swarmed across the province in concentrations never before seen. In August, clouds of the insects descended upon Regina and blanketed the city. Escape from the pests was impossible as they crawled, chewed and perched on every available surface.

In 1937, Saskatchewan reached the lowest point of the Dirty Thirties. Wheat production averaged a miserable 2.7 bushels per acre, less than a third of 1936 levels, then the worst year to date. Net farm income spiralled into the red again, exceeding even the extreme losses of 1931. Thousands of farm families, who had hung on thus far, threw in the towel and set off in search of someplace with a future. The governments of Ontario and Alberta warned the Saskatchewan refugees to stay out of their provinces.

The residents of Prince Albert, alongside the still flowing North Saskatchewan River, could almost pretend that the misery of southern Saskatchewan did not exist. But the provincial leader of the Conservative Party, when he drove his Buick sedan down into the rural constituencies, or to Saskatoon or Regina, entered a bleak and different world. The ditches and fence-lines were piled with tumbleweed and filled with blow-dirt. The landscape was grey and forbidding.

In the first year of his leadership, John Diefenbaker's sensitivity to his German name was reactivated by an allegation that he was sympathetic to Nazi Germany. The summer following his trip to Europe, the *Western Producer*, a farm weekly, carried an "Open Letter" from a reader who forwarded an extract from an extremist magazine published in Quebec:

"What has happened in Quebec is typical of the policy now striven for by the reactionary Tories all over the country. It is no accident that Mr. Diefenbacher [*sic*], the provincial leader of the Conservatives, attended the Nazi conference in Nuremburg, Germany, last September, and maintains a regular and intimate connection with the Nazis."

The reader wanted to know if Diefenbaker "went to the convention of his own free will, whether he was sent by the Conservative party, or whether an invitation had been extended to him by his Nazi friends?"

Diefenbaker threatened to sue, and both the *Western Producer* and its contributor promptly apologized and retracted the allegation. For his part, Diefenbaker silently abandoned any of the favourable impressions he had formed while visiting Berlin the year before.

Diefenbaker valiantly struggled to rebuild the Conservative Party. If the Liberals, now under Premier William J. Patterson, followed the traditional four-year cycle, an election was due in a year. The defeated Conservatives were far from fighting trim.

In fact, the party was so demoralized by its defeats that it did not even contest any of four provincial by-elections held late in 1935. The CCF, with five members in the legislature, was dangerously close to supplanting the Conservatives as the alternative to the Liberals. The Social Credit missionaries of Alberta Premier William Aberhart remained in Saskatchewan after the 1935 federal election, and were another growing threat.

The province was a maelstrom of political upheaval and activity as traditional voting patterns disappeared. The level of interest was acute as much of the idle time imposed by the Depression was devoted to public affairs. Radio, just coming into its own, was a natural medium for the swift dissemination of new political theories.

In this struggle for political survival, the Conservatives and John Diefenbaker were the underdogs. The party had no office, no staff, no riding organizations, no candidates — only the fiction of a provincial organization, and no money. Worse, there was no policy that could compete in Depression-weary Saskatchewan with the alluring remedies of socialism and monetary reform offered by the CCF and Social Credit.

The CCF was the real enemy, although that was not at first apparent. The new party, very grassroots-effective, took advantage of the Conservative weakness and burrowed busily into much of the constituency formerly occupied by the old-line party.

Diefenbaker did what he could, with only the help of Bert Keown, who succeeded him to the party presidency. The two tried to enlist a slate of candidates, but the party's prospects were so poor, there was little to attract good election material. The biggest problem was lack of funds. The Conservative treasury was empty, and there was no chance of replenishing it in the Saskatchewan of 1937. Diefenbaker sought financial aid from the Ontario Conservatives to help him reestablish the western wing of the party. No help came.

Fully aware of the tenuous situation of the Diefenbaker organization, the CCF watched carefully. It was in their interest that the Saskatchewan Conservatives remain weak, but not so weak as to provoke intervention by the Ontario group.

T.C. "Tommy" Douglas, later premier of Saskatchewan, but then a member of Parliament, wrote from Ottawa to provincial CCF leader George H. Williams: "If we make it too tough on fellows like Perley [the lone Saskatchewan Conservative MP] and Diefenbaker who are, I believe, sincere, we may very well have a Conservative in almost every constituency, with strong financial backing from the group here [Ontario], who are endeavouring to get the Conservative party on its feet again."

Douglas's fears did not materialize. Diefenbaker was able to patch together the appearance of an organization, not enough to be effective, but sufficient to justify the decision of the Ontario Conservatives to keep their money at home.

Diefenbaker needed to pick a seat for himself. Prince Albert was out. If he could not beat T.C. Davis in 1929, when the Conservatives were riding high, it was unlikely he could do so in 1938. After surveying the rural ridings within reasonable distance of Prince Albert, Diefenbaker eventually settled on Arm River. One hundred and twenty-five miles south of Prince Albert, the seat contained a strong Conservative vote. The terrific by-election battle of October 1928 had identified the party's supporters, and the skeleton of an organization was still in place. The Conservatives won Arm River in 1929 and, although it slipped back to the Liberals in 1934, the margin was fewer than three hundred votes. Just as important, the 1934 election left the Conservatives with over 38 per cent of the vote in Arm River, more than ten points above their provincial average. And the Liberal member was a newcomer, a crusty Scandinavian named Herman Danielson, who appeared to be vulnerable.

Diefenbaker's party was riven with dissent. The legacy of the "true blue" revolt still lingered. Federal and provincial factions developed. Several constituency associations refused to nominate Conservative candidates, preferring to negotiate "saw-offs" with the CCF, in the hopes of defeating the Liberals. Three ridings nominated "Unity" candidates (a CCF-Conservative coalition); one was a former Conservative candidate and one had been a minister in the Anderson government. Other former Conservative candidates chose to run as Independents. The three major cities, Saskatoon, Regina and Moose Jaw, all two-member constituencies, delivered full slates of candidates to Diefenbaker. After that, it was hit or miss throughout the rural ridings.

Premier Patterson called the election for June 8, 1938. When nominations closed, the Conservatives had fielded candidates in twenty-four of fifty-two ridings — not bad, considering the much better organized CCF had only thirty-one. The steam-rolling Social Credit nominated forty. Only the Liberals had a candidate in every riding.

Diefenbaker and his Conservatives were almost completely ignored during the spring election campaign. The Liberals, Social Credit and CCF regarded themselves as the real contenders. Both the Liberals and the CCF turned on the invading legions of Alberta Premier Aberhart, describing the apostle of the A plus B Theorem — the economic principle that supposedly made Social Credit work — as a conquering dictator in the style of Mussolini. The Liberals declared the Social Credit threat so serious that "upon the result of this election will depend whether or not Canada is to continue as a united British nation."

In the face of such hyperbole, Diefenbaker, who had turned his law practice over to Cuelenaere so that he could throw himself into the campaign, had difficulty making himself heard. It did not help that he adopted a novel and somewhat restrictive campaign posture. Declaring what he described as his "philosophy of party leadership," Diefenbaker asserted that "only such political promises should be made as are capable of performance." It might have been the wrong campaign to attempt such a responsible program. The air was full of Aberhart's wild monetary promises, and even the more restrained projections of the CCF signalled that the status quo was going out of style.

The official Conservative platform was distributed by a pamphlet bearing a photograph of a stern "John G. Diefenbaker, M.A., LL.B., Leader of the Conservative Party of Saskatchewan." It promised the introduction of the transferable ballot and the refinancing of the provincial debt at lower interest rates, and made a bid for the vote of the teachers. During the Depression, many teachers had received only a portion of their salaries. The Conservatives offered to pay all arrears within a year.

"Continued drought, insect ravages, hail, rust, and abnormally low prices for farm products demand an equitable adjustment of existing debts," the platform stated. It further promised that "debts shall be reduced so that the creditor shall share with the debtor the loss occasioned by crop failures and abnormally low prices."

His 1938 platform contained two features that stayed with Diefenbaker more than twenty years: the promise to study a system of crop insurance or acreage indemnity payments, and support for the principle of state medicine, approved two years earlier by the legislature, but not implemented because of lack of funds.

Diefenbaker set up a heavy schedule of schoolhouse and town hall meetings in support of his candidates. He received only modest coverage from the press, but his speeches were not the stuff of headlines. Those were stolen by "Wild Bill" Aberhart and his promises to rid Saskatchewan of "the tyranny of finance."

Diefenbaker condemned the Liberals for their record on relief administration, and for "adopting a policy that too easily lends itself to political influence." He attacked the Patterson government for its "Soak the Poor" policies and for the use of civil servants in the campaign: "Every man or woman in civil service, regardless of political belief, creed or race, has a right to security of tenure, if efficient, but I warn those who participate in politics that they are thereby endangering their position...."

At the major party rally in Regina, Diefenbaker spoke of his campaign in Arm River. "Government inspectors in Arm River are so thick they have been ordered to wear a distinctive ribbon in their lapels so they will not go around asking each other for their vote," he said.

In Saskatoon, Diefenbaker denounced the Liberal campaign promises: "No more brazen attempt to buy the electorate with its own money has ever been made," he declared. "You shall not eat, you shall not drink, and you shall not be clothed unless the Patterson government is returned — that's what they say."

Premier Aberhart drew audiences in the thousands, setting political records that still stand. When the Social Credit bandwagon reached Prince Albert, 3,500 people poured into the armoury to hear his fiscal evangelism. Aberhart promised a $25 monthly dividend to all. Diefenbaker claimed that some local candidates were, on their own initiative, raising that to $125.

Nature smiled upon Patterson and his Liberal government. The drought broke and the rains returned, so much so that wet roads made campaigning difficult. The summer of 1937 was the last cruel twist of fate, and then the weather returned to normal. Fall rains and plenty of snow restored the soil. In the spring of 1938 crops were sprouting and hope was in the air, omens that an incumbent administration prays for. The crop, the first in years, fell victim to rust, but that was well after the election.

On June 8 the voters, too, smiled upon Patterson, and returned his government with thirty-eight members and 45 per cent of the vote. Social Credit was rejected; it elected only two candidates. The CCF remained the official opposition with ten members and 19 per cent support. Diefenbaker and the Conservatives were also-rans. None were elected, and their share of the vote dropped to 12 per cent, less than half of the 1934 level. In Arm River, in a two-way battle, the crusty Herman Danielson had prevailed, not as vulnerable as had been thought. Diefenbaker succeeded only in reducing Danielson's majority by ninety-seven votes. Danielson went on to win five more elections in Arm River, but always regarded his victory over Diefenbaker as his greatest achievement.

Saskatchewan Conservatives did not hold John Diefenbaker responsible for their second total defeat. At the party convention in Moose Jaw on October 26, they rejected the leader's proffered resignation, and confirmed him in office.

Diefenbaker gave an account of his efforts to organize the party for the election. The situation had looked hopeful in the spring, he said, "but along came a political fungus [Social Credit] that destroyed the Conservative hopes, as rust did the 1938 crop." The leader decried the situation in several ridings where local Conservatives refused to nominate candidates, hoping to defeat the Liberals by getting behind the CCF: "I could not overcome that feeling," Diefenbaker said.

"Financial institutions in Eastern Canada placed their money on the Liberal party, and against the Conservative party. Great corporations took the stand that, regardless of the consequences, Social Credit must be defeated, and they placed their money on the party with candidates in every constituency," he went on. "The lesson for Conservatives," he concluded, "is that there must be no temporizing with third parties, no matter what they may be."

The Conservative treasurer reported that the party had raised $1,500 in the province, $6,000 outside Saskatchewan, and had a bank balance of $39.06.

Diefenbaker was finally discouraged. He had worked hard during his two years as Conservative leader, and the results were zero. As he told the Moose Jaw convention, the party fought three elections — in 1934, 1935 and 1938, two provincial and one federal — and succeeded only in electing one member of Parliament.

Certain that his political ambitions were never to be realized, Diefenbaker turned once more to his Prince Albert law office.

But early in July, a month after the Saskatchewan election, the Conservative Party of Canada met in Ottawa to choose a successor to R.B. Bennett. Murdoch A. MacPherson of Regina entered the leadership contest and, with Bennett's support, made a very strong showing before losing to Robert J. Manion.

MacPherson had never sat in Parliament, and was no longer a member of the provincial legislature. A western lawyer without a seat, he came close to succeeding another western lawyer as leader of the national party.

John Diefenbaker filed that information. There was always hope.

14

The Edge of Opportunity

One of Canada's best known imposters died at Prince Albert in April 1938. International fame as an author, lecturer, naturalist and conservationist had come to the man known as Grey Owl, who lived in the Prince Albert National Park. Only a few days before his death, Grey Owl had returned from a lengthy lecture tour of England and the United States.

Grey Owl claimed Indian ancestry, presenting himself as the son of a Scots father and an Apache mother. After his death, the facts emerged and he was identified as Archie Belaney — an Englishman, of all things. After the initial reaction of dismay at the discovery of Grey Owl's fraud, recognition eventually came his way for his contribution to the cause of conservation.

Despite the remoteness of his residences, Grey Owl's career included a number of women. One was Anahareo, with whom he lived for several years and by whom he had a daughter, Shirley Dawn. A year and a half before his death, he went through a ceremony of marriage with another woman, Yvonne Perrier, at Montreal. Perrier was living with Grey Owl when he died.

The bogus Indian was a close friend of Prince Albert lawyer A.C. March, K.C., who drew up a will for him. He divided his estate between Shirley Dawn and Yvonne Perrier, and made a modest provision for Anahareo. Grey Owl's books and lectures brought him financial success. He left an estate valued at more than $14,500, quite respectable by the standards of 1938.

Unfortunately, Grey Owl was not only an imposter but a bigamist. He left a wife and three children at Temagami, Ontario, and Samuel J. Branion, K.C., filed a claim against the estate on behalf of Angle Belaney. Angle, an Ojibwan, had married Archie Belaney in 1910 and borne three children to him. It was from Angle that Belaney first learned the native culture that enabled him to develop his later career.

Belaney left Angle in 1925. She had no further word from him, but watched his growing prominence. Angle raised their three children by, as she said, "cutting wood, picking berries in season, doing some trapping and domestic servant work as I have opportunity to obtain it."

Yvonne Perrier, to her surprise, was no longer a lawful widow, but she was still a beneficiary under Belaney's will. So was Shirley Dawn. Any allowance that might be granted to Angle Belaney would reduce their shares. Perrier, and Shirley Dawn's guardian, hired John Diefenbaker to protect their interest in Grey Owl's estate.

Angle Belaney's claim was under the Widows' Relief Act. Adultery on the part of a widow was a defence to such a claim. Diefenbaker arranged to have Angle examined under oath at North Bay, Ontario.

During that examination, Angle freely admitted that, eleven years earlier, she had given birth to a child that lived only three months. The birth, she testified, was the result of being raped by another Indian, one Charlie Potts, who attacked and overpowered her late one night as she returned to her cabin. Potts denied the story, but said that, some years after the alleged rape, he had committed adultery with Angle twice, and had paid for the service. Diefenbaker had struck pay-dirt, and with that evidence the case went to trial.

Mr. Justice P.M. Anderson, who had opposed Diefenbaker during the Bryant Charges Commission hearing, had been on the bench not yet a year in October 1939 when Branion and Diefenbaker appeared before him with their contest over Grey Owl's estate. Mr. Justice Anderson took a kindly view of Archie Belaney's great fraud: "Though somewhat of a fascinating masquerader, Grey Owl was not essentially a charlatan, but, with an instinctively histrionic bent and vision, he intuitively saw that an Indian in moccasins, clad in leather trousers and beaded leather coat, his long straight black hair in two braids, surmounted by a crown of feathers, his face highly colored with paint, would strike the imagination of the public much more impressively and would fit more harmoniously into the picture of the northern wilds than a well-dressed Englishman fitted out with the quiet but perfect clothes of a Bond Street tailor. He was par excellence a grand poseur."

The judge also looked kindly upon Angle Belaney, and did not believe Charlie Potts: "Suppose, even, that Angle Belaney did commit adultery on the occasions mentioned, it would not change the result, in my disposition of this application. Archie Belaney left his wife in 1925, promising he would return. For many years, docile, patient and pathetically faithful, she waited and expected his return. He did not communicate with her nor did he return. He forced her under great difficulties and hardships to rear and educate his three children without any assistance from him. If she went astray on a couple of occasions during those thirteen years of his continued wilful desertion and neglect while he was living in continuous adulterous relations with Anahareo and Yvonne Perrier, he was the effective cause of her erring conduct."

Mr. Justice Anderson awarded one-third of Grey Owl's estate to his deserted widow. Then he spoke kindly of John Diefenbaker, heading off any criticism for his having contested Angle Belaney's claim: "I think counsel for Shirley Dawn and Yvonne Perrier was justified in defending this issue."

As Conservative leader, John Diefenbaker contended throughout the 1938 election campaign that the Liberal government was improperly interfering in the administration of relief in the province. As a lawyer after the election, Diefenbaker became convinced that he was right, that the Liberals were granting relief on the basis of political allegiance. The biggest scandal in the history of relief administration in Saskatchewan erupted at

Wakaw. Diefenbaker was called in to defend several of those accused of participating in the fraud.

The rural municipality of Fish Creek, near Wakaw, had been victimized by the wholesale use of false and forged relief applications and orders. Julius Syroshka — son of the municipality's secretary, employed as its relief director — and William Mandryk, a local merchant, were the kingpins of the scheme. Syroshka forged approved orders for groceries which Mandryk processed. The two split the proceeds.

The fraud expanded, taking in the reeve of the municipality, several of its councillors and a large number of local farmers who had filed false relief applications. In November, the provincial government stepped in, suspended the entire municipal council and placed its affairs under an official administrator.

The government sent in William M. Rose, K.C., of Moose Jaw, as special prosecutor. Rose laid 296 charges of forgery and uttering (passing forged documents) against Mandryk, and 60 charges against Syroshka. Syroshka pleaded guilty and agreed to testify for the Crown. Mandryk retained John Diefenbaker.

Mandryk's preliminary inquiry was held in Wakaw's town hall in December 1938, before Magistrate J.E. Lussier. It ran for four days, was adjourned into January, and then ran for several more. It was the biggest legal show in the history of Wakaw. By the time it finished, 102 witnesses had testified.

Rose was trying Mandryk, but Diefenbaker was trying the Liberal government and its handling of relief administration. As he said in correspondence with the editor of the Regina *Daily Star*: "All the prosecution does in the case is bring out the evidence against Mandryk, and the record of wrong-doing so far disclosed has been brought out by myself in cross-examination...all of the evidence that is brought out is strong condemnation of the Government and its inspection system in the matter of relief and of political interference in the matter of relief."

Chagrined at having been squeezed out of the headlines during the 1938 election, Diefenbaker was careful to ensure that he did not lack publicity in the Fish Creek trial — or ever again for that matter. During this trial he gave some special assignments to E.N. (Jiggs) Davis (no relation to the T.C. Davis clan), a law student whom he had hired in September 1938. When the editor of the Regina *Daily Star* inquired about the news value of the case going on at Wakaw, Diefenbaker replied: "I think it very essential that you be represented at the preliminary hearing, but if you feel that it will be too costly, you could get full coverage from Mr. E.N. Davis from my office who has already agreed to report for the Prince Albert Daily Herald, and I have no doubt that you could make arrangements with him to forward you copy from day to day."

Julius Syroshka's testimony was the highlight of the case. He explained how he and Mandryk developed and operated their scheme of processing forged relief orders, including even a system of code phrases they used for communicating.

Diefenbaker was more interested in the larger area of Syroshka's work as Fish Creek relief director. What directions had he received from Regina, the lawyer wanted to know?

Relief officials in Regina frequently overruled him, Syroshka testified, and sometimes this resulted in increased payments to the applicants. The reeve, for example, had one child, but drew relief for eight persons. Another farmer was placed on the Fish Creek relief rolls although he lived in the next municipality. Sometimes, Syroshka stated, he was directed to give out relief and not mark it down in his books.

The headlines rolled, but William Mandryk was not pleased at the way his defence was conducted. Committed for trial, he discharged John Diefenbaker and engaged Peter Makaroff, K.C., of Saskatoon, another prominent defence counsel. Ultimately convicted, Mandryk was sentenced to thirty months imprisonment.

Karl Novosad was the proprietor of The Honey Bee Café on Prince Albert's River Street, notorious for its questionable nightlife. Above the café were seven or eight rooms which

Novosad rented out whenever he could. The rooms were not sumptuous.

In January 1939, the police raided The Honey Bee, arrested Karl Novosad and charged him with living off the avails of prostitution. Two young ladies, residents of The Honey Bee rooms, confessed that they shared the income they derived, from what was then known as "illicit activities," with the café proprietor. Their tariff was two dollars. If the customer did not pay Novosad fifty cents on the way up to the rooms, the young ladies were required to make payment directly to their landlord.

Prince Albert was scandalized. Although everyone "knew" that sort of thing went on down on River Street, it was something entirely different to read about it in the *Daily Herald*. John Diefenbaker was retained to defend Novosad. Jiggs Davis went to work on the case.

Novosad's trial came up before Mr. Justice Donald Maclean and a jury on April 19. Diefenbaker, with the help of Davis, struggled to find a defence. The two girls were only nineteen and seventeen years old. Although he strongly suggested their stories were fiction, the defence lawyer could go only so far in cross-examination without looking like a bully to the jury. In addition, there was strong corroboration from employees of The Honey Bee.

The *Daily Herald* in its coverage pointed out that both girls were white and "both white men and Chinese came to them." George M. Salter, K.C., prosecuted as if he was on to an international white slavery ring. "It is always the higher-ups who are the last to be caught," the Crown counsel told the jury, looking fiercely at the proprietor of The Honey Bee.

Diefenbaker trotted before the jury every defence he could see in the case, hoping that the six men would bite on something. "A completely manufactured tale," he opened. "You may not be able to get high class witnesses in a case like this, but you can get truthful witnesses. What is there to prevent these girls from charging the hotelkeepers of other hotels they frequent with also living on the earnings of their prostitution?"

If the jury preferred to believe the girls' testimony, then, Diefenbaker contended, the fifty-cent payment to The Honey Bee proprietor should properly be construed as rent of the room, not coming from the earnings of prostitution. Finally, the defence fell back upon eloquence.

"This is a court of law, not of morals," Diefenbaker exhorted the six men. "The accused must be tried on the charge for which he was arraigned, and not for anything else he might have done.

"When the proof is not there, the accused is entitled to your verdict of not guilty. The proof is not here," he concluded.

Nothing worked. The jury considered the matter over lunch, and came back with a verdict of guilty. Jiggs Davis felt sick. It was his first criminal jury trial.

Mr. Justice Maclean recognized his duty. After adjourning overnight to give himself time to reflect upon the case, he passed sentence. "I take a very serious view of this matter," he began. "This is too serious a matter, especially in view of the fact the accused conducted a café which the public was invited to patronize....I sentence you to three years in the penitentiary," His Lordship concluded.

Karl Novosad sucked in his breath and turned pale. Jiggs Davis nearly fainted. He had worked so hard on this case that he had come to believe passionately in Karl Novosad's innocence. Three years. Jiggs could not believe what he heard.

That was the end of the legal career of Jiggs Davis. Diefenbaker appealed their client's conviction and sentence, but Davis did not care. He decided he had no stomach for the harshness of the law. The young student resigned his articles, left Diefenbaker's employ and moved to Ontario to pursue a career in business.

The Court of Appeal rejected the Novosad appeal; conviction and sentence were confirmed. The proprietor of The Honey Bee served his time.

By 1939, John Diefenbaker had been in Prince Albert fifteen years, but he was not yet fully accepted by the community.

Rather, his fellow citizens regarded him with something akin to amused, but not unaffectionate, detachment. As is often the case with a flamboyant criminal defence attorney, Diefenbaker's trial success had not brought him complete respectability in the eyes of the city's financial and social establishment. Although his firm became more secure each year, it had not succeeded with the corporate clients solicitors seek — the banks, trust and mortgage companies.

Diefenbaker participated in Prince Albert service clubs and fraternal lodges, but seemed to encourage others to maintain a distance. During their ten years together, Edna had greatly softened his personality, but still he took himself very seriously; he was aloof and remote. As he strode down Central Avenue, stiff and formal, Diefenbaker was very much the city's pre-eminent trial counsel. There was about him none of the *bonhomie* of the hustling politician. On the street, he frequently curtly ignored even John Cuelenaere, his associate for six years.

Prince Albert did not take John Diefenbaker quite as seriously as he took himself, but accepted his air of importance as part of his somewhat quaint personality. His political activities in recent years had all been outside the city and were regarded locally as in the nature of an unusual hobby. The Conservative Party had not quite fallen to the level of a garden club, but it was an almost forgotten political force. This was particularly true in Prince Albert, where Prime Minister Mackenzie King and Attorney General T.C. Davis reigned federally and provincially as if by feudal right.

The lawyer worked hard at promoting himself. His list of clubs, service organizations and lodges is impressive: the Canadian Legion, the Kiwanis Club, the Great War Veterans' Association, the British Veterans Old Comrades of Canada Association, the Canadian Club, the Prince Albert Historical Society, the Horticultural Society, football clubs, sports clubs, the Motor Club, even something called the Saskatchewan Social Hygiene Association. He was also a loyal lodge man and belonged to the

Loyal Order of Orange, and the Elks. There was very little more that Prince Albert had to offer.

Yet, in the midst of all this activity, Diefenbaker was somehow just off-centre, like the child at the birthday party who, although present, is not quite included in the games.

In June 1939, W.B. Kelly, the president of the Lake Centre Conservative Association, was trying to organize a nominating convention. August would mark four years in office for Mackenzie King's government and an election was expected in the fall.

Ernest E. Perley, MP for Qu'Appelle, could attend on Thursday, June 15. Kelly got busy on the telephone to the other Conservative officials. He called provincial leader John Diefenbaker and found him at Humboldt, tied down by a major arson case. Diefenbaker called John Cuelenaere, who was just barely able to come down to Humboldt and fill in, while the senior counsel drove to the nominating convention in Imperial, Saskatchewan.

The 1933 federal redistribution had extended the eastern boundary of the federal Long Lake riding and changed its name to Lake Centre — an appropriate choice, as the seat lay dead in the centre of the populated southern half of Saskatchewan. Its borders were almost identical to the provincial constituency of Arm River, but Lake Centre was somewhat larger, extending southeast to take in the rural area between Regina and Moose Jaw. Like Arm River, Lake Centre had a history, almost a tradition, of non-resident Conservative candidates. Stewart Adrain, a Regina lawyer who ran twice in Arm River, represented the party in the 1925 federal election. In 1930, the seat was won for the Conservatives by Dr. Walter D. Cowan, also of Regina. It was not until 1935 that the party turned to a local candidate, Allan Peters, who lost to Liberal John Frederick Johnston.

Lake Centre had inherited a Ku Klux Klan presence from the 1928 Arm River by-election. Cowan was the Saskatchewan treasurer of the Klan and W.B. Kelly, who called the 1939 nominating convention, was the Kligrapp (local president) of the Klan organized at Imperial.

The Lake Centre Conservatives were considering nominating another non-resident in 1939, even before John Diefenbaker arrived in Imperial on June 15. Three Regina residents attended the meeting: Franklin W. Turnbull, K.C., a former MP; Claude Burrows, K.C.; and Cliff Thurston. All were interested in the nomination. So were George Haggerty and Charles Harlton, both of Belle Plaine at the southern reach of the seat, and W.B. Kelly, the meeting organizer.

All six allowed their names to go into nomination. So did John Diefenbaker. Everyone briefly addressed the meeting, but then all but Diefenbaker withdrew. The Conservative leader, who had harboured no such plans when he left Humboldt, became his party's candidate for the fifth time.

Two weeks later, T.C. Davis resigned as attorney general and MLA for Prince Albert in favour of a seat on the Saskatchewan Court of Appeal. The man who stood between John Diefenbaker and political power in Prince Albert had stepped down. The way was open. Could the leader of the Conservative Party in Saskatchewan, resident in Prince Albert, fail to contest the up-coming by-election and maintain political credibility? The mission was suicidal. After the 1938 election, it was clear that Conservatives could not be elected at the provincial level, not yet.

Diefenbaker was saved from the decision by the accident of the Lake Centre nomination. He was committed, and unavailable to run in Prince Albert.

Two months after Davis's resignation, on September 1, 1939, Adolf Hitler invaded Poland. On September 3, Britain and France formally declared war upon Germany. Seven days later, Canada followed. The world was in conflict.

On September 18, a week after Canada's declaration of war against Germany, RCMP Constable Phil Hughes and a companion were hunting grouse near Cookson, north of Prince Albert. A woman, dressed only in a slip, approached the two men. Her husband, she said, had shot himself.

Henry Emele was lying in his farmyard in a pool of blood. "Who's responsible for this?" Hughes asked.

"She gave me the works," Emele replied.

"Who is 'she'?"

"My wife."

Henry Emele died in Hughes's car on the way to the hospital. Isobel Emele was charged with his murder. She called John Diefenbaker.

Russ Brownridge had joined Diefenbaker and Cuelenaere on September 1 as an articling student. He was assigned to sit down with Mrs. Emele and take a written statement of what happened.

Brownridge took Isobel Emele's version of what had happened in the farmyard to John Diefenbaker. When the firm's senior counsel finished reading, he smiled.

"I shouldn't have much trouble crying our way out of this," he told Brownridge.

15

Rex v. Isobel Emele: The First Trial

Isobel and Henry Emele's fifteen-year marriage had gone bad almost from the beginning. They had not slept together for more than ten years. Henry had been twice convicted of assaulting his wife, but, after she left him for a time eight years before, he had not again struck her. They lived in constant tension on Emele's one-section bush farm beside the Prince Albert National Park, sixty miles north of the city.

Since the rise of Adolf Hitler their relationship had worsened, if that was possible. Henry, born in North Dakota of German parentage, was a fan of the Nazi chancellor. Isobel, a fiery immigrant from Northern Ireland, was a champion of the British Empire. When Hitler invaded Poland, Emele was elated. England, and then Canada, would be next, he said. "Hitler will run this country and you'll learn to like it," Emele threatened his wife.

E.J. DesRosiers, still in the Prince Albert RCMP detachment, but now with the rank of detective-sergeant, did not get out to the Emele farm until late in the afternoon of Monday, September 18, 1939. Other members of the detachment were already combing for clues, and Constable Buchanan was taking a statement from Isobel Emele.

Emele must have committed suicide, Isobel said. "I believe my husband to be insane. He has been acting very queer lately for about a year or more and has gradually been getting worse."

The farm wife claimed she had been working in the kitchen just before noon when she heard Emele on the outside step. Then she heard a shot. Frightened, she hesitated a moment, then panicked and ran out the kitchen door and across the yard and road to a neighbour's home. As she went down the kitchen steps, she saw Emele with a gun in his hands. He was wobbly on his legs but she did not notice any blood.

The neighbours were not at home. The terrified woman, clad only in her slip, ran up the road where she found the grouse-hunting Constable Phil Hughes.

Emele must have been delirious when he claimed she had shot him, Isobel said. "All I can say is that my husband shot himself — I certainly didn't do it."

DesRosiers and his men were unable to locate a firearm anywhere near where Emele had collapsed. They spotted blood on the walk leading to the kitchen steps and dug up a couple of stained flagstones for evidence. DesRosiers detailed two men to stay all night at the Emele farm. "Keep an eye on her," he ordered.

The next day the police took Isobel to Prince Albert. She would have to identify Emele's body, they explained. Isobel told them she would like to talk to John Diefenbaker. "As soon as we get through at the morgue," she was promised.

But that promise was not kept. After viewing her late husband's remains, Isobel was driven straight back to her farm home. The police continued to keep a close eye on the widow. A neighbour woman was brought in, "as a matron," they later admitted. Isobel's four children were taken to a nearby farm. She was alone, and almost a prisoner in her own home.

By the morning of the third day, Isobel was an emotional wreck. She then confessed to Buchanan and DesRosiers that she had killed Emele.

Relations between the two had been unusually strained for two or three days, she now told them. Emele, a notorious tightwad, refused to allow his wife to hire a girl to help with the harvest crew expected soon, and — as he so often did — stopped speaking to her. A burst of misery flooded Isobel. On sudden impulse, when she heard him on the step, she seized the rifle from behind the kitchen door, poked it through a hole in the door, and fired. She showed DesRosiers where she had thrown the gun, a .30 calibre Remington.

The hole in the door had been caused by the removal of the lock. The police tested it with the Remington and found that it was not quite large enough to enable the muzzle to pass completely through. DesRosiers examined the hole. The outer rim was stained with a black smudge. He cut out the door panel and sent it down to Regina for examination. According to DesRosiers' measurements, the hole was exactly forty-five and three-eighths inches above the top of the floor. It coincided with the hole in the right side of Henry Emele's chest.

By the time Isobel Emele made contact with John Diefenbaker, DesRosiers had what seemed to be an airtight case.

The Emele case came to Diefenbaker at an extremely busy and crucial time in his career. He had a heavy trial schedule, and he needed to get organized in Lake Centre. There was also the problem of the Prince Albert by-election brought about by the resignation of T.C. Davis; in the end, neither the Conservatives nor the Social Credit fielded a candidate, leaving Liberal Harold J. Fraser, who had defeated Diefenbaker for the Prince Albert mayoralty in 1933, to succeed to Davis's seat by acclamation. John Cuelenaere was brought in to help with the Emele defence.

Isobel Emele's preliminary inquiry began on October 6 and, after an adjournment in November, was completed on December 5 when she was committed for trial at the February 1940 King's Bench sittings at Prince Albert.

On January 25, 1940, Mackenzie King unexpectedly called an election. The vote would take place on March 26, 1940. John Diefenbaker was in another election campaign.

The Conservative candidate for Lake Centre was trapped. He was booked before the Supreme Court, his first appearance in that court, on February 6, and he would just be able to get back from Ottawa in time for the Emele trial a week later, on February

13. The first half of the two-month campaign period was shot. There was nothing else to do; Diefenbaker carried on.

When the Emele case opened, the first item to be dealt with was the appointment of counsel for the accused. Isobel was without funds and the court appointment would authorize a very modest fee to be paid by the government. It was a version of our present-day legal aid system. The trial judge, Mr. Justice P.M. Anderson, took judicial notice of the election in which Diefenbaker was a candidate: "I am appointing you and Mr. Cuelenaere in case one of you are called away, and that will enable one to carry on, so I appoint you and Mr. Cuelenaere, and probably when I come to fix the fee, I will consider it as one."

As the trial of Isobel Emele began, the world was waiting for Adolf Hitler and Nazi Germany to launch the second phase of the war. Mobilization was under way and 90,000 Canadians were already on active military service. That same day, Associated Press reported: "Upwards of 700 Jews, routed from their homes in Stettin on 6 1/2 hours notice for mass removal, were on trains today, presumably headed for Poland, although their exact destination was undisclosed." The Holocaust had begun.

What caused John Diefenbaker to smile when he read articling student Russ Brownridge's account of their client's story was the statement that Henry Emele was not only a Nazi sympathizer, but an organizer for the German *Bund*, a Nazi support group. The Crown could try Isobel Emele if it liked; Diefenbaker would try Henry Emele, the deceased Hitler-lover.

He began with the first witness Crown Attorney George Salter put on the stand, fifteen-year-old Dorothy Emele, Henry and Isobel's daughter. When Dorothy had testified in the fall, she had quickly admitted her father's pro-Nazi sentiments and activities and the defence lawyer had brought this out in detail. Over the winter, the girl became sympathetic to her deceased father, and Diefenbaker had to take her back time after time to her earlier evidence. Slowly, painstakingly, he built before the jury the image of an autocratic, miserly bully who gloried in the conquests of Adolf Hitler.

Dorothy reluctantly admitted that, when her mother needed clothes, Emele bought her four fifty-cent dresses. Isobel's only coat was the one she brought from Ireland sixteen years before.

"And in order to make some money your mother made butter and sold butter?"

"Yes."

"Is it not a fact that the groceries that were got in to supply the threshing gang were bought with the money your mother made out of the butter?"

"Yes."

"Now, did your dad tell your mother when Hitler got control she would be shown her place?"

"He said when Hitler gets control he will show the people on relief and didn't work. He would show them their places."

When Salter re-examined, Mr. Justice Anderson commented: "I notice, Dorothy, that you answer a lot faster for Mr. Salter than for Mr. Diefenbaker."

But Diefenbaker had what he needed.

The second thrust of the defence was to knock out Isobel Emele's confession on the grounds that it had not been voluntarily given. Diefenbaker and Cuelenaere contended that the police, by refusing her request to see her lawyer and by moving into her home, had subjected their client "to a subtle third-degree" designed "to break her down."

Cuelenaere cross-examined RCMP Constable John Kerr, who had been at the Emele home throughout the investigation. Kerr, like Dorothy Emele, was less frank than he had been at the preliminary and, again, the earlier thoroughness paid off. Cuelenaere reminded the policeman of his testimony the previous fall.

"So you and Constable Buchanan remained there on guard overnight, that is a fair enough statement?"

"Yes, that is fair enough."

"It would be fair enough to say there was an eye kept on her all the time?"

"Yes, sure."

The defence had another problem, the matter of the accusations made by the dying Henry Emele that his wife had shot him. Constable Hughes, whose grouse-hunt had been interrupted by the killing, took the stand to tell of the deceased's last words. The jury was sent out while Diefenbaker and Salter argued the admissibility of those statements.

"She gave me the works," Emele had said.

"Who is 'she'?"

"My wife."

Later, Emele had elaborated.

"I was out digging potatoes, went in for dinner. The door was fastened on the inside. She said: 'wait a minute' and she shot me through the door."

Isobel was present as her dying husband spoke.

"He is out of his mind. He does not know what he is saying," she protested.

The rule against hearsay evidence excluded Hughes's testimony about Emele's last words unless they could be brought within one of the many exceptions. Mr. Justice Anderson accepted John Diefenbaker's submission that the rule prevailed.

"The only way in which it might be admissible would be as an indirect admission of the accused. The accused must practically have accepted that as her admission, or, in substance, that she admitted it," the trial judge explained. "In my opinion, the accused did not accept these statements that were alleged to have been made. In fact, she contradicted them. I have no hesitation in saying, so far as I am concerned, these statements are not admissible."

Henry Emele was not allowed to speak to the jury from the grave. George Salter recorded an objection to the ruling.

Clear of that hurdle, Diefenbaker went after Constable Hughes about the confession Isobel Emele had given. The lawyer was blunt.

"Do you stick yourself in people's houses and make yourself a self-invited guest when making investigations?" he demanded.

"In certain cases I would."

"You were instructed to stay around the placc and keep it under observation?"

"Yes, and continue investigation."

"And keep her under observation."

"Yes."

"And if she had endeavoured to leave the place, you would have stopped her?"

"I think possibly I would have."

"So that you will agree with me now, Constable, that, although no charge had been laid against this woman on Monday or Tuesday, she was not a free agent to go where she pleased."

"During the time I was watching her, no."

Then Diefenbaker tackled the policeman for refusing Isobel's request to see a lawyer.

"On the 19th of September, didn't she ask you and tell you she wanted to see Mr. Diefenbaker?"

"She said she wanted to see Mr. Diefenbaker."

"Did you give her an opportunity to see the solicitor?"

"No."

"And it is a rule in the RCMP that, when a request is made to a police officer on investigation, asking for a solicitor, that that information is passed on to his superior?"

"Well, they are given opportunities to communicate with a solicitor if they ask for it."

"And, during your experience as a constable, in your own personal case, any time an accused asked for a solicitor he has got a solicitor?"

"Yes."

The police refusal of Isobel Emele's request to see her lawyer was fatal to the confession they had won from her. Diefenbaker summed up for Mr. Justice Anderson the position his client had been in:

"I will just point out a few of the surrounding circumstances that are striking. The police officers come into this woman's home and occupy a portion of her house. Her children are removed from her, they are not there. She is placed in charge of a matron. All through she had a tight surveillance around her. If she attempted to leave, she would have been followed.

"Here is this woman alone with police officers and a matron, five police officers from time to time, two overnight. Then they bring her into Prince Albert, on official request. She asks for a lawyer. She is told, 'After you have viewed the body.' She is taken then over to the morgue, down to the morgue in the basement, and sees the body of her husband.

"What was she taken there for? It wasn't identification. She wasn't told. She is then taken away and she is taken back to her home, and the children are not there. She is alone among strangers, and she goes out to feed the hogs, the police officers are along, every moment is under surveillance. Everything she does is under the eye of the law.

"We know she was tired, and she had been through a very horrible experience with her husband when he was still conscious.

"After she has again asked for a lawyer, she is left alone without an opportunity to do what she had a right to do, to communicate with her solicitor. She finally says to a police officer, 'I just do not know what to do. I want to do what is best for the children'...."

Mr. Justice Anderson interrupted. He had heard enough.

"Mr. Diefenbaker, in my opinion, so far as any confession is concerned after Mr. Diefenbaker was asked to come, I am of the opinion that anything after that is not admissible for the reasons you have mentioned here.

"It is important, as everyone knows, that she be given the full rights of defence, and what counsel would have told her would be: Don't under any circumstances give or sign any confession of any kind. That would be one of the first things the defence counsel would tell her, and I am not going to let any confession in after Mr. Diefenbaker was asked to be got in touch with so that she could have the benefit of his advice.

"I hope I am right in my decision, but if I am wrong there will have to be a new trial in this case, but that seems to me to be the correct decision."

From the defence point of view, the case could not be going better. There remained, however, two major elements of serious concern to Diefenbaker. First he questioned Sergeant DesRosiers about his measurements of the Emele kitchen door.

"Could you tell the court the distance of the doorknob down to the platform?"

"No."

"Did you yourself experiment with the opening of the door? Did you try the handle?"

"I do not think I did."

"So that you would not be able to tell us the position a person's body would be in in bending forward to turn the knob on the outside?"

"That is correct."

It would not be apparent until later what the defence was up to with this admission.

Dr. Frances McGill, the provincial pathologist, had performed the autopsy on Henry Emele's body. While she was on the stand, George Salter tried to head off a defence he suspected might be coming forward.

"Now, did you form any opinion from your examination of this man, taking his size into consideration, whether or not that wound could be self-inflicted by holding the rifle...?"

"I object to that, My Lord," Diefenbaker interjected, "as she is not an expert in gunnery."

Mr. Justice Anderson allowed the question, and Dr. McGill responded.

"Personally, I do not think it could be self-inflicted — that the gun could be held without touching the body and without a contact wound."

Salter tried to press his advantage.

"Well, then, having regard to the distance from the end of the barrel to the trigger of the rifle...." Diefenbaker was on his feet again.

"That is just what I am objecting to. That is a matter for the jury to conclude upon, and not a matter for a medical practitioner, however proficient they may be."

This time the trial judge sided with the defence. Salter went no further with that line.

Diefenbaker had some questions for Dr. McGill.

"By the way, Doctor, in regard to the question of powder burns, this is perfectly clear, isn't it: that in view of the fact that the clothing surrounding the wound was saturated with blood, that even if there had been powder burns, they might very well not have been ascertained?"

"I think that is possible."

That was not quite good enough for Diefenbaker and again he referred to the preliminary transcript. He read a portion of Dr. McGill's testimony to her.

"'The whole region is stained with blood so it is impossible to say whether there were any powder burns.' That is correct?"

"That is correct."

Now the defence was able to tackle its second area of concern. Diefenbaker was interested in another feature of Dr. McGill's examination, the angle taken by the bullet as it passed through Emele's body.

"And it went inwards and downwards?" Diefenbaker asked.

"And backwards. It went backwards towards the back of the body to the left. It was only three inches from the midline at the back, and eight inches from the line, and slightly downwards — an inch and an eighth down."

"The declivity was an inch and an eighth?"

"Yes."

When Dr. McGill stepped down, court adjourned for the fourth day of the trial. Rex v. Emele had opened on Tuesday, February 13, and now moved into Saturday, February 17, its last day. Out of respect for the funeral of the Governor-General, Lord

Tweedsmuir, in Ottawa on February 14, Mr. Justice Anderson delayed opening that afternoon session until 3:30. Two witnesses remained to be heard on Saturday.

James Churchman was the RCMP ballistics expert. He had performed some experiments firing the .30 Remington through holes in wood similar to the one in the Emele kitchen door. The result was a smudged area matching the one on the Emele door. Churchman explained that the smudge was caused by "the gases leaving the muzzle and coming in contact with the wood after the bullet has passed out."

Churchman had also examined Emele's shirt and the bullet hole in the front. Salter tried again to head off any suggestion of a self-inflicted wound.

"Could you tell whether or not that hole was made as a result of a contact bullet or not?"

"That is not a contact bullet hole of entrance. A contact hole would show evidence of tearing, it would be larger than this hole and quite ragged."

Diefenbaker and Churchman had wrestled at the preliminary and the expert had conceded the points that were important to the defence. In cross-examination, Diefenbaker swiftly reminded the witness of the limits of his findings.

"It is correct, isn't it, that you cannot swear that the shot went through Exhibit P-14 [the Emele door]?"

"That is correct."

"All you were able to find were some nitrates?"

"Yes."

"And nitrates could be there as a result of the door having laid [sic] on the ground, that is correct?"

"Yes."

"Or from being where manure was?"

"That is correct."

Mrs. Mary Morris had been a friend and neighbour to Isobel Emele ever since the accused woman had arrived in Canada from Ireland. At noon on the Wednesday, two days after the shooting of Emele, Mary Morris had visited the Emele farm at Isobel's request. Isobel had just confessed to the murder of her husband, was under arrest and on her way to Prince Albert.

"I killed him. I know I shouldn't have done it, but I'm not sorry," Isobel told her friend.

Now Mary Morris stood in the witness box, ready to repeat that conversation to the jury. Diefenbaker and Cuelenaere had their objection and argument ready. This was the last critical hurdle they faced in the evidence.

Mr. Justice Anderson had ruled out the confession Isobel Emele had given the police on the grounds that its voluntary nature had not been established. In criminal cases there is a concern that an accused might concoct a confession to a policeman, or a person in authority, to escape improper pressure. But Mary Morris was not a person in authority. Why would Isobel's comment to her friend not be admissible, Mr. Justice Anderson wanted to know?

Because, Diefenbaker, argued: "the police officers were still on the premises...this is a continuing transaction. Unless the Crown can show that the circumstances which actuated the accused in giving the first statement, the involuntariness of that statement, had been removed from the mind of the accused."

"My learned friend's argument is wrong," protested George Salter. "Everyone knows Mrs. Morris wasn't a person in authority."

Diefenbaker and Cuelenaere had come up with an ingenious argument, and it worked. Mr. Justice Anderson was still critical of the police for refusing Isobel's request for a lawyer and "that same condition of affairs prevailed."

"I haven't got a case exactly on this point, but I prefer to err on the side of the accused, and I refuse to allow the statement in," Anderson ruled.

Again Salter recorded his objection. But John Diefenbaker had won the third crucial debate over the admissibility of evidence highly prejudicial to his client. It was time to put what was left of the Crown's case to the jury.

It was nearly four o'clock Saturday afternoon when George Salter rose to address the jury. A prosecutor in the great tradition of high-minded fairness, he carefully reviewed the evidence he had succeeded in placing before the jury.

Only two people, he stressed, were known to have been on the Emele farm the morning of the shooting, after the children left for school. "Henry Emele," Salter charged, "had been coming home for lunch. Instead of food, he received a bullet in the chest from a rifle fired through a hole in the kitchen door."

The prosecutor cautioned the jury about speculating that Emele might have committed suicide. "Emele was not a tall man," he pointed out, "Dr. McGill's measurements showed that he was but five feet, seven and one-quarter inches in height. It would have been impossible for him to have turned the rifle upon himself."

Physical and mental stamina are essential requirements for criminal defence work and John Diefenbaker, although never robust, was well supplied with both. At 5:00 p.m. he rose from his place at the counsel table and approached the jury box. Fully alert, his voice charged with dedicated purpose, it was his eyes that commanded the attention of the six listening men as they fixed each one in turn.

Seizing the .30 calibre Remington from among the exhibits, Diefenbaker challenged Salter's contention that Henry Emele could not have turned that weapon upon himself. Holding it at arm's length, the lawyer reversed the rifle, pointing it at his own chest, as he demonstrated how suicide could have been accomplished.

"Never mind how tall Henry Emele was. The length of the arms is what counts. And," he correctly pointed out, "there is no evidence before this court as to the length of that man's arms.

"If Mrs. Emele committed murder, she must have handled this gun," he continued, waving the rifle at the jury. "And if she handled this gun, where are the fingerprints the police found on this gun?" Diefenbaker's voice rose to a cry as he completed the question. Again he had correctly pointed out a gap in the evidence. Nothing had been said about fingerprints.

The defence counsel then swung into his standardized description of reasonable doubt and the onus of proof that lay with the Crown. "It is not the duty of the defence to prove anything in this case — nothing. The onus is upon the Crown to prove murder. They have not proved one thing that can tie the accused up with the death of her husband."

The reason for Diefenbaker's concern with the door measurements and the angle of the bullet wound now became apparent. Had the shot come through the hole in the door, he argued, the rifle barrel must have been at right angle to that door. If it had been pointed down to produce the bullet path that had been proven, the bullet would have struck the outer rim of the hole. Henry Emele, the defence contended, had not been shot upon the kitchen step, but somewhere else, probably on the walk leading to the steps. And, if that was so, he could not have been shot by Isobel Emele, as the Crown contended.

Diefenbaker reviewed the evidence of the morning's activities on the Emele farm.

"On the morning of the shooting, Mrs. Emele hauled water for the morning wash. She took off the dress she was wearing to put in that wash. She prepared grouse and cooked them for dinner for her husband and herself. And she laid places for two at the kitchen table.

"That," he declared, swinging his eyes from man to man across the jury box, "does not look like premeditated murder to me."

Mr. Justice Anderson followed right along. Without even a short adjournment, he proceeded to charge the jury although it was after 6:00 p.m.

In his charge, Anderson raised two aspects of the case that had escaped Diefenbaker and Cuelenaere. Respecting the smudge in the hole in the door, which the Crown contended had been caused by a gunshot, Anderson pointed out: "There is no evidence that showed when that smudge was put in the old piece of wood, whether it was there two months ago, or six months ago, or eight months ago, or whether it was recent or not."

Then the trial judge injected another possible theory into the case: "There is no evidence that anyone thought there was some other man around, but, after all, who saw the accused shoot, and might there have been another man around? This deceased evidently was a quarrelsome man."

The jury foreman did not think it would take long to settle their end of the case. Shortly after 7:00 p.m., when Mr. Justice Anderson concluded, he asked: "Would you like to have your dinner first, gentlemen of the jury?"

"Give us five minutes, and if we haven't come to a decision, we will go to dinner," the foreman replied.

As it turned out, more than five minutes was required, but not a great deal more. After dinner, at 9:00 p.m., the jury came back with a question. Had the rifle been loaded when it was found? No one knew. The evidence was searched out. It had been loaded; a live round was in the chamber.

That was all the jury needed. This time they were back in five minutes. Verdict: "Not Guilty."

The courtroom was filled with loud applause from the crowd that had awaited the jury's return. "Unprecedented," court officials called the outburst.

Isobel Emele had been in custody since her arrest on September 20. The strain of the trial had been too much for her. She thanked Diefenbaker and Cuelenaere, hugged her children briefly, and then was whisked away for medical attention.

The Conservative candidate for Lake Centre took off his gown. On Monday morning he was in his constituency.

16

From Courtroom to Commons

John Diefenbaker was not the only candidate trapped by the suddenness of the 1940 election. Prime Minister Mackenzie King had sandbagged the entire Conservative Party, all of Parliament in fact, with a snap election.

The previous fall, King had promised another session of Parliament. Instead, within a few hours of the opening of the session on January 25, he called for dissolution and went to the country. Conservative leader Robert Manion called King's move "an act of autocracy."

Diefenbaker found himself running as a "National Government" candidate. The Conservatives, in an attempted replay of Prime Minister Borden's Union government of 1917, were promoting a scheme for a coalition government to prosecute the war. As things turned out, Manion was no Borden, and 1940 was not 1917.

When the Prince Albert lawyer was finally free to take part in the campaign only five weeks were left in the election. But he had a natural advantage in Lake Centre that more than offset the time loss.

Diefenbaker had waged an effective campaign in Arm River just two years earlier, and Arm River made up almost two-thirds of the federal seat. The dormant election organization was easily restructured and put to work. More important, John Diefenbaker had a high profile in the constituency, and needed very little introduction. His highly-publicized victory in the Emele case was more valuable than expensive campaign advertising.

The countryside in which John Diefenbaker campaigned in 1940 was, although the same geographically, very much different from that of 1938. The drought had broken and the Dirty Thirties were over. The crop of 1939 was the best since 1928. Stubborn hope was replaced by still timorous confidence. Nature began to repair the ravages of the duststorms.

But the effects of the Depression remained for years. Saskatchewan farms staggered under a stupendous burden of debt. Prince Albert, after finessing its way through the fiscal nightmare of the 1930s, defaulted upon its debenture indebtedness in 1940. Moose Jaw, in default since 1937, took years to recover.

The emotional scars borne by those who suffered the slow, grinding misery of the Saskatchewan Depression remain even today. John Diefenbaker escaped personal financial crisis, but he, too, carried wounds upon his soul. As he campaigned in 1940, the lawyer discovered that he possessed a special rapport with the other survivors of the bleak decade.

Edna Diefenbaker was the Lake Centre candidate's greatest asset on the hustings. It was still her warm and friendly way, her memory for names and faces, that made a success of their personal campaigning. For his part, the candidate by now needed little advice on how to conduct himself on a platform.

Mackenzie King's nomination as the Liberal candidate in Prince Albert at the end of February 1940 was a civic celebration, a "homecoming" that Diefenbaker, campaigning in Lake Centre, could not help but notice. Special trains brought the faithful in from all over northern Saskatchewan. The prime minister told his constituents he was sorry that affairs of state had prevented him from visiting his riding since the 1935 election and spoke proudly of his government's war effort.

The Lake Centre Conservative candidate added some planks of his own to the Conservative Party's National Government platform. They were specially tailored to the western farm vote.

"We intend to enact legislation to raise the price of your [farmers'] produce at least 40 per cent," Diefenbaker announced at a meeting in his riding. "The farmers today pay too much for what they buy in proportion to the price paid to them for their produce. We intend to equalize prices and give the farmers a break."

Radio was used extensively in the 1940 election and Diefenbaker, as Saskatchewan Conservative leader, was selected to represent the party in a fifteen-minute CBC national broadcast. Speaking from Prince Albert, he returned to some of the themes he had used in his 1925 and 1926 campaigns.

"The Liberals," Diefenbaker charged, "are waging a cruel campaign. They are engaged in the work of putting race against race, class against class. They are spreading propaganda among western Canadians of central European origin that a vote for Robert Manion will mean their oaths of allegiance and naturalization papers will be made scraps of paper."

The use of wartime censorship by the King government, he went on, "is displaying a marked tendency towards dictatorship. Dictatorship is founded upon the principle that people shall only be allowed information which the government considers is good for the people to know."

Diefenbaker strongly attacked the CCF for its pacifist policy. He ran a prominent advertisement that quoted CCF leaders M.J. Coldwell and J.S. Woodsworth, who were encouraging Canadian youth to avoid enlisting. The ad concluded: "In the interest of Canada, you should not vote CCF. If you vote CCF you are doing your part to elect the Liberal candidate."

In Lake Centre, Liberal John F. Johnston, in a radio address, accused his Conservative opponent of being a conscript in the First World War. Diefenbaker angrily replied and felt that Johnston's false accusation helped his campaign.

In 1935 the Conservatives, under R.B. Bennett, had been soundly defeated, winning only 39 seats to the Liberals' 178. Only three of their seats were on the Prairies, one each in Saskatchewan, Alberta and Manitoba. Something of a comeback in 1940 was a reasonable minimum expectation.

It was not to be. The Canadian voters saw nothing in Robert Manion to attract them away from the dull but businesslike government of Mackenzie King. On election day, March 26, a late spring blizzard swept across Saskatchewan. Roads drifted over and that night voting returns were slow. When the votes were counted across Canada, hardly a seat had changed hands. The Conservatives still had thirty-nine seats in total, still twenty-five in Ontario, still three on the Prairies.

In Lake Centre, final returns were held up by the weather. John and Edna Diefenbaker waited out the results at home in Prince Albert, joined by a few friends and law partner John Cuelenaere. They eagerly totalled the poll counts telephoned to them by the Conservative organization in the riding.

At midnight, their figures gave John Diefenbaker a small lead, about 150 votes, but the reports from several polls were missing. Nothing was conclusive, and no final tabulations could be had. The radio reports ignored Lake Centre. Returning offices and committee rooms closed for the night. The election was over, and John Diefenbaker could not find out if he had won or lost.

Finally, John Cuelenaere, an active Liberal, telephoned his party's offices in Regina. The Liberal organization could be counted on to have up-to-the-minute and accurate election tallies. They did, and confirmed that Lake Centre was lost to the Liberals.

John Diefenbaker won. By just 280 votes out of more than 16,000 cast, Lake Centre elected John Diefenbaker to join Saskatchewan's other Conservative MP, Ernest E. Perley of Qu'-Appelle.

Before Diefenbaker took his seat in the House of Commons, he had an acquittal to defend. On March 8, the Crown filed an appeal in the Emele case, its argument being that Mr. Justice Anderson had erred in rejecting the accused's confession to the police and her admission to Mary Morris. The case came before the Court of Appeal on May 6. Herbert Sampson and George Salter appeared for the Crown. Diefenbaker and Cuelenaere, for the defence, repeated the arguments they had used so successfully at trial.

The four appellate judges disagreed with Mr. Justice Anderson. The failure of the police to grant Mrs. Emele's request to see a lawyer was not, in their view, fatal to the voluntary nature of her confession. It was, they said, "but one of a number of circumstances requiring consideration in determining that question."

The appeal court was more firm respecting the conversation between Isobel Emele and Mary Morris:

"We are clearly of the opinion that the ruling rejecting the statement made by the respondent to Mrs. Morris was erroneous," the judgement went on, "and consequently there must be a new trial."

The appeal decision came down on June 1, 1940. Isobel Emele was again arrested and placed in jail to await her new trial. That would not be until the fall jury sittings in Prince Albert.

By October 15, 1940, when Isobel Emele again came to trial, the Second World War had been raging for more than a year. The United States had not yet entered the war, and England and her European allies recoiled desperately as German armies conquered almost at will. The Battle of Britain, Hitler's attempt to secure air supremacy preparatory to his invasion of England, had been underway for two months. Anti-German feelings, already high, were inflamed by patriotic propaganda.

Mr. Justice Donald Maclean, a veteran of eighteen years service on the bench, had been assigned to the case. Always a "no-nonsense" trial judge, Maclean was determined to ensure that Isobel Emele was tried according to law, not prejudice, however patriotic.

Passion entered the case from the opening moments. The shock of her re-arrest and incarceration and the prospect of another trial had nearly destroyed the accused woman's emotional stability. On the arm of a police matron, she entered the courtroom sobbing uncontrollably, in full view of the entire panel from which her jury would be selected.

The murder indictment was read to Mrs. Emele, and the clerk of the court continued with the required ritual.

"How say you?" he asked, "Are you guilty, or not guilty?"

"Pardon?" the poor woman replied.

"How say you? Are you guilty or not guilty?"

"Not guilty," she managed, and the trial was underway.

Salter changed the order of his witnesses from the first trial, perhaps hoping to minimize the emotional features of the case. He began with his police evidence. Dorothy Emele would testify last.

Isobel Emele's confession went into evidence quickly. Mr. Justice Maclean, following the Court of Appeal, saw nothing significant in the police refusal to let her speak to her lawyer.

Fortunately, Isobel had been loquacious when she had given her statement to Constable Buchanan, and he dutifully wrote down all she said. Her comments covered several pages.

"I looked thru the hole in the door and saw my husband was quite close to the kitchen door. After pointing the rifle in the general direction of where I saw him close to the kitchen door — I pulled the trigger of the rifle and it fired.

"After I fired the rifle I opened the kitchen door and noticed my Husband Henry staggering on his feet and slightly bent over...I ran."

After describing the shooting, Isobel went on: "The first two years of our married life was not to [sic] bad and Henry and I got along pretty good....

"After the second year it has been like living a continual hell with my husband Henry; he has been unreasonable, bad tempered and spiteful and is jealous of all the neighbours."

Isobel had been beaten by her husband.

"I forget when these things happened there were so many of them, meaning that he, my husband Henry abused me so much. On one occasion my husband threw a claw hammer at me and hit me on the side of my body."

Then the Ulsterwoman continued into the story that had first caused John Diefenbaker to smile.

"And to top it all recently, within the last few months he has been upholding Hitler strongly and generally he is in favour of

Nazi Germany. You see I am very British and very proud of it and I cannot bear to hear anyone run down our Country and uphold such a man as Hitler and his Nazism. We have had a number of quarrels about this and when he loses his temper he picks up the first thing that comes to his hand and strikes me with it.

"My Husband Henry Emele has been very queer lately and has frightened me, the way he talks to himself, and gestures to himself as if he was talking to someone, when no one has been around and has been this way for about two years and gradually getting worse and by his attitude and manner I have been afraid he was going to kill me and the children.

"I felt very badly this morning of the 18th September 1939 as I had my Menstrual Period — and felt very low, and combined with the disappointment of not being allowed to have a girl to assist me during threshing and continuous living with my Husband in misery, and all what I have stood for during the last 13 years made me decide on the spur of the moment just as I heard my Husband Henry approach the kitchen door, to shoot him...."

The jury would likely agree that Henry Emele had not been a man who would be much missed, but murder is murder. With that statement in evidence, Diefenbaker and Cuelenaere had a very different case on their hands than the first time around.

More critical evidence was yet to come. Mr. Justice Maclean agreed with Mr. Justice Anderson's exclusion of Henry Emele's last words, so the second jury, too, would not hear of that accusation. But, the Court of Appeal had also approved the admission Isobel Emele had made to Mary Morris: "I killed him. I shouldn't have done it, but I'm not sorry."

John Diefenbaker was ready for Mary Morris, a long-time friend of his client. He attacked her credibility.

"I put it to you," the lawyer accused, "that at the trial in February you expressly stated that Isobel Emele 'should hang by the neck'?"

"I did not," was the vehement denial.

"Did you not, in this courtroom, in the presence of a number of ladies, and Dorothy Emele, state, in these words, 'We'll hang her, won't we, Dorothy'?"

Mary Morris was apoplectic, but John Diefenbaker was relentless.

"Do you deny that, in conversation with one Alex Steiger, you stated, 'It's a damn shame that the law should be like that. She should hang by the neck'?"

"I certainly do. I don't even know an Alex Steiger."

Diefenbaker turned from the witness towards the frozen audience. He gestured at a man seated in the crowd. The man stood.

"Do you deny knowing this man?" The lawyer whirled back to Mary Morris, his long arm pointing at her like a rapier.

"I do. I don't know that man." But her repudiation was somehow not quite equal to the dramatic accusation. A question remained in the minds of the listeners.

When Dorothy Emele was called, Mr. Justice Maclean made a suggestion that would have sunk the defence. The judge had read the transcript of the evidence given at the first trial.

"I don't think it should be necessary to hear this girl," the trial judge said. "I can't see where her testimony will produce anything relevant to the case."

Diefenbaker and Cuelenaere were thunderstruck. Only from Dorothy could they get before the jury the full story of Emele's miserable character and pro-Nazi sympathies, unless they put Isobel in the stand. To call their client would certainly be fatal.

Maclean was probably technically correct. The evidence the defence needed from Dorothy was not related to the charge, but it was vital to their case. The judge's proposal came close to being an unwarranted interference with counsel's conduct of the trial. Salter was quite willing to call the girl.

Diefenbaker rose to his feet, thinking quickly. He needed a reason for Dorothy to be on the stand that he could justify on legal grounds. He could not rely upon his real reasons.

"Provocation, My Lord. Part of the defence is that the accused was so provoked by the conduct of the deceased and his treatment of her, that she acted in the heat of passion. The defence requires the opportunity to cross-examine the girl on the conditions in the Emele home that might have contributed to the emotional state of the accused."

It worked. Maclean relented and Dorothy Emele took the stand.

Isobel's daughter had changed her attitude since the first trial. She was no longer reticent and unco-operative, but willing and frank as she described the tension between her parents and its causes.

The witness's mother, in the prisoner's dock, wept silently as Dorothy testified.

The jury listened intently as John Diefenbaker brought out the story of Henry Emele's support for Adolf Hitler and his conquests, his work on behalf of the German *Bund* and his miserly and brutal treatment of his wife.

Salter and Diefenbaker ran through the evidence in two days, just half the time required at the first trial. On the morning of October 17, the prosecutor faced the jury.

"It is not a pleasant task to ask a jury to convict a person accused of murder," the gentlemanly Crown attorney began, obviously sincere. "All the evidence points to the truth of the accused's own version of the killing," he went on. "She pointed the rifle through the small, round hole in the kitchen door and shot Emele when he came to the house at the noon hour. There is no evidence to show that Emele committed suicide."

Then Salter hit the real issue in the case dead on. "Henry Emele's pro-Nazi sympathy provides no excuse for his murder. If he was a Nazi, there are ways of dealing with that."

The courtroom was jammed when Diefenbaker began his address to the jury at 1:30 p.m. The Emele case had become a sensation and other lawyers crowded into the audience. Chief Justice J.T. Brown, Diefenbaker's first trial judge, happened to be in

Prince Albert on other business and arranged for reports on the defence lawyer's performance to be sent to him.

The new member of Parliament disappointed no one. With his client weeping quietly behind him, Diefenbaker unleashed a storm of passion on her behalf. For an hour and twenty-five minutes he thundered and wept, stoking the emotions of not only the six men on the jury, but everyone in the courtroom.

Isobel Emele's confessions were nothing but the product of a mind so distraught as to be bereft of reason, the lawyer claimed. She spoke to the police as she did only to escape the pressure of their improper confinement of a woman in her own home, to ensure the safety of her children so rudely taken from her. The testimony of Mary Morris was beyond belief, the vengeful words of one shown to be spiteful and dishonest.

The condition to which the accused had been brought was also the product of years of misery and maltreatment at the hands of the deceased Emele. Little wonder that life with such a man had caused her to lose her grasp upon reality, the impassioned counsel implored.

Diefenbaker could not suggest that Henry Emele deserved killing, although he had done his best to create that impression throughout his cross-examinations. But as he concluded his address he subtly reminded his listeners of that feature of his case. The lawyer turned to a peroration that he had used before, but never so effectively as he did in front of the second Emele jury.

"Remember," Diefenbaker challenged the jurors, "remember, that you cannot find this woman guilty unless you are prepared to go home tonight and say, say to your neighbours, your friends, your family, 'I convicted her.' You cannot say, 'they convicted her.' You cannot even say, 'we convicted her.' You must, if you are to find guilt here today, be fully prepared, each one of you, to admit when you leave, 'I convicted her.'"

With that, Diefenbaker stood for a moment before the jury, then slowly returned to his seat at the counsel table. He knew he had struck all the right chords.

Mr. Justice Maclean tried to return the case to legal principles as he charged the jury.

"Even if a person is a Nazi, an individual may not go out and kill him and be justified under the laws of the land," the trial judge emphasized. There was no evidence of a third party who might have shot Emele, he said, and the defence theory of suicide was insupportable. Mr. Justice Maclean wanted to see justice done, and he was not so sympathetic to the defence as Mr. Justice Anderson had been.

But the jury concluded that justice had already been done. It returned at 9:45 p.m., after five and a half hours of deliberation. Verdict: "Not Guilty."

The courtroom erupted in a deafening, enthusiastic burst of applause. It was, the *Daily Herald* reported, "a wild, impulsive demonstration of applause that was a reflection of public opinion in both the city and district."

Mr. Justice Maclean was not amused. He dismissed the jury, saying, "I have no comment to make."

"You have heard the verdict?" he asked Isobel Emele.

"Yes, My Lord," she responded faintly.

"You are now dismissed."

"Thank You, My Lord," Isobel said.

"Don't thank me, or anybody," Mr. Justice Maclean finished curtly, and he adjourned court.

John Diefenbaker went to Isobel Emele in the prisoner's box to reassure her. "God bless you," she said, and again began to weep.

The crowd pressed forward to congratulate the lawyer, among them the *Daily Herald* reporter. That night the legend of John Diefenbaker's invincibility was born.

Speaking to the reporter, the new member of Parliament announced that Mrs. Emele was his seventeenth and eighteenth client tried for murder — figures that more than doubled the actual statistics! That number became fixed, even in his own mind, and was added to as later cases came.

The legend that was born that night in the Prince Albert court house quickly grew and travelled well beyond the borders of Saskatchewan.

At the conclusion of the Isobel Emele's first trial, John Diefenbaker had taken off his gown and gone to campaign in Lake Centre. After the second Emele acquittal, the victorious lawyer, now a member of Parliament, ventured onto the stage that was all of Canada. There, John Diefenbaker cultivated and burnished his hard-won reputation until he achieved the image and legend he craved.

And, to the entire nation, he became "The Man From Prince Albert."

Epilogue

On May 27, 1940, eight days after he first took his seat in the House of Commons, John Diefenbaker rose to make a suggestion to the minister of national defence. The Emele case, which he had argued in the Court of Appeal just three weeks before, was still on his mind.

The people of Saskatchewan, the member for Lake Centre stated, were "demanding that the government do something towards controlling the Nazi influence within their province."

"I point out," Diefenbaker said, "that today there are areas in Saskatchewan where Nazi activities are continuing in a manner which would not be credited elsewhere in the Dominion. People in the province are asking for action.

"The people of Saskatchewan are not hysterical, but they want measures to be taken at once to offset and control this menace in their midst."

Diefenbaker raised the issue of two militia units in Prince Albert which had not been mobilized.

"I ask the minister of national defence whether, in view of the critical situation — I call it critical advisedly — arising from subversive activities in Saskatchewan, he will consider the immediate recruitment to full strength of the Prince Albert infantry and artillery units. Otherwise, there will be no protection in northern Saskatchewan against enemy activities."

It was wild overstatement; there were no "enemy activities" in Saskatchewan. The province was likely of less interest to Germany than any region of Canada. But it made good news. The press gallery knew of John Diefenbaker's presence in the House of Commons almost from the day he arrived.

The firm of Diefenbaker and Cuelenaere was uncertain how to deal with the absence of the senior partner during the lengthy sittings of Parliament. Concerned that Diefenbaker's election might cause a loss of business, the partners decided against bringing another lawyer into the office, at least for a while, and Cuelenaere carried on alone during Diefenbaker's entire first term in Parliament. Not until another successful election and the end of the war did assistance arrive. In 1946 Roy Hall, a 1943 graduate of the University of Saskatchewan, joined the office upon his release from the RCAF.

By then John Cuelenaere was an overworked lawyer. He had become prominent in his own right and had developed a strong clientele. An alderman for several years, Cuelenaere was elected mayor of Prince Albert in November 1945.

The senior partner of Diefenbaker and Cuelenaere still received the largest share of the firm's profits. With the return of some prosperity to Saskatchewan, the office then earned about $10,000 a year, of which 60 per cent went to John Diefenbaker.

All during the more than fifteen years that John Diefenbaker spent as a private member of Parliament, he continued the practice of law as best he could. Required to be in Ottawa from fall until early summer, Diefenbaker returned to Prince Albert as often as possible — usually for Christmas and Easter breaks — and carted files back and forth. Travel was by train, and Diefenbaker secured special boxes to accommodate both his legal and political material. To the staff in the law office who packed them, the boxes quickly became the "coffins." Many files made the round-trip between Prince Albert and Ottawa several times, and some received no attention other than the packing.

Prince Albert noticed a change in the personality of John Diefenbaker when he became a member of Parliament. Edna had worked a considerable improvement over the years, but suddenly her husband became a "mainstreeter." On Central Avenue, he now had a greeting for every passerby. He developed his new technique until his promenades along Prince Albert's downtown street became a local tradition.

John Diefenbaker did not permit his new political career to supplant his professional life. He maintained his interest in the law and regularly attended the annual meetings of the Canadian Bar Association. In 1942 he was elected to a three-year term as vice-president of the national body.

Diefenbaker's connection with the ill-fated Anderson government and the 1929 election followed him to Parliament. In 1942 he was attacked by Dr. Harry R. Fleming, the Liberal member from Humboldt — the same Dr. Fleming whom Diefenbaker had cross-examined in Rex v. Wysochan at Humboldt in 1930. Fleming accused his fellow Saskatchewanian of having been: "closely associated with the late Anderson government that assumed office on an appeal to race and religion. That party slandered French-Canadian priests and sisters and placed upon the statute books of Saskatchewan a law that prescribed what form of dress the nuns should wear when teaching in the schools of Saskatchewan."

Diefenbaker did not defend the Anderson government, but denied that he had been associated with it. He demanded, and got, a withdrawal, saying, "It is true that I was a candidate, but I had nothing to do with the drafting of any legislation of any kind."

Fleming fell back on an allegation that Diefenbaker had been: "associated with the Ku Klux Klan. I am sure the honourable gentleman cannot deny this."

Diefenbaker replied hotly. "I want an unequivocal withdrawal of that statement. It is false in every particular."

Fleming tried to continue: "I know this man was associated with the Ku Klux Klan, because they had meetings all around Prince Albert."

Upon the direction of the Speaker, Fleming withdrew.

Some years later, John Diefenbaker again faced allegations arising from his past. In 1948 he made a second try for the leadership of the Conservative Party, running against the Ontario "Old Guard" who supported George Drew. The contest grew dirty, as such contests will, and a "smear campaign" caught the attention of Canadian Press. It reported rumours that Diefenbaker was "in ill health, was a former member of the Ku Klux Klan, and was of German origin."

Diefenbaker denied all the accusations.

The unique intertwining of the lives of John Diefenbaker and T.C. Davis continued. In 1940, Prime Minister Mackenzie King appointed James Gardiner Minister of War Services. Davis took a leave of absence from the Saskatchewan Court of Appeal to serve as Gardiner's deputy minister. Both Prince Albert lawyers took up residence in Ottawa. In 1942 Davis was appointed high commissioner to Australia and went on to serve as Canadian ambassador to China, West Germany and Japan. He spent fifteen years away from Canada and did not return until 1957.

Once elected, Diefenbaker proved to be unassailable. He held Lake Centre in 1945 against a CCF tide that seized eighteen of the twenty-one Saskatchewan ridings, including Mackenzie King's in Prince Albert. In 1949, in spite of a redistribution that removed much of his traditional support, he won again, this time with a majority of more than 3,400 votes.

Ten days after that 1949 election, on July 7, the re-elected member of Parliament was in Creighton, across the Saskatchewan border from Flin Flon, Manitoba, appearing for the accused in a murder preliminary. John Diefenbaker was, after all, still a lawyer.

Joseph Albert Rolland Boudreau Graveline was charged with the stabbing death of Herbert Magill Williams at Creighton, Saskatchewan, on June 5. It was John Diefenbaker's last Saskatchewan murder case.

The trial came before Mr. Justice Adrien Doiron, formerly the Humboldt prosecutor, on October 4, at Melfort. But first there was the question of whether Graveline was mentally fit to stand trial.

The thirty-six-year-old accused, from St. Boniface, Manitoba, had a history of mental illness. When Roy Hall interviewed him in the cells, Graveline showed strong indications of being out of touch with reality.

He was able to converse with the flies in his cell, Graveline told Hall. The flies, he said, were reincarnations of all his former lovers. They advised him spiritually and provided him much comfort.

A jury hearing was held to determine Graveline's mental capacity. A psychiatrist from the North Battleford Mental Hospital where Graveline had been examined testified that, in his opinion, the accused was fit to stand trial. Diefenbaker cross-examined.

Did the doctor know about the accused's strange belief in flies? he asked.

Yes, the doctor was aware of Graveline's conversations with his cellmates, but, nonetheless felt that he was capable of appreciating reality and conducting his defence.

Mr. Justice Doiron thought otherwise and imparted his views to the jury. They agreed with the trial judge and Graveline was remanded back to North Battleford "until the pleasure of the Lieutenant-Governor be known." That was the quaint way of saying that the accused would be kept in the mental hospital until such time as he might become fit to stand trial.

Some time later, Roy Hall ran into the psychiatrist on another matter. How, Hall inquired, did the doctor square the story of the flies with his opinion on Graveline's capacity to stand trial?

Easy, replied the doctor. The judicial system sent the mentally unstable accused to his institution, where he would recover. Then he would be sent back to trial, the trauma of which would bounce him right back to North Battleford. Might just as well try him right off and get it over with, was the doctor's view.

And that is just what happened. A year later, in October 1950, Graveline stood again before a jury. This time he was found fit to stand trial and the Crown proceeded with the evidence.

Creighton was a rough, northern town. A Saturday night drinking party at Graveline's home had degenerated into fistfights. Bottles were smashed and someone was thrown through a window.

In one of the fights, Graveline had been bested by John Holmes. Holmes decided to leave the party and got behind the wheel of his truck. As he did so, Graveline ran into the house and seized a butcher knife.

While Graveline was in the house, the unfortunate Williams pushed himself into the driver's seat of the truck, shoving Holmes out of his way. Someone — everyone assumed it was Graveline — jammed the knife into Williams's chest. Graveline was seen returning the bloody knife to his kitchen.

The confusion continued. Holmes tossed the injured Williams into the back of his truck and headed for the hospital in Flin Flon. Another participant, William Novosel, rode with Williams.

Speeding through the bush, Holmes lost control of his truck and ran into a pole. Novosel popped right out of his boots, flew into the pitch-dark bush, and disappeared. Holmes carried on. The boots and Williams remained on board. Williams was dead on arrival at the hospital.

Meanwhile, back at the party, Graveline was threatening to lay charges against Holmes for beating him up. He actually walked to a neighbour's house looking for a ride to go to the Flin Flon police detachment for that purpose.

That it had been one hell of a party was evident from the blood-alcohol test performed on Williams. His liquor consumption had been only average for those in attendance, but he registered .272. That was beyond the point where stupor normally occurs, and three and a half times today's legal limit for driving.

Diefenbaker saw defences galore in the case — insanity, drunkenness, provocation, even a bit of self-defence mixed with mistake. He eschewed them all. The defence he chose was to pose the question, Who put the knife in Williams?

It was self-confidence bordering upon conceit. But unlike his early defences in Wysochan, Pasowesty and Bohun, John Diefenbaker now possessed supreme forensic skills, particularly in cross-examination and handling juries. His political prowess added to his courtroom presence, and he utterly dominated the Graveline trial. He pulled it off.

Diefenbaker's cross-examinations of the hapless party participants were lethal. Memories, fuzzy at the time and made more so by the year and a half delay to trial, became confused and conflicting. The accounts of that Creighton Saturday night dissolved into an imbroglio.

Even the police and crime laboratory testimony came under attack. It seemed that Mrs. Graveline had cut her hand upon the same butcher knife earlier that night, and John Diefenbaker managed to throw doubt upon the blood tests taken from the handle.

And, of course, why was Graveline looking for a policeman to charge Holmes? The Crown's case was that Diefenbaker's client had stabbed Williams, who was behind the wheel of Holmes's truck, thinking he had attacked Holmes, his earlier assailant.

Addressing the jury, Diefenbaker heaped scorn and doubt upon the Crown evidence. They had not heard the sort of testimony needed to support a conviction for murder. Was there not a reasonable doubt in their minds that, in the drunken mêlée of that night, it was Graveline who had wielded the murder knife?

There was a doubt, the jury agreed, and Graveline was acquitted. He returned to St. Boniface.

The prediction of the North Battleford psychiatrist soon came to pass. Diefenbaker began to receive strange calls from Graveline in the middle of the night. He finally reported the problem and Graveline was popped back into the institution. Diefenbaker did not hear from him again.

It was a win without glory. In the ten years since John Diefenbaker's last murder trial, that of Isobel Emele, the press and public had become somewhat more sophisticated. Murder trials, particularly the garden-variety sort, were no longer front page news. Graveline attracted little attention compared to Diefenbaker's earlier capital cases.

John Diefenbaker needed another major trial, a headliner, one that would cement his still-growing reputation of invincibility.

Just a month after the Graveline trial, an event occurred in the Canadian Rockies that turned into the most sensational case in John Diefenbaker's career.

On November 21, 1950, a troop train — Canadian National Passenger Extra No. 3538 West — rumbled through the Rocky Mountains headed for Vancouver and Fort Lewis, Washington. There, its passengers — more than three hundred members of the Royal Canadian Horse Artillery — would marshall with the remainder of Canada's Special Brigade before shipping across the Pacific to the Korean War.

At Canoe River, Bill Tindill and Harry Patterson were loading poles at the siding. They looked up as they heard the whistle of the troop train approaching from the east. In horror, they saw a passenger liner, Transcontinental Number 2, roar around the curve from the west.

Tindill waved frantically, trying to flag the Transcontinental. Smiling, the fireman returned Tindill's greeting.

The two locomotives met head-on and leaped into the air, then exploded and fell back into a jumbled tangle of steel and steam. Both engine crews died instantly.

The two trains continued to move upon each other, carried onward by their weight and momentum. The cars were flung off the track or telescoped by the pressure of those behind. The all-steel cars of the Transcontinental withstood the terrific forces, but the older, wooden-sided cars of the 1,500-foot-long troop train were crushed. Seventeen soldiers died and dozens were seriously injured.

When the terrible grinding and tearing finally stopped, more than 500 feet of train had been compressed into 130 feet. The mound of wreckage rose 35 feet into the air. The shaken survivors turned to the grisly work of rescue. It was 10:40 a.m.

At Red Pass junction, fifty miles east of the wreck, Jack Atherton, a telegraph operator, received the news. White-faced, he turned to the agent.

"There's been a collision. A head-on."

"What hit?"

"No. 2 and the passenger extra."

A moment later, Atherton reached for his copy of the orders he had handed to the crew of Extra No. 3538 when it passed through Red Pass earlier in the morning.

"Well, my orders are O.K.," he said, "I'm in the clear."

But, there was a problem with train order No. 248 as delivered by Jack Atherton to the conductor on the troop train. The order had been issued by the dispatcher in Kamloops over the telephone simultaneously to both Red Pass and Blue River, a station west of Red Pass. The Kamloops and Blue River versions of order No. 248 contained two words not found in Atherton's copy.

The order, as received by the troop train instructed it: "Passenger Extra 3538 West meet Number 2, Engine 6004, and Number 4, Engine 6057, Gosnell." This cleared the troop train down to Gosnell, where it would clear the track for the eastbound Transcontinental passenger trains Numbers 2 and 4.

But the order, as issued by Kamloops, had read: "Passenger Extra 3538 meet Number 2, Engine 6004, *at Cedarside* and Number 4, Engine 6057, at Gosnell."

Cedarside was the siding at Canoe River where the troop train should have been sitting in safety as the Transcontinental was cleared through.

Somehow, the critical two words that would have prevented the tragedy had failed to make it into the copy of order No. 248 that Jack Atherton handed to Extra 3538.

Yet Canadian National rules required that each operator write down his orders, then read them back to the dispatcher, spelling out each number to prevent the possibility of mistake. What could have happened?

Two days after the wreck, the RCMP interviewed Jack Atherton. A bad telephone line, the Red Pass operator suggested.

"I am very certain that the words 'at Cedarside' did not reach Red Pass Junction," he said.

When he read back the order as he had written it, Atherton claimed, Kamloops and Blue River, who should have been checking word for word, "did not catch my serious mistake."

In December the Board of Transport Commissioners, sitting in Edmonton, held a formal inquiry into the accident. When those proceedings were over early in January the RCMP charged Jack Atherton with manslaughter. Just one of the twenty-one deaths was chosen for the charge, that of Henry Proskunik, the fireman on Extra 3538.

The twenty-two-year-old Atherton was a native of Saskatoon, where his parents still lived. They wanted John Diefenbaker to defend their son.

At first, Diefenbaker declined. Tragedy had struck his life, and even such a case as Atherton's held no interest for him.

For several years, Edna Diefenbaker's health had been a serious worry to the couple. Her condition seemed to be a form of depression and with treatment she appeared to recover. Shortly before the Graveline trial, however, Edna was diagnosed as suffering from leukemia. Now she was in hospital in Saskatoon.

Edna did not recover. On February 7, 1951, she died in her husband's arms.

John Diefenbaker was truly grief-stricken. The loss of Edna was the greatest of his life thus far, eclipsing all of his political defeats.

Before her death, Edna secured John's promise that he would undertake the defence of Jack Atherton. He would do so.

As he had so many times in the past, John Diefenbaker pulled himself together and carried on. He was fifty-five years old, and much of his life lay before him.

The Atherton preliminary inquiry was scheduled to begin on March 13 at Prince George, BC. Diefenbaker arranged to be admitted to the British Columbia bar, paying a $1,500 fee for the privilege.

Roy Hall undertook the basic preparation of the Atherton defence. He attended the inquest, conducted interviews, reviewed the evidence called before the Board of Transport

Commissioners and studied the railway's rules and procedures. By the time they reached the preliminary inquiry, Diefenbaker and Hall had a thorough grasp of the case.

The defence posture would be an old Diefenbaker classic. While casting doubt upon the Crown's allegation that Atherton had been negligent, he would point to the Canadian National as the villain, the real cause of the tragedy.

Diefenbaker, although still in grief at the loss of Edna, was powerful and exacting in cross-examination at the preliminary. Over three days, witness after witness, almost all C.N.R. employees, conceded detail essential to the defence.

Temporary fade-outs on the telephone line over which order No. 248 had passed were not uncommon, Diefenbaker established. One lineman was very co-operative and the lawyer took full advantage of his opportunity.

"With your experience you have seen a lot of stoppages in telephone communication?"

"Yes."

"Wet snow does it?"

"Wet snow will cut it. Heavy wet snow."

"A bird lighting on the telephone wire will do it?"

"Birds flying into the wires may cause them to short."

"There have been cases like that?"

"Lots of times."

Diefenbaker pressed for more.

"You had a fish on the line up here?"

"That's occurred quite a few times. A bird picks up a wet fish and lays it on the line. That will cause a short, a good wet fish."

It would be great evidence when repeated before a jury.

John Diefenbaker's style was something new to Prince George. Interest in the case was high and the court room was packed as the Prince Albert lawyer seized the offensive. He went straight at the railway officials.

The subdivision in which the accident occurred was the third most dangerous in British Columbia, the senior engineer admitted. Yes, an automatic signal system would likely have averted the collision.

Except for the engine crew on the Transcontinental, all the deaths and serious injuries had been found on the troop train. And those, Diefenbaker drew out, were in the wooden cars with steel underframes only. Worse, the wooden cars had been mixed between all-steel cars, contrary to good railway practice.

"Isn't it a fact that these poor soldiers that were killed were in wooden coaches, or wooden coaches with...?"

"With steel sheeting and steel underframes. They were not in an all-steel car."

"Is it not a fact that it was the soldiers in the first two or three sleepers that were badly, seriously injured?"

"Yes, sir."

"Those men, those unfortunate men, were in those wooden cars?"

"Those class of cars."

"And is it also a fact that, any of the soldiers that were in the cars that were of steel construction, there were no injuries to them, no serious injuries?"

"That is right."

H.W. McInnes, K.C., of Prince George handled the preliminary for the Crown. When the prosecutor closed his case after twenty-one witnesses, Diefenbaker made a brave but futile pitch for Atherton's discharge.

The gross negligence required to support the charge of manslaughter was far more than the absence of reasonable care, he argued.

"Here is this boy, twenty-two years old, two years with the railroad and no training, not sent to a school, and yet given a responsible job on the main line.

"This boy, his future gone, with no black marks and a clear record, should not be committed to stand trial for manslaughter."

McInnes was gracious with his closing remarks. He paid tribute to "the forensic ability and outstanding oratory" of John

Diefenbaker. "I deem it an honour to have opposed him in his first appearance in a British Columbia court of law."

Atherton was committed to stand trial at the spring assizes of the Supreme Court of British Columbia at Prince George, due to commence in May.

Roy Hall went up to Prince George a few days before the trial to check out the jury list with W.D. Ferry, a local lawyer who served as co-counsel. When Mr. Justice A.D. MacFarlane called Rex v. Atherton on May 10, Diefenbaker relied on Hall's and Ferry's recommendations as the jury was selected. After the case was underway, Diefenbaker leaned over to Hall and complained.

"I don't think you did much of a job with this jury. Half of them are railroaders and the other half are former servicemen." Diefenbaker was concerned that both groups would be vindictive towards Atherton.

Hall assured his senior partner that, when it came to Jack Atherton against the Canadian National, the railroaders would be with Atherton. The former servicemen, also, would come in handy, Hall promised.

The prominence of the Atherton case drew the attention of Colonel Eric Pepler, K.C., Deputy Attorney General of British Columbia. Pepler, a one-legged veteran of the First World War who continued to carry his rank, assumed the position of senior Crown counsel. The Colonel was the perfect foil for John Diefenbaker

The defence lawyer seized the initiative — and the headlines — on the first day of the trial. Following the line he had developed at the preliminary, Diefenbaker went after the senior C.N.R. engineer about the use of wooden cars. Pepler objected.

"The C.N.R. is not on trial here. There is only one question here, was the accused guilty of criminal negligence, or was he not."

"There could have been an indictment against the C.N.R. for lack of safety measures," Diefenbaker snapped, "but there was not. It was against my client."

The press leaped on Diefenbaker's accusation. "C.N.R. Should Stand Trial, Hints Atherton Counsel," the headlines reported.

In his experience, the engineer admitted, the only passengers not carried in steel cars through the mountain regions were soldiers.

"Do you know why soldiers are required to ride in wooden cars?" Diefenbaker demanded.

"I do not."

Pepler objected again, pointing out that the indictment against Atherton referred only to the death of fireman Henry Proskunik. Then he continued with a most unfortunate remark.

"We here are not concerned with the death of soldiers."

Diefenbaker leaped at the opportunity.

"Oh! Colonel! Oh!" he said scathingly, with a meaningful glance and gesture at the jury.

That evening, Roy Hall was dining in a local restaurant, one with high-backed booths. Three or four members of the jury, not yet sequestered, were in the next booth discussing the trial. Hall could not help but overhear their conversation.

"I was a corporal in the First War," said one juryman. "I always thought those officers didn't give a damn about the men, and now I know they don't."

Diefenbaker never relinquished the edge Pepler had given him. He maintained relentless pressure on both the Crown and the C.N.R.

Some witnesses, particularly the co-operative lineman, were less helpful than they had been at the preliminary. Diefenbaker uncovered the fact that all C.N.R. witnesses had been called to a meeting in Jasper a few days prior to the trial. Present at the meeting had been the C.N.R. general manager and a company lawyer, who had reviewed with each witness the evidence given at the preliminary.

"A school," the defence lawyer described the meeting, and contended that C.N.R. employees were unable to give honest testimony for fear of losing their jobs. Diefenbaker's careful work at the preliminary became invaluable as he referred again and again to admissions made there, but since retracted.

When he arose to address the jury on the fourth day of the trial, John Diefenbaker had the case in hand, but he spared neither Pepler nor the C.N.R. He referred to the lineman's testimony:

"He admitted at the preliminary hearing that words would be lost over the telephone, if there was a short in the wires, but it took him a long time to say it again here. He had been to 'school' since then, been to C.N.R. 'school' at Jasper, and the C.N.R. brass were helping."

Diefenbaker began reading to the jury from the preliminary transcript, a questionable tactic, and Pepler rose and objected. But to interrupt opposing counsel's address to the jury is a serious step, and Mr. Justice MacFarlane said so.

"I do not think you should object like this," he suggested. Pepler persisted, and the trial judge lost his patience.

"Please, just stop this," he roared.

Pepler hastily took his seat, but continued to mumble.

"You are growling," Diefenbaker told the Colonel.

"Yes. I am growling. I'm objecting, too," Pepler retorted.

It was an unseemly performance, particularly for such senior counsel, but Diefenbaker seemed to enjoy it. He gave Pepler another lick.

"I sat and suffered while my learned friend misconstrued the evidence," he stated, referring to Pepler's own summation to the jury.

Turning back to the jury, Diefenbaker contended that the faulty train order came about through a short circuit in the telephone lines between Kamloops and Red Pass. "A pause, a moment of silence, was not unusual in the transmission of a message," he claimed.

For two and a half hours, Diefenbaker reviewed the evidence and castigated the C.N.R. He concluded with the powerful plea: "No small men shall be made goats by the strong or the powerful in this country."

Roy Hall's assessment of the jury was correct. They were back in forty minutes with a verdict of "Not Guilty." A sob of relief came from Jack Atherton's mother, dressed somberly in black and sitting in the front row of the spectators. Dozens of onlookers flocked around John Diefenbaker, complimenting him on his defence.

That the C.N.R. had lost a case in which it supposedly was not involved was clear from comment carried by the Prince George *Citizen*: "There is no travesty of justice more pitiful to watch than a man with a home and family trying to give honest evidence about his employer's operations while representatives of that employer are jotting things down in notebooks only a few feet away."

The *Citizen* also reported the opinion of a prominent Prince George Liberal about the Atherton defence counsel: "For a Conservative, that man seems pretty intelligent."

The Atherton trial, although covered by the Vancouver papers, was mostly disregarded by the eastern press. John Diefenbaker helped cure that oversight when he returned to Parliament Hill. He was interviewed by some of the columnists.

"John Diefenbaker, K.C., famed lawyer and House of Commons critic, returned to his duties yesterday with another legal victory in his briefcase," the Ottawa *Citizen* reported. "Among the numberless trials in which the brilliant John Diefenbaker, M.P., has participated, none were more dramatically successful than this far-famed counsel's triumph at Prince George last week," said another paper.

Diefenbaker, as he had after his victory in Emele, boosted the actual statistics considerably and announced that the Atherton case had been his 581st jury trial.

The railroaders of Canada, and many of the military, needed no newspapers to tell them of the Atherton trial. They were quite aware of John Diefenbaker's work on behalf of Jack Atherton, and the way in which he had belittled the C.N.R. Their appreciation showed in later years.

One final major trial remained to John Diefenbaker, again on behalf of a Saskatchewan lad in trouble in British Columbia. This time he overplayed his theatrical talent.

The call for Diefenbaker came on behalf of twenty-six-year-old Donald Cathro, from Radville, Saskatchewan. Cathro was charged with a murder in Vancouver. In fact, he had already been convicted, and Cathro and his family were desperate. His conviction had been upheld by the British Columbia Court of Appeal, and the last hope was the Supreme Court of Canada, an avenue open because of two dissenting judgements in the Court of Appeal.

Cathro and three others — Chow Bew, Eng Git Lee, and Richard Wong — had planned and carried out a robbery on Ah Wing, a corner groceryman. Cathro, whose job was to keep Ah Wing quiet, seized the elderly man around the neck but failed to stop his screams for help. Chow Bew took over, threw Ah Wing to the floor and put his knee to the groceryman's throat. Ah Wing's voice box was fractured and he strangled. The jury convicted Cathro of murder, refusing his plea for the lesser offence of manslaughter.

Cathro was defended by Craig Munroe, a graduate of the University of Saskatchewan law school, who was happy to be joined by the eminent John Diefenbaker. Both lawyers appeared on the appeal to the Supreme Court, Diefenbaker's second, and last, appearance before Canada's highest court.

In November 1955, the Supreme Court agreed with the dissenting judges of the Court of Appeal. The first trial judge had committed an error with the jury. A new trial was ordered, and John Diefenbaker won a chance to persuade a fresh jury that Donald Cathro had not been a party to the murder of Ah Wing.

The new trial came before Mr. Justice J.V. Clyne of the British Columbia Supreme Court. Diefenbaker's defence was that Cathro, who had come to rob but not to murder, had intervened between Chow Bew, the real villain, and Ah Wing in an attempt to rescue the groceryman. In the struggle, Ah Wing fell, with Cathro on top of him, and the death was accidental.

Mr. Justice Clyne described John Diefenbaker's last jury address in his memoirs, *Jack of All Trades, Memoirs of a Busy Life*:

> Diefenbaker produced a very tense moment in court when he said, "And now, gentlemen of the jury, I shall show you how it happened." With his gown flying in the air, the future prime minister of Canada rushed across the court and threw himself on the floor in front of the jury box and almost under the counsel table.
>
> The assize room in the old court house was a large room, and it was crowded during this trial. The judge's bench stood quite high above the counsel table and the rest of the court room, so that, in fact, Diefenbaker had practically disappeared from my sight. There was dead silence in the room.
>
> I, of course, could not allow this sort of nonsense in my court room, so I said, "Mr. Diefenbaker, if you will come out from underneath the table, I will be able to follow your argument more clearly."
>
> The courtroom burst into laughter and Diefenbaker concluded his address somewhat sheepishly.

The jury did not accept Diefenbaker's theory. Cathro was again convicted of murder and sentenced to be hanged. A recommendation for clemency from Mr. Justice Clyne helped Diefenbaker secure a commutation of the sentence. Paroled some years later, Donald Cathro did not turn away from bad companions. His body was found floating in Vancouver harbour.

In December 1956, the year of Donald Cathro's second trial, John Diefenbaker, on his third attempt, finally won the leadership of the Conservative Party of Canada. In the election of June 10, 1957, he achieved his greatest ambition, and succeeded to the office of prime minister. His days as a trial lawyer were over.

But he never lost his interest in the law. He followed events in the courts, particularly in Saskatchewan, and enjoyed every opportunity to chat with old friends still active in the profession.

And he carried with him into the prime minister's office his memories from his time as an outstanding gladiator in the arena of Saskatchewan law and politics.

Chief Justice J.T. Brown, the long-serving Chief Justice of Saskatchewan's Court of Queen's Bench, retired in 1956. The office was still vacant when John Diefenbaker became prime minister. Mr. Justice George Taylor thought it would be appropriate that he be promoted to Chief Justice for the remainder of his time on the bench (federal judicial appointments were then for life). Taylor wrote the new prime minister, suggesting his promotion and mentioning the many pleasant trial experiences he and Diefenbaker had enjoyed together.

Prime Minister Diefenbaker remembered those experiences very well, all the way back to the Pasowesty trial in Wynyard in 1929. He did not have the same fond recollection that Taylor described.

"Can you imagine?" the prime minister sputtered to M.A. MacPherson, Jr., of Regina, (later himself Mr. Justice MacPherson of Saskatchewan's Queen's Bench). "Can you imagine me appointing that old bastard to anything?"

Taylor died in April 1959. He was succeeded on the court by Russell L. Brownridge who, as a law student, had interviewed Isobel Emele in September 1939. Brownridge was later promoted to the Saskatchewan Court of Appeal.

Early in 1957, John Diefenbaker's old adversary, the Honourable T.C. Davis, Canadian ambassador to Japan, retired and took up residence in Victoria. One last encounter remained to be fought between the two old political warriors. This time, Diefenbaker won.

Davis was a shareholder in Radio Station CHAB in Moose Jaw. The station had been purchased some years before by his brother, W.L. Davis, the publisher of the Prince Albert *Daily Herald*.

By this time television had arrived. In cities across Canada, television broadcasting licences were granted to prominent radio stations. In June 1957, CHAB applied for the Moose Jaw licence. The application was approved, and forwarded to Cabinet for final clearance. There it stopped.

"They'll not get it," said the new prime minister, "and no one by the name of Davis will ever get it."

And so it was. The Davis family understood the reality of politics better than most. They sold CHAB and the new owners picked up the television licence.

T.C. Davis died in Victoria on January 21, 1960.

In December 1962, Roy Hall, who had worked so effectively with John Diefenbaker on the Graveline and Atherton trials, was appointed to the Saskatchewan Court of Appeal.

John Cuelenaere remained the longest-serving associate in John Diefenbaker's legal career. But, at the end of his life, he fell out with his long-time senior partner.

In 1964, Cuelenaere was elected to the Saskatchewan legislature, and became a minister in the government of Liberal Premier Ross Thatcher. Cuelenaere spent his last days in Prince Albert. He refused to see John Diefenbaker, in spite of emissaries sent by the former prime minister, and died without speaking to the man with whom he spent his entire professional life. Cuelenaere gave no specific reason for his embitterment. Stricken with cancer, he died on February 12, 1967.

The John M. Cuelenaere Library stands in downtown Prince Albert. In front of city hall is a statue of the former prime minister, the other member of Diefenbaker and Cuelenaere.

John Diefenbaker bequeathed $275,000 to the city of Prince Albert, to be placed towards a civic centre to bear his own name. The monies were paid in 1982. In 1987, it was discovered that the city had failed to earmark the funds — they had been taken into revenue and disbursed upon ongoing expenditures. Following a protest, the city replaced the bequest, which now sits in a special fund awaiting sufficient additional contributions to undertake the project.

John Diefenbaker died in Ottawa on August 16, 1979. Following arrangements he had carefully worked out, the funeral was held in Ottawa's Christ Church Cathedral. The body was then carried by special train to Prince Albert, and on to Saskatoon. On August 22, the former prime minister was interred on the campus of his *alma mater*, the University of Saskatchewan.

The eulogy was delivered by Joe Clark, another former Conservative prime minister:

> In a very real sense, his life was Canada. Over eight decades, he spanned our history, from the ox cart on the prairies to the satellite in space. He shaped much of that history — all of it shaped him.
>
> Now that life, that sweep of history, has ended. And we are here today to see John Diefenbaker to his final place of rest.
>
> It is appropriate that it be here. For, while John Diefenbaker was all of Canada, he was, above all else, a man of the prairies. His populism was inspired in this open land. His deep feelings for the needs of individuals were shaped by what he saw and felt during the Depression years. The South Saskatchewan Dam, one of his physical legacies, reflected his determination that farmers in the region should never again suffer dust when there should be grass. It was from Prince Albert that he looked North and caught the vision with which he stirred the minds and hearts of all of us.
>
> And so, we commit his mortal remains to the prairie soil, here on the campus where he studied and was Chancellor, above the river which was a route of our first westward pioneers, in the province which formed him.

Index